S. Giridhar and V. J. Raghunath have been friends since 1984 when they worked at Carborundum Universal's factory at Chennai and played city cricket tournaments together. Raghunath, now 76, was a left-handed batter and a fearless close catcher who rubbed shoulders with some of India's best cricketers of the 1960s and '70s in the first division leagues of Chennai and Mumbai. Giridhar, now 66, bowled leg spin and was also an agile close catcher, though he did not play at the same level.

Apart from *Mid-wicket Tales*, they have also jointly written *From Mumbai to Durban: India's Greatest Tests* (2016). Giridhar, whose work with Azim Premji Foundation over the past 21 years has taken him to remote corners of the country, also did a detailed study of government schoolteachers for a moving and inspiring book, *Ordinary People, Extraordinary Teachers: The Heroes of Real India*.

Praise for *Mid-wicket Tales*

Mid-wicket Tales...[delves into] the game's rich history, exhaustive technicalities, [and] varied personalities...to carefully explore the nuances of the game's core elements...Flip through the pages of the book randomly, and you are sure to whet your cricketing appetite. —*Wisden India*

Mid-wicket Tales is a wonderfully put together book. This book will ensure that its readers never forget the traditions of cricket and the players who have gone to painstaking efforts to uphold the culture of our great game. —Matthew Hayden, Australian Test cricketer

I loved reading about so many fantastic players who played the great game of cricket. It is so well researched and there are so many fantastic statistics throughout. I particularly liked the section on sublime left handers. —Mike Hussey, Australian Test cricketer

Giri and Raghu [bring] a lot of erudition to their essays...but they also [have] a feel for the history of the game, its characters, its romance... They could put things into perspective and that is why this book covers a wonderfully wide range of issues. —Harsha Bhogle, cricket commentator and writer

S. Giridhar [and] V. J. Raghunath...are...'incurable cricket romantics' who believe that 'much that is noble about the game will remain unsullied by the passage of time', and in that spirit they have written an altogether charming and engaging book...[which] would cheer anyone up. —Gideon Haigh, journalist and cricket historian

The book has left me bowled over. Facts, snippets and anecdotes gracefully come together in this one-of-a-kind book. I applaud the special effort the authors have made to feature many brilliant cricketers who were just not lucky to become stars. Analytical and insightful, thought provoking but not controversial, this book brings both smiles & tears. —Javagal Srinath, Indian Test cricketer

This book is for all genuine lovers of cricket. It has a lovely mix of statistics, technical analysis and stories that enable us to marvel at the past and appreciate the present. The narrative brings alive the game to the reader, animated cricket as I would call it, with such a unique warmth that you will go back again and again to your favorite passages. —E. A. S. Prasanna, Indian Test cricketer

A nostalgic journey through Test cricket...*Mid-wicket Tales* is an unabashed ode to Test cricket...It is also an antidote for the cynicism of today...The optimism is infectious and remarkable for a book about cricket in the modern era...And there might be a lesson in that for fans. That watching cricket is supposed to be a labor of love. —*Firstpost.com*

The duo makes you see things you hadn't thought about. Did you know, for instance, that Kapil Dev, whose natural instinct you would swear was to dispatch the cricket ball into the stadium seating, was a judicious batter for whom rotating the strike was as crucial as hocking the ball for a six?...The book is well worth reading for some unexplored insight into India's world of celebrity cricket. —*Business Standard*

Mid-wicket Tales is one of a kind in modern times. The anecdotes don't just make you smile, but thanks to the wonderful narration, also help you visualize the action being relayed. The book has you hooked from the very first page...[T]he writers make you wish how you were a part of their rich discussions. Test cricket devotees will find the book quite enjoyable. —*The New Indian Express*

Reading *Mid-wicket Tales*...is a mandatory requirement in order to win back what Giridhar and Raghunath so passionately talk about—win it back from the commerce and the spin. And put cricket back into the heart of the game again. —Sharda Ugra, *ESPNcricinfo*

MID-WICKET TALES

A Century and More of Cricket

S. GIRIDHAR
V. J. RAGHUNATH

SPEAKING
TIGER

SPEAKING TIGER BOOKS LLP
125 A, Shahpur Jat, New Delhi 110049

First published in 2014 by Sage Publications India
This edition published by Speaking Tiger Books 2023

ISBN: 978-93-5447-598-6
eISBN: 978-93-5447-600-6

10 9 8 7 6 5 4 3 2 1

Typeset in Sabon Roman by SÜRYA, New Delhi
Printed at Shree Maitrey Printech Pvt. Ltd., Noida

*Raghunath dedicates this book to his mother
Lalitha Jayaraman who introduced him to the game.*

*Giridhar dedicates the book to his father T. K. Subramanian
with whom he watched countless cricket matches
from the age of seven.*

CONTENTS

LIST OF TABLES

PREFACE TO REVISED EDITION

It is a wonderful life, *Mid-wicket Tales* would say, because when its original publishers closed and one feared the book would fade away, it found a new home with the kind and gracious Ravi Singh and Speaking Tiger Books. So, nine years after being published, here is *Mid-wicket Tales*, freshly washed and combed, ready for another tilt at cricket lovers' hearts.

When *MWT* was first published, what moved us immensely was the reception it received. From cricketers like Rahul Dravid and Matthew Hayden, cricket writers like Gideon Haigh and Suresh Menon, to cricket literature loving readers, the book received warm and generous reviews. When the late Sidhanta Patnaik reviewed the book, he spotted some factual errors. But the book also tempted him into becoming its proofreader so that the subsequent edition could be error free. If all this does not make a book feel blessed, what will?

And because the original *Mid-wicket Tales* had the angels on its side, we decided that even in the new edition, we would retain the essays as they were first published. What we wrote then on catching and captaincy, on pace and spin, on batting and the changing complexion of a complex sport, was as we saw it then. To try and update each story to be in tune with 2023 might hurt the soul of the original. And at the pace at which the game is moving, it would anyway be like climbing an escalator that is coming down.

Instead, we have added a potpourri of new essays. One is on how video analytics has become integral to not only cricket strategy but also commercially critical for television viewership. We have added an essay we wrote during World Cup 2019, tracing the strategic acumen of various captains from the inaugural World Cup. We have essays that mark the seamless handing of the baton from Dhoni to Kohli and an essay on Mahatma Gandhi and his connection with cricket that we wrote for the great man's 150th anniversary.

Women's cricket has captured the hearts of cricket lovers in recent times. The unadulterated joy and skill with which the women cricketers play, provides viewers with a fresh perspective on how to enjoy watching sports. Mithali Raj, Harmanpreet Kaur, Smriti Mandhana, Jhulan Goswami, and others are now household names and on every advertising company's chase list. We are delighted that Karunya Keshav, who has followed and written extensively on women's cricket, has contributed a special feature to this edition of *MWT*.

We have wrapped up this new edition with what one would call the concluding chapter. This is where we have tried to collate and synthesize all the significant developments in the game in the nine years since the book's first publication. Writing this commentary on the important turning points, on cricketers who in this period have earned a place in cricket's hall of fame and on all the technical developments in the game, we wondered if this has indeed been a decade of great and rapid change.

1

THE THRILL OF CLOSE-IN CATCHING

Two uniquely thrilling visuals of Test cricket have not changed with time. One is the first morning of a Test match—new ball, fresh wicket, three slips and a gully and a leg gully, alert and ready as the fast bowler comes thundering in to bowl. The other is the last day of a Test match—dusty wicket with cracks and warts, and slip, silly point, gully, forward short leg and leg slip waiting like vultures around the bat as the spinners weave their web. Will backward short leg have time to react as the inside edge comes from behind the front pad? Is slip standing too deep or too close? Every ball is fraught with excitement, and the possibilities are endless. Close-in catching is an indescribable thrill that transcends the ability to explain in mere words. It is strangely more difficult to describe than the cover drive or the googly. From the bat to hand, the ball takes a fraction of a second. Most times it is off the edge; sometimes it is flush of the middle of the blade, as the slash to gully or the flick or even a pull to leg. Eknath Solkar arguably the greatest forward short leg ever, when pressed repeatedly to explain how he made those catches, helplessly said, 'I don't know, I see it and I up it!' There is something so uncanny about the sharp close-in catch, it seems to come more naturally to some, but we know that is mere illusion for behind it is a lot of practice.

Great slip fielders do not dive, lunge or grab. They see the edge a fraction earlier, move smoothly to the right or left with soft hands in front of their body and take the catch bending just enough to ensure the hands are at a comfortable height. Their anticipation and balance make the catches they take seem easy, almost always. If the ball comes very low and away from them, it is then that they dive to complete the catch, roll on to their shoulder and are up effortlessly. If you have seen Bobby Simpson, Colin Cowdrey or Mark Waugh dive to take a catch in the slips, you can be certain that most other ordinary mortals would not have even got their fingertips to the ball as it flew past them.

Most slip fieldsmen have been specialist batters as they are trained to concentrate ball after ball for long periods and therefore are ready when that edge finally comes behind the wicket. However, history serves us this deliciously ironic information that the first great slip fielder was actually a fast bowler—Australia's Jack Gregory in the 1920s. It is said that Gregory read Arthur Mailey's googly better than even his wicketkeeper Bert Oldfield and that there were instances of him running around from slip to leg slip to catch inner edges of Mailey's googly! He was not the only fast bowler to field superbly in the slips. Keith Miller, one of the greatest all-rounders, was amazingly good at slip. He brought the same insouciance to his slip catching as he brought to his batting and bowling. With Miller it was all style. Miller stood erect, legs apart and didn't crouch like most others did at slips but was quick and a natural who timed his movement to catch the ball instinctively. There is also Ian Botham who, standing closer than others, made second slip a position all his own as he pouched everything effortlessly.

Australia, South Africa and England have always had very good specialist slip fielders to support their battery of fast bowlers. It was natural that countries with the best fast bowling attacks had good slip and gully fielders. The two Australians Mark Waugh and Mark Taylor are among the greatest slip catchers in cricket history. Since they played in modern times, we have seen them in live action—either on television or on India's Test grounds. The best English slip catchers were Wally Hammond in the 1930s and Cowdrey in the 1950s and 1960s. Both were heavy men and moved as if in slow motion but were always at the right place at the right time. When South Africa came back to Test cricket in the 1990s, Brian MacMillan was as brilliant as Taylor and Waugh. Jacques Kallis made second slip catching look absurdly easy. Mahela Jayewardene and Stephen Fleming are a couple of other names from the last 20 years that come readily to mind while discussing slip catching. The greatest slip catcher of them all has to be Bobby Simpson.

He had his own unique style. While the bowler—Alan Davidson, Graham McKenzie or Neil Hawke—ran up to bowl, he would be squatting on his haunches, left knee lower than the right. As the bowler delivered the ball, Simpson would come up. He hardly ever dropped anything and rarely dived or lunged to take a catch. His catches per match ratio is still the highest ever in Test history. India's best close catchers were naturally those that supported our spin quartet in the 1970s. Ajit Wadekar, S. Venkataraghavan, Eknath Solkar and Syed Abid Ali formed an umbrella field to give the cutting edge to make our spin bowling truly dangerous. As B. S. Chandrasekhar would run in to bowl and the Calcutta crowd's roar reached a crescendo, the batter would already be on edge. At pick pocketing distance from him was Solkar. Out of sight just behind him, was Abid Ali. Out of the corner of his eye he could also see Venkat, bucket-sized hands, chewing gum, supremely confident at close gully. Wadekar seemed to be lounging at slip but would not drop anything that came his way. The pressure on the batter was unimaginable.

As we were writing this piece, it seemed to make perfect sense that we talk to Rahul Dravid, very good at first slip and also the holder of the record for the highest number of catches in Tests about slip catching. Why was he good at it? Reminiscent of what Venkat told us, Dravid says drill and practice is the only way.

> You would never ever have seen me without a ball when I was a child. I was always bouncing and catching it from any surface all day long. Right since my school boy cricketer years, fielding and catching practice is like a ritual day after day. Of course, I also have big hands.

Giridhar immediately measures his hand with Dravid in a high five mode and Dravid's hand is a clear inch bigger! Dravid rates Mark Waugh, Mark Taylor, Freddie Flintoff, Ricky Ponting and Mohammad Azharuddin as the best slip catchers he has seen. Azhar, he says was sheer joy to watch. He had soft hands and the way he took catches was almost as though he was divinely blessed and then describes a catch that Azhar took at second slip as Dravid watched transfixed from his own position at first slip.

The formation of the slips and gully has a certain rationale. First slip stands about six feet away from and three feet behind the wicketkeeper while second and third slip stand in line with the wicketkeeper, an arm's length separating them from first slip. First slip is deeper since only a faint edge would go in that fine a direction and since he does not have the advantage of gloves like the keeper. Gully ought to be clearly two steps ahead, closer to the batter; the idea is to stand at a distance from the batter such that an edge from a forward defensive stroke would carry to you at knee height and also close enough to take the ball that pops up of the shoulder of the bat. That means the slips and gully should vary their distance from the batter, based on the bounce and pace of the wicket, and the speed of the bowler. One thing that puzzles both of us is that these days, we do not see fielders adjusting their position according to the pace of the bowler or the carry of the pitch. They seem to stand deeper to comfortably catch the slashed edge off the back foot and consequently many snicks off the front foot prod fall well short of the slip fielders. More surprising, even when this has happened a few times, the slips do not move up. Gully fielders too stay back deep and that almost seems like a semi-defensive option to stop the fierce slashes from going to the boundary than to grab the edge from a well-bowled outswinger.

Fielders who excelled at gully are Aussies Richie Benaud, Ashley Mallett and Mike Hussey, England's Paul Collingwood and of course India's own Venkat. At gully, multiple abilities are called for: the ability to spring up like a tiger to catch the high slash or go low either side to pluck the edged square drive or spring forward to take the lob. Crouching to spring with anticipation is perhaps the key. Benaud was absolutely the best there in his days. Mallett fielded at gully to the demonic speed of Jeff Thomson and Dennis Lillee. Both Benaud and Mallett stood closer to the bat than other gully fielders and that created catching opportunities for them.

Eknath Solkar—one of the greatest short-leg fielders
Photo Courtesy: Kasturi & Sons

It is a paradox that while one-day cricket and T20 cricket have raised the standards of fielding beyond recognition, one of the great casualties has been catching at short leg. There seem to be no more short-leg specialists. The freshest new Test player is asked to man the position as if it is a punishment posting for new recruits. It was not so earlier. The earliest short leg for spin bowling was Jack Fingleton taking catches off Bill 'Tiger' O'Reilly's fast bouncing leg-breaks and googlies. Fingleton would sometimes be joined by a second short leg, the skipper Vic Richardson himself. After World War II, the best known short-leg fielders were Tony Lock, Garry Sobers and Eknath Solkar.

Tony Lock sharpened his reflexes in the 1950s, fielding to the deadly spin of Jim Laker and Eric Bedser at the Oval where Surrey won eight successive County Championships. Between 1952 and 1956, Stuart Surridge captained Surrey for five seasons when they won the Championship all the five years. While they had champion players like Bedser, Laker, Lock and Peter May, the cutting edge for their success was the captain's example and special emphasis on fielding, especially close catching. Surridge and Lock led a band of exceptional catchers making a difference to the team's success never witnessed before in County cricket. Till then only wicketkeepers had pouched more than 50 catches in a season, but between Surridge and Lock, in those five seasons they took 449 catches and in three of those seasons, Surridge took more than 50 catches.

Good fielders adjust their position after a few balls seeing the bounce and the turn and how a batter is playing at short leg and silly mid-on. Some bowlers and captains are very particular about where exactly they want their fielders to stand. Bill Bowes in his book, *Express Deliveries*, tells this lovely tale of Wilfred Rhodes who adjusted Bowes at short and wide mid-on, in fact coming over and marking the exact spot for Bowes. In the next over, the batter hit a ball so hard and straight to Bowes' tummy that he had to catch it to save his life. So close catching is not only about practice, skill and courage but also about planning, strategy and an understanding between Captain, bowler and fieldsman.

Garry Sobers was marvelous at short leg to the bowling of Lance Gibbs. Even as captain, Sobers would field there. One remembers at Madras, Sobers scurrying back a few steps instead of turning his back when the batters attempted to pull/sweep and in the bargain diving forward to catch what turned out to be an inside edge off the pad. Vivian Richards was brilliant anywhere close in and one of your authors was lucky to witness two absolutely stunning catches that Richards took standing very close at forward short leg at Bangalore in 1974. First Farokh Engineer and then when Sunil Gavaskar clipped off his toes, Richards threw out his left hand, knocked the ball behind, turned, ran two steps and dived to take the falling ball inches off the ground. The absolutely awesome effort late that evening left all of us speechless and shaken. The fearless Solkar and Abid Ali also took full-blooded hits as well as bat-pad half chances in spectacular fashion. All these are stories of days when there were no protective helmets or shin guards. Today's short-leg fielders, even with the full protective paraphernalia, cannot take those catches since they instinctively take evasive action and therefore cannot watch the ball. For a brief while in 2003–2004, India had an excellent forward short leg in Aakash Chopra; he was clearly a specialist who relished the position.

Why are some more comfortable in the slips, others at gully and some inclined to stand at suicidal short leg or leg slip? There is good reason. Slips watch the ball from bowler to the bat and its edge. Gully concentrates on the edge of the bat, anticipating the hard low edge. Short leg watches the back of the batter's legs as the ball is being delivered. Only with constant practice, does one start feeling comfortable in a position and as one takes some good catches in that position; it becomes a preferred choice and one develops a lot of pride in that specialist role.

And so the close-in catcher waits, concentrating ball after ball, for what he makes of the chance that comes his way could decide the course of the match. He hitches up his trousers, crouches and waits.

INDIA'S BEST FIELDERS BEFORE THE ONE-DAY INTERNATIONAL (ODI) ERA

India had few good fielders before the advent of one-day cricket. We wrote about this in ESPNcricinfo.com in August 2009.

Madras, 1956: India versus New Zealand, Polly Umrigar Catches Bert Sutcliffe

Sutcliffe is the mainstay for the Kiwis. If India gets him, they have won half the battle. Well set, Sutcliffe goes for a pull off Jasu Patel and the ball soars high to square leg. Polly Umrigar stationed near the square leg umpire, turns and sprints back 25 meters, looking over his shoulder, all the while making good ground to finally take the catch. Next morning *in The Hindu*, S. K. Gurunathan wrote that unfortunately for Sutcliffe, he hit the ball in the direction of the only fielder in the Indian team who could have attempted and made the catch!

Madras 1964: India versus Australia, Rusi Surti Catches Bill Lawry

Bob Simpson and Bill Lawry are trying to build a sizeable lead and set India a goodish target. Tiger Pataudi, the captain, has Bapu Nadkarni at one end, keeping them on a leash. Patrolling the deep is substitute Rusi Surti, perhaps India' s best outfielder ever, swooping in on everything coming his way and throwing back in one action. When Nadkarni tosses one up, Lawry puts his right leg out and on bent knee swings Nadkarni hard and high to the square leg fence. At the end of the Nadkarni over, Pataudi, Nadkarni and Surti meet mid-pitch and a plan is hatched. They walk away and an over is bowled from the other end. Nadkarni now resumes his next over to Lawry. The third ball is tossed up a bit more; Lawry goes for the big shot again. Even as the ball leaves Nadkarni' s hand, Surti from deep long leg starts sprinting toward his right, deep square leg. Running flat out,

Surti takes a sensational catch and the crowd rises to its feet spontaneously.

Oval, 1971: England versus India, Eknath Solkar Catches Alan Knott

Chandra has ripped the top order of the England team in the second innings. If India gets the troublesome Knott out, victory is theirs. Venkat—Chandra's spin partner in that series—has the usual cordon around the bat. Crouching low at forward short leg is one of the finest in cricket history. Eknath Solkar does not take his eye off the ball ever. As Knott plays forward to Venkat, it is the merest of inside edges—hardly a chance—but Solkar diving full length forward miraculously takes the ball. The innings folds up and India goes on to record their first ever Test win on English soil.

Sydney, 1978: Australia versus India, Madan Lal Catches Peter Toohey

Toohey the outstanding batter in a depleted Aussie side hooks Karsan Ghavri to long leg. Substitute Madan Lal—he had lost his place in the side to Ghavri—takes off from fine leg, 25 yards of the finest sprint, and even as the ball is falling to the ground a yard inside the ropes, dives, somersaults and comes up triumphantly holding aloft the ball. Readers will instantly recognize that to dive after a sprint is extremely difficult, to catch the ball diving like that is miraculous. Next day, Bill O'Reilly in the Australian media simply called it the greatest catch he had seen.

To embark on an exercise to shortlist the best Indian fielders of the times before the advent of ODIs in the 1970s may at best yield a dozen names. India in the 1950s–1970s threw up some gifted batters and bowlers but the great fielder was almost an apparition. The most often heard comment on radio those days when a boundary was hit off an Indian bowler was 'and the fielder escorts the ball to the boundary.' Grounds on which we learnt our cricket were bumpy and grassless. We grew up playing cricket on gravel grounds and our natural instinct for self-preservation ensured that by the time we reached college we had developed an aversion for diving to stop the ball. So while being self-deprecating about our fielding, we are not without empathy.

So, before the ODI era, who were the Indian fielders good enough to be bracketed with the best fielders of their times? The first 20 years of India's Test cricket, the era of Colonel C. K. Nayudu, Vijay Merchant and Lala Amarnath—yield just a couple of names—Syed Mushtaq Ali, the cavalier opening bat and Gul Mohammed an outstanding fielder and easily the best for India in his time. When Test cricket resumed after World War II, India's fielding was marginally better. Luckily we had a sprinkling of players from the Services—all fit and agile—and that helped India look better on the field. Hemu Adhikari easily the best among them and his colleagues C. V. Gadkari and V. M. Muddiah showed the benefit of training and serious fielding drills. An electric cover point, Adhikari later was the first Indian team manager to put a premium on fitness and fielding.

In the 1950s, our fielding came to be represented by Polly Umrigar. Back then, when Subhash Gupte, Vinoo Mankad and Ghulam Ahmed bowled spin for India they had just one special catcher, Polly Umrigar. The tall Parsi was absolutely precious and probably the only one who could be counted upon to take difficult catches both in the outfield and close in. Madhav Apte in the outfield was the other good fielder. Later into the 1960s, we had Nadkarni close in, and, Surti, Pataudi and Chandu Borde in the outfield. It was the advent of Pataudi in 1960 that put a stop to that depressing spectacle of Indian fielders jogging to merely fetch the ball back from the ropes. Pataudi the young captain, despairingly surveying his team told them, all I expect from you is to see dirty trouser knees at the end of the day. Pataudi set the example, and apart from his electric fielding also plucked astonishing catches from his position at covers or mid-wicket. In the Delhi Test match of 1964—we recall this as though we saw it yesterday—a cover drive by Mike Smith, the Marylebone Cricket Club (MCC) captain, struck sweetly flew just inches off the ground. Pataudi swooped forward and took the ball even as it was dying in front of him. Some wickets must be credited only to the fielder—this was one.

As Indian cricket came of age in the early 1970s it had a formidable close-in cordon manned by Solkar, Abid Ali, Venkat and Wadekar. It was the Solkar era. When Solkar passed away, the most moving tributes came from the spinners who knew that he provided them a unique cutting edge standing at forward short leg. Solkar had courage, anticipation, reflexes and the God-given ability to go for anything with both hands thus giving him a better chance to make catches. There has been none like Solkar. Venkat had equally good reflexes and the ability to spring up from his crouching position at gully or in the slips and took overhead catches with nonchalance. And Gavaskar too was pretty safe at first slip and folks would remember he pouched four catches in that memorable World Cup final against West Indies in 1983.

Picking the good Indian fielders of that pre-ODI era might be an effort. Unfortunately, to pick the poor fielders of those day s is not at all difficult—Ghulam Ahmed among the worst; Vijay Merchant, Rusi Modi, Vijay Manjrekar and Dilip Sardesai all poor fielders. A whole lot of them were short and portly—Chandu Sarwate, Vinoo Mankad, Subhash Gupte, Pankaj Roy, the list goes on—and were not quick movers. Some who looked lithe and elegant—M. L. Jaisimha for instance—unfortunately did not take their fielding seriously enough.

It was only since the advent of one-day cricket in the 1980s that India's cricketers ran up laundry bills. And the late 1970s and 1980s threw up a line of excellent fielders—Brijesh Patel, Madan Lal, Yashpal Sharma, Yajurvindra Singh, Kapil Dev, Azharuddin and some others.

Fielding is something one can work on and get consistently better at. As we get better, we begin to enjoy it even more. Both of us found catching drills so thrilling that even when we were into our forties and playing nothing but office cricket, we would exult like children while holding a difficult catch. Raghunath for instance would forever be indebted to his league captain Rangan who gave such intensive close catching practice that he became an absolutely fearless short-leg fielder. Our grounds have improved and diving in the outfield is no longer fraught with risk. Although even today we do not have a fielding side that is comparable to the South Africans and Australians, we are capable of putting up a good fielding outfit with the likes of Suresh Raina, Virat Kohli, Ajinkya Rahane, Yuvraj Singh, Ravindra Jadeja and others. The one glaring weakness is at short leg. There is no one fit to tie the shoe laces of the peerless Solkar.

2

THE LESSER KNOWN FACETS OF KAPIL'S BRILLIANCE

This is one of the more difficult essays we have attempted. So much has been said and written about Kapil Dev that the reader might well skip this piece, saying, 'Oh we have heard and read it all before.' But we think we are going to discuss a couple of facets of Kapil Dev's wondrous abilities that have not received adequate attention. So bear with us while we unfold our story and we hope it is worth your time.

Whenever Kapil is mentioned, Indians usually recall two images. One is that of Kapil sprinting back many yards that summer evening at Lords to take the most important catch in Indian cricket history. The other is that of Kapil, 1,000 watt smile, holding aloft the World Cup and his endearingly inept attempt to open and spray the champagne. If you prod some more, other images will follow—of this great spell of bowling or that fantastic innings or those four sixes in an over from Eddie Hemmings and so on. This story hopes to jog other memories of Kapil in readers' minds. The two facets of Kapil's genius (the only time we will use the word in this essay) that we will discuss here, pertain to batting. The first of these is the ability to rotate the strike. Kapil in this aspect of batting was on a pedestal all on his own. Kapil, for many readers, will conjure up images of big hits for six or booming drives for fours. This is not illusory because Kapil had an awesome strike rate of 95.1 in ODIs which meant he certainly biffed them a long way. But hidden or lost behind such imagery is the Kapil who hardly took a minute to settle down and before you knew it had already pushed along with a single here and a couple there, with not a sniff of violence. Why was Kapil so uncannily good at this? Quite simply because he had an innate sense of timing and a God-given gift for placing the ball. Rarely would he push the ball straight to the fielder. It was always a few yards to the left, right or short of the fielder. He was able to do this because he was technically sound and never was this more evident than when he drove the ball. This ability of his to rotate strike was there for all of us to see in both Test cricket and ODIs. Was he really that good? Do the figures support our fulsome praise? You bet they do!

In ODIs, Kapil faced 3,979 balls to score 3,783 runs for that strike rate of 95.1. Of these, he hit 291 balls for fours and 67 for sixes. If you remove these 358 balls that Kapil dispatched for fours and sixes, you will find that he scored the remaining 2,217 runs of 3,621 balls. In other words, he ticked along at a strike rate of 61.2 even of those balls which had not gone for a four or a six. What this kind of a rotating strike rate ensured was that there were fewer dot balls; the score board kept moving; he turned over the strike regularly to his partner. In fact, he was peerless at this facet of the game and we say this after studying similar statistics for the other three all-rounders of his time—Ian Botham, Imran Khan and Richard Hadlee; the best one-day batters and finishers of his time—Dean Jones, Javed Miandad and Viv Richards; and the best finishers of modern times—Michael Bevan, Mike Hussey and Mahendra Singh Dhoni. Just for a lark, we also compared Kapil's rotating strike rate with that of Adam Gilchrist and Virender Sehwag. None of them has a rotating strike rate that is better than Kapil. The nearest to Kapil in this respect are Hussey, Bevan and Dhoni, who are considered as super finishers. Interested readers could perhaps extend this by comparing the rotating strike rates

Kapil Dev in action during the year 1991
Photo Courtesy: Kasturi & Sons

of great batters like Sachin Tendulkar, Ricky Ponting, Brian Lara and others and in case any of them exceeds 61.2, we will be very interested!

The other facet of Kapil's batting acumen that has somehow escaped attention has been his absolutely wonderful running between wickets. One aspect of cricket that is best appreciated sitting at the ground rather than in front of the TV is running between wickets. Both of us have had the pleasure of watching Kapil Dev's Test hundreds at Chennai against Australia and West Indies. Kapil always had so much time even for the sharpest single that we cannot recall him having to do anything desperate. Alive and alert to the single he would simply lope across with a big grin on his face. What was particularly laudable was that he did that in a team where only Mohammad Azharuddin among his teammates those days was a gazelle. Kapil would force the laid back Dilip Vengsarkar and Sandeep Patil to run with him, both for his runs as well as theirs. Kapil would twirl his bat at the end of the run; Vengsarkar would lean on his bat to catch his breath. And yet Kapil's judgment of a run was so good that one cannot recall a run out. Judging a run was something innate; something completely natural to him. How good was he? In a word, simply sensational. In 184 Test innings, Kapil was not run out even once. It is a track record that obviously cannot be bettered! We would like to go out on a limb and state that he would have been involved in very few run outs of his partners too. In ODIs, Kapil was run out 10 times in 221 innings. On this parameter he is behind Gilchrist, Botham, Hadlee and Richards but ahead of the other batters whom we have taken for comparison.

Kapil was ahead of his time. He added so much more value to his hitting through his running between wickets and the rotating of strike. His strike rate of 95.1 of course stands the Test of time—only the likes of Shahid Afridi, Sehwag and Gilchrist have a strike rate better than his. Kapil's rotating strike rate is superior to all even today. Even at a time when Indians are world champions at the one-day game, they know that rotating the strike and running well between wickets are two aspects where they could do better. The import of Kapil's phenomenal ability in these two facets of batting cannot be lost.

We finish off with this precious nugget: Kapil Dev never missed a Test match because of injury or fitness reasons in a career that spanned 131 Tests spread over 16 years. It is another facet of his career—this astonishing fitness for a fast bowler—where he towers over his contemporaries as well as present day pace bowlers. We leave you with some ODI figures to mull over in Table 2.1.

TABLE 2.1: Kapil—Marvelous at Rotating the Strike

Sl. no.	*Player*	*Career span*	*ODI innings*	*Strike rate*	*Rotating strike rate*	*% Run outs*
1.	Kapil Dev	1978–1994	225	95.1	61.2	5.1
2.	Mike Hussey	2004–2009	119	86.2	57.4	6.3
3.	M. Bevan	1994–2004	232	74.2	56.3	9.2
4.	M. S. Dhoni	2004–2009	145	90.2	56.0	6.3
5.	Viv Richards	1974–1991	187	90.2	53.0	3.0
6.	Imran Khan	1971–1992	175	72.7	52.7	8.6
7.	Dean Jones	1984–1994	164	72.6	52.6	11.2
8.	Richard Hadlee	1973–1990	115	75.5	51.1	3.1
9.	Javed Miandad	1975–1996	233	67.0	50.7	11.0
10.	Chris Cairns	1991–2006	215	84.3	49.3	8.8
11.	Adam Gilchrist	1996–2008	287	96.9	47.3	3.9
12.	Ian Botham	1976–1992	116	79.1	43.7	2.6
13.	V. Sehwag	2000–2009	205	101.9	42.9	8.0

Source: Data from espncricinfo.com. Analysis and tabular compilation by authors.

3

FAB FOUR: ONCE IN A LIFETIME LINEUP

There is something extremely seedy about the way the inexorable finish to the glittering careers of India's finest ever quartet of middle order batters is being dissected with complete insensitivity. Compare this to the time when we peacefully bid adieu to the other fab four 30 years ago, the incomparable and finest ever quartet of spinners.

Ah but those were different times! The mind goes back to the 1960s and 1970s—the era of this unmatchable spin quartet. No live television coverage for almost the entire part of their career, those were the days when the fruity voice of Pearson Surita and the nasal drone of Ananda Rao in India, and the vivid description of John Arlott in England and Alan McGilvray in Australia brought them into our lives. Remember Arlott in the summer of 1971 describe S. Venkataraghavan and B. S. Chandrasekhar 'Here comes Venkat, tall, slightly flat footed, five languid steps, left hand reaching for the sky...' and 'Chandra, shirt tail flapping in the breeze, sleeves buttoned down, turns, begins his run, 1, 2, 3...11, past Umpire...'

Yes, romantic times those...we won a match or two now and then and were happy to hug those memories. And then we won some more and we realized that these four magicians were in fact setting up opportunities for victories more frequently than ever before. And so this quartet was forged over 15 long years. Erapalli Prasanna the eldest came into the Indian side in 1962, Chandra in 1964, Venkat in 1965 and Bishan Singh Bedi in 1966. Each of them made their debut at age 20 or earlier. For their entire careers four spinners, brothers in arms, but fighting forever for three places in the team.

Each was poetry in motion...fluid, smooth, economical of action and with unending guile. Bedi the supreme artist, warm hearted, always the first to applaud the sixer from the batter but owner of the best arm ball in cricket history; Chandra the least demonstrative, quiet, magical, unplayable destroyer; Prasanna, cunning, cocky, plotting all the time to make a fool of the batsman; Venkat, of fierce tigerish resolve, almost a fast bowler's temperament to complement his spinner's brain, bowling for team satisfaction than for his own ego...

By the time the Indian team went to Pakistan in 1978—to resume cricket ties after 18 long years—it seemed that these four icons had been playing for ever. Prasanna was 38, Venkat and Chandra 33, and Bedi just a year younger. And between them they seemed to have bowled a million overs! They had bamboozled Garry Sobers and Clive Lloyd, lulled Ian Chappell and Doug Walters to doom; toyed with Keith Fletcher and John Edrich...They seemed to have taken every wicket for India in the last 15 years! But 15 years is a long time and these intelligent men knew that they were approaching the end of illustrious careers.

What they did not know was that in a matter of weeks, just three Test matches to be precise, the quartet would hurtle from the twilight of their careers to oblivion. What these maestros received in Pakistan was a hiding of soul searing proportions from Javed Miandad and Zaheer Abbas, Asif Iqbal and Majid Khan. No newspaper devoted columns to discuss the imminent demise of the quartet. The end was almost instantaneous for three of the four spinners. Prasanna never played again after returning from Pakistan. Bedi and Chandra made a token appearance in a couple of Tests and were dropped. Venkat, the warrior, kept plugging away for a few more years but must have been a lonely man missing his three comrades till he too faded away. There is perhaps a lesson for us here from the way the spin quartet went out of our lives. None of the fab four spinners ever announced their retirement from the Test cricket. They were fearless samurai; when the time came for them to be dropped they accepted this with dignity and the press gave them the space and the respect that they deserved.

When four great spinners with 900 wickets between them could go with grace and dignity, is it too much to ask that four great batters with 35,000 runs between them also go the same way? We live in noisy strident television rating point (TRP) times, but surely we can lower our tones, stand aside, and salute them as they go back to the pavilion one last time. Sachin Tendulkar, Rahul Dravid, Sourav Ganguly and V. V. S. Laxman, rare gems all and for all four to be playing at the same time for India.... We will never know how blessed our country was till they are all gone.

4

MEN LIKE DRAVID: TRUST THEM WITH YOUR LIFE

Some of the best of cricket writing in recent times have been the essays about Rahul Dravid after he announced his retirement, each a genuine tribute to a man and cricketer who left the game richer than he found it. For Indian cricket, Dravid was their Horatius on the Bridge, the defiant hero whom India trusted the most when cricketing honor was at stake. Steely purpose, unwavering resolve, fierce concentration, limitless patience, courage, skill and above all that sweat on the brow—there was an entire lesson in life in his batting. Even as Dravid erected a barricade for his beloved India, his movements were always classical and graceful. When he unfurled the cover drive, it would be picture perfect; when he drove into the onside, it was a sight for the gods. In simple cricketing terms, if one were to list the five best onedrop batters of all time, Dravid would be among them. If you were to rank them on style and elegance, Dravid would be there and if you were to rank them on their demeanor and conduct on the ground, he would perhaps top the list. Every which way, quite simply, Dravid is among the world's greatest batters of all time and also among the finest ambassadors of the game.

Don't you want to hear about him from himself? We agreed to meet at the Clubhouse at the Chinnaswamy Stadium in

Bengaluru at 10.30 a.m. Dravid in fact turns up a few minutes early for our meeting. Welcoming us with a smile, he insists on ensuring we are seated comfortably and have our coffee before beginning our conversation. Dravid has that special quality of creating an atmosphere of 'saukhya' (sorry, we cannot find an appropriate word in English), and the conversation flows comfortably and amiably. Everyone knows that Rahul is intelligent, erudite and articulate, but to hear him speak was to understand that he was also blessed with wisdom.

We asked Dravid about his batting.

There is no magic formula or mantra. I was born with a good temperament and concentration came naturally to me as a kid. Even before I became a professional cricketer, I made this attribute count because I knew it is important. I had the determination to make good. I practice for long hours and I get a routine going to help me focus ball by ball. I had an ingrained value for my wicket. I was my school's best batter and therefore right from those days you know how important your wicket is for the team. The other key thing is to relax off the field so that I conserve emotional energy.

About the technique and methods of practice.

To begin with I was born with some talent for the game; it is a God-given gift. I find net practice invaluable. I am personally not a great fan of the bowling machine although I have of course used it. It is just that I find purposeful practice hugely beneficial. A lot of kids practice a lot but is there a focus on learning from the practice? I call purposeful practice as being 'cricket smart'. Technique is important and my own coach in my early years stressed on it. I am by nature an analytical person and think about my game a lot. But in time, I also recognized not to overdo it and realized one has to trust oneself and one's game. Experience teaches you and it is critical that one is watching and learning all the time. And what is important is also to recognize that there will be some areas which you will never crack and be comfortable with that realization.

Rahul Dravid standing his ground during the third day of the final India vs West Indies Test match, 2011

Photo Courtesy: Kasturi & Sons

How is it that Dravid, Tendulkar, Laxman, Kumble are such splendid ambassadors for India and the game?

Balance in life is the key; treating success and failure equally, and being able to treat fame, adulation and money with a sense of perspective and balance. We all came together at the time. We fed off each other; we admired each other, and found huge inspiration from each other's achievements. On the field, our responsibility is paramount because we represent the country and we must ensure that we adhere to the code of conduct and code of honor. We have a certain responsibility in the public domain because we are the nation's cricketers but people should be realistic in their expectations from their cricketing heroes. We never tried to be 'role models'; it is dangerous to be a role model for we are only human and make mistakes as much as the next person.

It is easy to predict that this man will have a distinguished second innings and play more important roles in society and nation.

We decide to extend this essay into a tribute to those batters who like Dravid were trusted the most by their country. Each country has their Horatius. Not all played the game as gracefully as Dravid or with his sense of fair play. Some were pugnacious, some ugly to watch but at the end of it what they shared with Dravid was that they simply refused to sell their wicket. They fought, scrapped and kept vigil to carry their country to safety when defeat threatened.

Our list of 'who will bat for me when my life is at stake' is not exhaustive but the fact that we want to name just a few implies that these are our first choices. The one departure from some of our other essays is that we will not go earlier in cricket history than the 1950s. In alphabetical order, they are: Ken Barrington, Allan Border, Shivnarine Chanderpaul, Andy Flower, Sunil Gavaskar, Jacques Kallis, Kumara Sangakkara and Steve Waugh.

Andy Flower was all that separated Zimbabwe from a rout every time they played. Downturned lips that gave him a permanently peeved look and 'I have booked bed and breakfast on this pitch' intent so plain for all to see that the fielding captains left him well alone and tried to dismiss batters at the other end. Flower has a much higher percentage of unbeaten innings than most batsmen, because he was left stranded at the end of the innings. Deft and skillful, he was more the tragic last man standing than triumphant hero because Zimbabwe was the weakest team and went down often despite Flower's fiercest defense.

Similarly, Shivnaraine Chanderpaul was the lone man among the ruins more times than we can remember during the last decade for the West Indies. When he made his debut against England, Ted Corbett wrote that the helmet was so big for his small head that it settled down around his ears. But he made 50 after 50, every time he came to the crease. In many of India's games against West Indies, Chanderpaul has thwarted them. Five centuries and 22 fifties in his second innings against the best of opposition show how he prized his wicket and fought tooth and nail. He might have looked ungainly, taking guard as though the bowler is delivering from mid-wicket but Mike Atherton—the former England captain and now a commentator and writer—in a memorable turn of phrase, said, 'you could balance an egg on top of his head' to describe how still Chanderpaul's head is when he plays the ball. No wonder, he kept notching up scores and many times twice the next highest score in his team. Chanderpaul came to Test cricket two years before Dravid and soldiered on for far longer. A team usually loses a match if it fails in its first innings. After that it is an uphill defensive battle—to bat long hard hours in the third or fourth innings of the Test match to prevent defeat on a wearing pitch. It is natural that our list would feature stalwarts who regularly put in sterling performances when the chips were down. Once in a few decades, a team will pull off an improbable win, and once in a century, conjure a victory like India did in Kolkata 2001. And if that reminds readers that Laxman is not on our list—well he is on the 'very very special' list of players who have snatched the most victories from positions of defeat. He is the Houdini, we are talking here of Horatius!

Kumara Sangakkara has a dozen centuries in his second innings—six on his homeland and six in the opposition territory. His greatest innings was 192 against Australia in Brisbane in November 2007. As Sri Lanka chased an impossible 516 runs in the fourth innings, Sangakkara almost raised visions of a victory till an error by umpire Rudi Koertzen ended his innings. At the end of match ceremonies, Koertzen apologized to Sangakkara, for he knew what Sangakkara might have achieved if he, Koertzen, had not felled him. Gifted with elegance and timing, Sangakkara is the best blend of style and substance. His batting average in the second innings on opposition soil is nearly 53—which only a handful of batters in cricket history can boast of. He of course shares something very special with Dravid. Both are extremely well read and erudite. Dravid's Bradman oration at Canberra in December 2011 and Sangakkara's MCC Spirit of Cricket Cowdrey lecture in July 2011 are two of the finest ever speeches by cricketers in the long history of the game.

Jacques Kallis had an average of less than 23 in his first 10 Tests but even then he had the calmness of a monk and such perfectly organized defense that it was obvious it would be most difficult for any opposition to prize him out. First innings or second, spin or pace, Australia or India, Kallis just grinds away and never ever looks like getting out. There is something so resolute and immovable about him at the crease that unless he is removed, victory for the bowling team is unthinkable. Six second innings centuries on every major cricketing opposition soil and a batting average of 56, which is nearly as good as his overall average of 57, is proof enough. His ability to soak up pressure and play the maximum number of balls as did Dravid, blunted the opposition attacks. If one asked any opposing captain, whose wicket you most wanted, the answer would be K.A.L.L.I.S

Allan Border made his debut in a disintegrating Australian team. For six years, Australia battled to save Test matches and Border was at the center of them all. In describing Border's heroics, it is almost impossible to separate batter Border from captain Border. Sleeves buttoned down, scruffy beard, an open shouldered stance, minimum back lift, a shuffle, ball dropped at the crease and ready for the next; almost similar movements, no flourish but the ball is put away to point boundary and he is ready for the next. Shepherding his flock, prodding them, growling at them, without Border that Australian team would never have climbed back so quickly. Border was less stylish than most of the left handers. But if there are two days to go in the Test match, the target an impossible 445 runs and Malcolm Marshall, Joel Garner and Michael Holding coming for the kill, whom do you want in your corner? Border always had to fight first innings and second innings. Here is a Border epic, the second Test between West Indies, the world's best team then and Australia at Port of Spain in March 1984. West Indies put Australia in to bat and knocked them over for 255. Border came to the crease at 16 for three, batted nearly six hours and returned unbeaten on 98. Rain had taken out a day's play, so when West Indies piled up 468 they declared so that they could have a day and more to try and bowl out Australia. Border thwarted them with a century that occupied five hours at the crease and a draw was achieved with the tail-enders providing him rare and precious support.

Ken Barrington was not the obdurate 'stonewaller' that he is most remembered as. He was actually a free stroke player, much like his jovial, happy self, off the field. But England in the 1950s and 1960s needed him to play the sheet anchor role and none could play that as well as he did. He averaged over 51 in his second innings outside England and had three hundreds, two of these in Australia. In dire circumstances, like in India in 1963–1964, he held an end up and ensured the rest did not have to pad up since they were all down most of the time with upset tummies!

Steve Waugh and Dravid's mutual admiration is famous. Dravid sought Waugh's advice throughout India's tour of Australia in 1998/99 and later Waugh insisted that only Dravid write the foreword to his autobiography. Like Dravid, his average for the second innings is much lower than his first innings, but both have done the rescue act innumerable times in the first innings. Waugh's transition to greatness began on the Australian tour to West Indies in 1995. He went there with glaring weakness against the fast bouncing ball. He won that battle—first with himself and then with the West Indian speedsters. Man of the series and a reputation as a warrior of the finest steel. Around 35 per cent of his runs have come batting at no. 6 or lower at an average close to 50 and that is another sign of a battler who never said die.

And now to the incomparable Sunil Manohar Gavaskar, bare headed, five feet four inches, squaring up to Marshall, Holding, Andy Roberts, Garner, Imran, Willis, Thomson and Lillee. How superbly organized he always was; never ever hit on the head; the classical straight drive, the clip off his legs, the quick single. Among the batters in our list, Gavaskar has the most staggering exploits. His second innings batting average on opposition soil is 61.45, while his average batting in the fourth innings is an almost Bradmanesque 72.21. Nine of his centuries have come batting second for India on foreign grounds with two double hundreds. India's first ever series win against West Indies in 1971 was secured and protected by Gavaskar's century in the fourth innings of the fourth Test at Barbados and his double hundred in the third innings of the fifth Test at Port of Spain denying the West Indians any chance of a comeback. If Gavaskar's phenomenal debut is Indian cricket lore, his double hundred at the Oval in 1979 as India chased 438 to win and fell short by 9 runs is a story scripted in heaven. Gavaskar and fourth innings heroics are inseparable. The most poignant of them all is his last Test innings. On a minefield of a pitch at Bangalore against Imran's Pakistan, Gavaskar played one of the greatest fourth innings. India fell agonizingly short by 16 runs. Pakistan knew the match was in their bag when Gavaskar was eighth man dismissed, caught off left-arm spinner Iqbal Qasim for 96. It was an innings of the greatest possible skill against the turning ball on a spiteful wicket.

Simon Barnes talking of Cowdrey in his book *A Book of Heroes* said:

> Perhaps heroism is at its best when it is futile—when a person is brave, makes sacrifices and is prepared to give everything-and-all to no avail.... Heroism is at its finest when there is nothing in it for the hero: only pain, humiliation and defeat. But the hero prefers to embrace such things, rather than take any of the easy options.

But it can be said of each one of the heroes in this essay.

Note: As the era of Kallis, Dravid, Ponting and others came to an end, they passed the baton to worthy successors, such as the impregnable but positive Steve Smith. Along with him, of course is, Kane Williamson, Joe Root and Virat Kohli, who carried the middle order on their shoulders with such composure and stylish stroke play that they never made it appear burdensome. And the 'Trust them with your life' club can also make place for dour and dependable fighters like Cheteshwar Pujara. It is an ever growing elite club.

5

ROLLS ROYCE AND OTHER TERRORS: RIGHT-ARM FAST

'Typhoon Tyson,' 'Whispering Death,' 'White Lightning,' 'Rawalpindi Express'—each is an epithet to describe that ultimate terror in cricket—the truly frightening fast bowler. Those who have watched cricket since the 1950s will swear that there was no more thrilling sight than Wesley Hall and Roy Gilchrist bowling together. Hall, shirt unbuttoned till the navel, gold cross glistening on ebony chest and a magnificent athlete's run of around 60 yards from near the boundary line for every delivery. His new ball partner, Gilchrist was shorter and smaller than Hall, but he was terrifying. Mean and vicious, he had a nasty bouncer and also bowled beamers at will. At Madras, in that Test in 1959, the unforgettable moments were when the West Indies after batting first, came to field. These two fast bowlers ran ahead on either side of the ground and there was a hush as each of them measured their run, almost to the boundary ropes. Both Hall and Gilchrist bowled bouncers that sailed over the leaping wicketkeeper Gerry Alexander's gloves for four byes. Even today as we relive those times, we can hear the crescendo of the Indian crowd as Hall and Gilchrist ran in to bowl. That unimaginable mix of thrill, trepidation, awe and anticipation is indescribable. There were no speed guns those days but surely Hall and Gilchrist must have bowled at close to 100 miles an hour.

We attempt to write on fast bowling with the humbling acceptance that only pale justice can be done to it in any one essay. Let us begin with some facts and figures* to place this in perspective.

- Right-arm fast bowlers alone have taken around 60 per cent of the Test wickets which implies that all other forms of bowling put together account for the remaining 40 per cent of Test wickets.
- In over 2,000 Tests played so far, right-arm fast bowlers have taken over 33,000 wickets.
- There are 270 right-arm fast bowlers with over 30 Test wickets. Of them, 85 have in fact over 100 Test wickets.
- Of the 10 best ever bowling performances in an innings, six belong to right-arm fast bowlers. Similarly, 9 of the 17 best ever performances in a Test match belong to right-arm fast bowlers.
- The best ever bowling average in cricket history belongs to Lohmann—an incredible 10.8.
- Unlike other forms of bowling, here one has to contend with the fact that there are serious sub-classifications: the tearaway fast bowlers, the fast medium accurate ones; the classical seam bowlers, the medium pacers and even those who run up to bowl what in current parlance is called the 110 km/hour bowlers. There is also a clear need to separately view bowlers of different eras.

We present in Table 5.1 a summary of fast bowling data in five eras: (a) from 1877 (when Test cricket began) to the beginning of World War I; (b) between the two World wars; (c) from 1947 to 1970; (d) from 1970 to 2000 and (e) since 2000. Each era too was so different: in rules of the game, the nature of the pitches, the equipment and gear available to players.

---

* The analysis presented here is based on the data that we downloaded when we wrote the essay. This caveat applies throughout the book, wherever we have presented statistics and analysis.

TABLE 5.1: Right-arm Fast Bowling across Five Eras: Figures That Tell a Story

	1877–1914	*1920–1939*	*1946–1970*	*1971–1999*	*Since 2000*
No. of test matches played	134	140	401	805	1,035
No. of matches played by bowlers>30 wickets	318	802	1,333	4,908	4,650
No. of bowlers>30 wickets	17	23	46	120	129
No. of bowlers>100 wickets	4	0	13	47	45
Total wickets taken	1,193	1,248	4,053	15,095	16,879
No. of 10 wickets/match	26	7	25	82	48
No. of 5 wickets/innings	94	70	185	645	561
Best bowling average	10.8	19.3	17.9	20.7	17.7
Best strike rate	34.1	43.3	49.4	36.9	35.3

Source: Data from espncricinfo.com. Analysis and tabular compilation by authors.

Some of these figures are stunning and we must address at least one incredible bit of statistics in the table. For example, what kind of a bowler was he with the bowling average of just 10.8 runs for a wicket? What kind of magician was he? Well, that is George Alfred Lohmann, born in 1865, who played his cricket between 1886 and 1896. He was just medium pace but seamed the ball both ways, with a lot of variations. The pitches those days were not of good quality and also left open to the elements and we must take this into account while reading into the bowling statistics of the early era. Lohmann was devastating. The best ever figures in an innings for a fast bowler belongs to him: 9 for 28. He played 18 Tests and he took 10 or more wickets in 5 of those Tests.

Who were the great fast bowlers of these eras? The task becomes progressively more difficult with each era but in Table 5.2 is our short list and then some analysis and discussion.

The first great fast bowler was Spofforth. Without being very fast, he still earned the name 'Demon Spofforth'. He was a match-winning bowler, taking 10 wickets in a match on four occasions and had an average of less than 20. He is also the first bowler in cricket history to claim a hat trick. Among bowlers of that initial era, his name has magic and mystique.

TABLE 5.2: The Great Right-arm Fast Bowlers from Spofforth to Steyn

In the first era, till 1914	Freddie Spofforth, G. H. Lohmann and S. F. Barnes
In the era between the two world wars	J. M. Gregory, Harold Larwood, Learie Constantine and Bill Bowes
Between 1946 and 1970	Alec Bedser, Keith Miller, Ray Lindwall, Brian Statham, Fazal Mahmood, Fred Trueman, Neil Adcock, Frank Tyson, Wesley Hall, Peter Pollock and Graham McKenzie, and Roy Gilchrist

Between 1970 and 1999	John Snow, Sarfraz Nawaz, Imran Khan, Dennis Lillee, Jeff Thomson, Richard Hadlee, Andy Roberts, Michael Holding, Bob Willis, Ian Botham, Kapil Dev, Colin Croft, Joel Garner, Malcolm Marshall, Terry Alderman, Courtney Walsh, Craig McDermott, Curtly Ambrose, Waqar Younis, Allan Donald and Javagal Srinath
Since 2000	Shaun Pollock, Dale Steyn, Lasith Malinga, Jimmy Anderson, Umar Gul, Shane Bond, Brett Lee, Andrew Flintoff, Glen McGrath, Shoib Akhtar, Makhaya Ntini, Mathew Hoggard, Stuart Broad, Pat Cummins, Mohammed Shami, Kagiso Rabada, Tim Southee, Josh Hazlewood and Jasprit Bumrah

Source: Data from espncricinfo.com. Analysis and tabular compilation by authors

When fast bowlers hunt in packs, they are devastating. West Indies dominated world cricket from the mid-1970s to the mid-1990s with the greatest galaxy of fast bowlers of all time. For those of us who want to understand how West Indies came to create their fearsome quartet, there can be no better source than the movie, *Fire in Babylon.*

Similarly Australia's 'Invincibles' under Donald Bradman had Lindwall and Miller. England had its best times when Trueman and Statham bowled together. Pakistan first became a force to reckon with when Imran Khan and Sarfraz Nawaz formed a genuinely good combination. And then there are many more.

There ought to be absolutely no doubt that the top dozen right-arm fast bowlers of the last 40 years are: Malcolm Marshall, Dennis Lillee, Glen McGrath, Dale Steyn, Waqar Younis, Richard Hadlee, Imran Khan, Curtly Ambrose, Michael Holding, Joel Garner, Allan Donald and Andy Roberts. But we must make room for Shaun Pollock, Ian Botham, Courtney Walsh and Kapil Dev too. Was the best of them Marshall? We think so. We saw him for the first time in 1979, making his Test debut—a callow youth of promise when he came with Alvin Kallicharan's team. By the time he came again in 1983, he was the world's best fast bowler. Shorter than his comrades, he had a bustling run to the crease, a whippy action and would bowl both in and outswing, from over and round the wicket. He was very quick, but because of his repertoire the speed became only the crowning glory. In fact it is this 'completeness' that raises Marshall to a pedestal of his own. But history tells us that he could face competition for this title from S. F. Barnes. Barnes, according to records and reports, was the finest exponent of in-cutters and inswing. Tall and strongly built, he was deadly accurate. He nailed batters repeatedly with his leg cutters and in-cutters and break-backs. They say that he never had even one off day in his entire career. With the ball he was England's most precious match winner.

For sheer poetry and grace of action, we need look no further than Holding. Umpires have sworn that when Holding ran in to bowl, they would know he had arrived at the bowling crease only as he went past them. He was called the Rolls Royce of fast bowling. It made perfect sense, because the classic Rolls Royce advertisement claimed that when the car ran at 100 mph, the only sound you heard was the ticking of the clock. Competition for Holding comes from Ray Lindwall.

Michael Holding, nicknamed the 'Whispering Death' in action

Photo Credit: Kasturi & Sons

Those who have watched Lindwall, insist that there was none to beat Lindwall for the classicism of his action. He delivered from a perfect side—on position to get late and accurate swing. We got a glimpse of Lindwall at Madras in 1956. Though past his best, Lindwall nailed seven Indian batters with a display of terrific fast bowling—the control, late swing and pace made him unplayable. There is a picture of Lindwall in Bradman's *Farewell to Cricket*. It is a side-on delivery stride of Lindwall just about to release the ball. The photograph captures the magic of his action.

It is instructive that some of these famed fast bowling combinations were forged only after those countries suffered heavy defeats. Lloyd created his feared battery of fast bowlers after his team was soundly defeated in a one-sided series in Australia in 1975–1976. Similarly, Ian Chappell, the piratical captain of Australia, formed his fast bowling battering ram of Lillee, Thomson, Max Walker and Gary Gilmour after Australia returned home from South Africa in 1970 with a 0–4 drubbing. Thomson was frighteningly quick with a slinging action while Lillee was classical. Lillee overcame career threatening stress fracture of the back to reinvent himself. From a tearaway fast bowler he became the complete bowler, and till Marshall came along, was considered the finest fast bowler. It is for Indians a real regret that we never saw Lillee and Thomson bowl in India.

Indian spectators also sadly did not see Fred Trueman in action. He reduced India to 0 for 4 in 1952 at Headingley, and Indian batters had never faced such pace before. Trueman had a lovely action and an ideal outswinger and all we have are pictures of Trueman's divine follow through, his mop of thick black hair falling over his eyes. Boycott, his teammate at Yorkshire and England, emphatically says that Trueman, Lillee and Marshall were the best fast bowlers he ever faced.

The quiet heroes are the relentlessly accurate fast medium bowlers who bowl long spells against the wind. They keep the pressure on from their end, not providing even a moment's respite. That is why Brian Statham of England is considered among the greatest of fast bowlers. Freddie Trueman might have spectacularly knocked over the stumps and sent batter scurrying back to the pavilion, but he did that because Statham made life miserable for the batters at the other end. Alec Bedser was another of those who bowled at less than express pace but carried England on his back for many years. He had the stamina of a horse and carried a huge work load. In fact in his Test career, Bedser bowled an average of 29 overs in an innings, which is more than anyone else with over 150 Test wickets.

Waqar Younis was perhaps the most effective bowler against the lower half of any batting side. He produced fast accurate yorkers at will and with the old ball reverse swung them to crush batters' toes. For a few years in the 1990s, all sides against Pakistan were virtually all out when their sixth wicket fell, for Waqar with Wasim Akram, simply polished off the tail in no time.

Australian fast bowler
Glenn McGrath in action, Cricket World Cup 1999
Photo Courtesy: Kasturi & Sons

Shaun Pollock, with that amazingly loose jointed action, took over 400 Test wickets and is the fifth highest wicket taker among fast bowlers. Pollock consumed most of his victims with subtle swing. He formed an awesome combination with Donald. Another excellent purveyor of swing bowling was Terry Alderman who shouldered Australia's bowling during its weakest years in the early 1980s after Lillee had gone. He reveled in England and Australia. Australia then was trying to come out of a trough and it would take Allan Border years to forge the resurrection. And for Border, the first signs of a climb to the top began when Craig McDermott and Merv Hughes—beer belly, unshaven, huge moustache—came together to give Australia a fighting fast bowling combination. That as we all know, acquired legendary proportions when McGrath came.

McGrath and Ambrose, without a doubt are right up there with Barnes and Marshall. These two epitomized the best of fast bowling—hostility, accuracy, variations, making the batter play every ball, fitness over long years of bowling, bagful of wickets, in short they were match winning spearheads for their country. Amid all the talk of fast bowlers' aggression, one of the striking features has been that the West Indian speedsters hardly ever sledged opposing batters. We have seen McGrath sledge batters (Tendulkar, the stoic master simply ignored this!) but apart from that one famous on pitch spat with Steve Waugh in West Indies, can one recall Ambrose talking? From his height of six feet and seven inches, he just had to glare at the batter. Somehow, we tend to associate Ambrose's great bowling with his height and bounce but he was such a superbly constructed bowling machine.

Fit, economical, accurate and with a marvelously calibrated use of seam movement, Ambrose on many occasions was unplayable. McGrath among all fast bowlers we have seen was the most accurate and relentless. He combined the unbridled aggression of a tearaway fast bowler (without being really fast) with an unmatched combination of discipline, tenacity and cunning. That cliché 'corridor of uncertainty' outside off stump—the batter's ultimate Test of judgment—belonged to McGrath. He made batters play every one of the 29,248 balls he bowled in Test cricket. He did not swing the ball as well as some others did but he was the best seam bowler ever. Many bowlers over a period of time had a graph where performance slowly tapered off as they came to end of their careers. Not so McGrath. He bowled as well in his 124th Test match and of course everyone knows how he signed off in great style at the 2007 World Cup. The only interesting variant is that for McGrath, it was his combination with leg spinner Shane Warne, rather than his fast bowling partners like Jason Gillespie and Brett Lee, that made Australia absolutely invincible for 15 years.

Dale Steyn too has joined these four as the greatest of fast bowlers. He had serious pace and a full repertoire, jewel among them the perfect outswinger. And his figures—wickets, bowling average and strike rate were right at the top, only improving with every Test match he played.

What do we say about India? We began promisingly in 1932 with the red hot pace of Mohammed Nissar and the skillful seam of Amar Singh, but quickly fell away. Medium pacers yes—Dattu Phadkar and Lala Amarnath for example—but it was finally in 1959 that we discovered Ramakant Desai. Tiny Desai, as he was nicknamed, had a beautiful run up, a lovely leap and also a good bumper. But after Desai, we had to wait till the peerless Kapil Dev emerged in 1978. Kapil had a lovely action, got close to the stumps and bowled a beautiful outswinger, but here is Boycott providing one of the best ever descriptions of Kapil Dev's action: 'The way he leapt into his delivery stride took him so far round you could see his back before he swiveled and let the ball go.' It is with the advent of Kapil Dev that pace came to have meaning in India.

At last, India was able to return fire with fire. We have said it before but we will say it again. Perhaps there was no equal to Kapil when it came to bowling fitness, for he did not miss a single Test match in his career because of injury. In fact he would have played all his 131 Tests in an unbroken sequence if he had not been dropped for a Test match in Kolkata in 1984. Javagal Srinath, followed in 1991, faster than anyone else and it was a sign of changing times that an Indian fast bowler relished the bouncy track at Perth as much as anyone else did. Among our medium pacers, Madan Lal and Roger Binny were precious in our one-day cricket but it was Venkatesh Prasad who did so well in the few years that he played for India. Prasad actually filled the place vacated by a canny street smart medium pacer called Manoj Prabhakar. Very cerebral, it was Prasad who brought the slow leg cutter into India's one-day game as a potent weapon. His resilience too had a positive effect on Srinath whose shoulders would droop when things got tough. What a good combination, briefly though, they made for India in the late 1990s.

While people born 100 years ago were lucky to have seen Trumper, K. S. Ranjitsinhji, Bradman, Hobbs and Hammond bat, they were perhaps not as lucky as our generation when it comes to fast bowling. We in the last 50–60 years have been lucky to have seen virtually every one of the greatest fast bowlers—from Lindwall and Trueman to Lillee and Roberts to Marshall, McGrath and Steyn. Our generation has also seen the greatest ever quartet of all-rounders playing at the same time. Botham, Richard Hadlee, Imran and Kapil Dev were colossal match winners and huge crowd pullers. All four were so good that they walked into their country's Test team on the strength of their fast bowling alone. What will the game be if it did not have the accompanying aggression and machismo of fast bowling? Almost on a whim we asked some of our friends who were not particularly close followers of cricket, what according to them was the best sight in cricket. And the unanimous answer was the sight of cartwheeling stumps! Can the knowledgeable cricket follower argue with that?

Note: In the last seven years, India's pace attack is among the best. Jasprit Bumrah, Mohammad Shami, Ishant Sharma, Mohammad Siraj and Umesh Yadav have ensured India is a dangerous side anywhere they play.

6

THE MAGIC OF LEG SPIN

It would be so tempting to begin this essay with Shane Warne's dismissal of Mike Gatting with the ball of the century. But on second thoughts we feel that it would be more appropriate to go back a 100 years to when the googly was discovered by the Englishman, Bernard Bosanquet. Bosanquet said:

> Somewhere about the year 1897 I was playing a game with a tennis ball, known as 'Twisti-Twosti.' The object was to bounce the ball on a table so that your opponent sitting opposite could not catch it. After a little experimenting I managed to pitch the ball which broke in a certain direction; then with more or less the same delivery make the next ball go in the opposite direction! I practiced the same thing with a soft ball at 'Stump-cricket.' From this I progressed to the cricket ball ...

Bosanquet, generously passed on the secret to a South African called Reggie Schwarz who in turn shared this with three compatriots. The result was that when England visited South Africa in 1906, the hosts greeted them with a team that included four leg break/googly bowlers and they routed England 4–1. In fact South Africa often opened the bowling during that series with a googly bowler.

Leg spin is infinitely and uniquely fascinating. Subhash Gupte and Bhagwat Chandrasekhar, Shane Warne and Abdul Qadir, and all those other artists have provided individual nirvana to millions of cricket lovers. Our love for leg spin is the love one has for an impish, unpredictable, clever child who will thrill, please, surprise and frustrate you depending on his mood. How do we convey this love to our readers? We have attempted this through a blend and weave of the bowling records and nuggets and stories of the many leg spinners who have graced the game.

So, here is the story of leg spin in two parts. The first part is a statistical assessment, keeping in mind that while numbers don't lie, they only tell half the story. The second part is a compilation of some of our favorite leg spin stories and anecdotes. This is how we went about it. In compiling our list of right-arm leg-spin bowlers, we decided to include only those who have played a minimum of five Tests and taken at least 40 wickets.* We excluded from our study the left-arm Chinaman bowlers such as Johnny Martin, Brad Hogg and Paul Adams, and the mystery spinners such as Sonny Ramadhin, Johnny Gleeson and Ajantha Mendis. We have devoted a separate chapter, all to themselves to this odd tribe who add vivid colors to the game. So our list of leg spinners is stacked up as in Table 6.1.

Does it surprise us that 40 per cent of the major leg spinners are Aussies? Perhaps not, for Shane Warne, Clarrie Grimmett, Arthur Mailey and Bill O'Reilly are never far from our memory. Why do New Zealand and West Indies have hardly any representation in such a compilation? Is it not striking that South Africa, who had a formidable quartet of googly bowlers till around the 1920s have not produced a single leg spinner in the last 90 years who makes it to the list. As long as cricket was largely played between Australia, England and South

---

* The data are taken from the espncricinfo.com website. The analysis and the 'effectiveness model' that we have experimentally created here is what we have used across the book. There might be some fallacies in the model but massaging numbers can also be fun!

TABLE 6.1: Leg Spinners Who Played At Least Five Tests and Have 40 or More Wickets

Sl. no.	*Player*	*Country*	*Span*	*Match*	*Innings*	*Wickets*	*Average*	*Strike rate*	*Five wickets/ innings*	*10 wickets/ match*
1.	S. K. Warne	Australia	1992–2007	145	273	708	25.41	57.4	37	10
2.	A. Kumble	India	1990–2008	132	236	619	29.65	65.9	35	8
3.	Danish Kaneria	Pakistan	2000–2010	61	112	261	34.79	67.8	15	2
4.	R. Benaud	Australia	1952–1964	63	116	248	27.03	77	16	1
5.	B. S. Chandrasekhar	India	1964–1979	58	97	242	29.74	65.9	16	2
6.	Abdul Qadir	Pakistan	1977–1990	67	111	236	32.8	72.5	15	5
7.	C. V. Grimmett	Australia	1925–1936	37	67	216	24.21	67.1	21	7
8.	S. C. G. MacGill	Australia	1998–2008	44	85	208	29.02	54	12	2
9.	Mushtaq Ahmed	Pakistan	1990–2003	52	89	185	32.97	67.7	10	3
10.	S. P. Gupte	India	1951–1961	36	61	149	29.55	75.7	12	1
11.	W. J. O'Reilly	Australia	1932–1946	27	48	144	22.59	69.6	11	3
12.	Intikhab Alam	Pakistan	1959–1977	47	78	125	35.95	83.7	5	2
13.	D. V. P. Wright	England	1938–1951	34	59	108	39.11	75.3	6	1
14.	A. A. Mailey	Australia	1920–1926	21	34	99	33.91	61.8	6	2
15.	W. W. Armstrong	Australia	1902–1921	50	80	87	33.59	92.2	3	0
16.	G. A. Faulkner	South Africa	1906–1924	25	43	82	26.58	51.5	4	0
17.	Mushtaq Mohammad	Pakistan	1959–1979	57	70	79	29.22	66.5	3	0
18.	R. B. Simpson	Australia	1957–1978	62	84	71	42.26	96.9	2	0
19.	P. A. Strang	Zimbabwe	1994–2001	24	38	70	36.02	81.7	4	1
20.	A. P. Freeman	England	1924–1929	12	22	66	25.86	56.5	5	3

21.	J. D. Higgs	Australia	1978–1981	22	36	66	31.16	72	2	0
22.	N. D. Hirwani	India	1988–1996	17	28	66	30.1	65.1	4	1
23.	A. E. Vogler	South Africa	1906–1911	15	28	64	22.73	43.1	5	1
24.	R. W. V. Robins	England	1929–1937	19	34	64	27.46	51.8	1	0
25.	K. J. O'Keeffe	Australia	1971–1977	24	40	53	38.07	101.5	1	0
26.	C. G. Borde	India	1958–1969	55	54	52	46.48	109.5	1	0
27.	D. A. J. Holford	West Indies	1966–1977	24	35	51	39.39	94.4	1	0
28.	Wasim Raja	Pakistan	1973–1985	57	69	51	35.8	80	0	0
29.	J. C. Alabaster	New Zealand	1955–1972	21	32	49	38.02	81.4	0	0
30.	Shahid Afridi	Pakistan	1998–2010	27	47	48	35.6	66.5	1	0
31.	L. C. Braund	England	1901–1908	23	38	47	38.51	80.9	3	0
32.	H. V. Hordern	Australia	1911–1912	7	13	46	23.36	46.6	5	2
33.	I. A. R. Peebles	England	1927–1931	13	20	45	30.91	64	3	0
34.	D. Ramnarine	West Indies	1998–2002	12	22	45	30.73	77.6	1	0
35.	W. E. Hollies	England	1935–1950	13	22	44	30.27	80.7	5	0
36.	A. Mishra	India	2008–2011	13	22	43	43.3	81.3	1	0
37.	R. W. Barber	England	1960–1968	28	42	42	43	81.5	0	0
38.	D. Bishoo	West Indies	2011–2012	11	20	40	39.55	76.1	1	0

Source: Data from espncricinfo.com. Analysis and tabular compilation by authors.

Africa, England seem to have consistently produced successful leg spinners but after England started playing other countries, they have completely dropped out of the leg spinner stakes. Both India and Pakistan have great representation in this elite list but Sri Lanka has none.

The bowling effectiveness model that we describe here is relatively simple and can be done with basic crunching on a spreadsheet. We have used the same model for analyzing the off spinners, the left-arm spinners and the fast bowlers too but it is only in this chapter that we will burden the readers with the details and logic of our model building. Our premise is that every aspect of bowling performance—wickets, strike rate (SR), bowling average, five wickets in an innings, 10 wickets in a match and the wickets taken in away matches—has a bearing on determining the overall value or effectiveness of the bowler. In order to arrive at a composite overall effectiveness index, we used the SR, bowling average, five wickets in an innings, 10 wickets in a match and the proportion of wickets taken away from home to create a relative index and converted each bowler's performance in each of these factors into his individual index score. To calculate the index for a particular parameter, let us demonstrate with the example of Warne's index for SR. His SR is 57.4. The cumulative SR of 38 players in our list is 2760.7 and so Warne's SR Index is 57.4 / 2760.7 expressed as a percentage which is 2.7. A similar index for each parameter is calculated for each of the players. The aggregate of the index for the five parameters—SR, bowling average, five wickets/innings, 10 wickets/match and proportion of away wickets—of each player provides us a score for each bowler. And as you would have noted from the way we calculated the SR Index, the lower this score the better is the bowler's rating; thus the one with the lowest score is best in class and the ranks would progressively go down as the individual index scores went up. Let us call this aggregated score as 'Bowler Index Score'.

But this 'Bowler Index Score' does not recognize or give

weightage to the number of wickets that a bowler had taken. The number of wickets reflects a bowler's longevity at the highest level of the game. Since 38 bowlers in our list range from an extreme high of 708 wickets to an extreme low of 40 wickets, we decided to convert the wickets to their logarithmic value. (Log W for 100 wickets has a value of 2.0, for 200 wickets would have a value of 2.3 and for 400 would be 2.6 and so on.) In order to retain consistency in the convention of lowest figures indicating highest degree of effectiveness, we created an overall Effectiveness Index by dividing the Bowler Index Score by the Log value of the wickets taken. Thus, Effectiveness Index = Bowler Index Score / Log W. Table 6.2 ranks the leg spinners by their Effectiveness Index. And so we have these players, each with an overall effectiveness index that ranges from the best of them all—Shane Warne at 2.21 to Chandu Borde at 6.12. We debated the merits of splitting this list into two separate categories or more—for instance would it be useful to have separate tables for bowlers with less than 100 wickets and those with more than 100 wickets. We also toyed with the idea of separating cricketing eras and have separate lists for players who were from the pre-1930 era and post-1930 era and so on. But finally we decided that we will retain all of them in one pool. There are obviously better and more sophisticated models that take into account the quality of opposition and the quality of wickets captured; the proportion of wickets against weaker teams; proportion of lower-order batters and tail enders in their bag and so on. Our purpose is to show that readers with an interest in statistics could easily try out simple models and then have fun comparing statistical assessments with perception and qualitative ranking.

When we stepped back from our efforts, we saw Warne, Grimmett and Chandrasekhar emerge at the top, something that would be greeted with unanimous agreement and would give credence to our methodology. On the other hand, we were disappointed to see Subhash Gupte, Bill O'Reilly and Abdul

TABLE 6.2: Ranking the Leg Spinners Using an Effectiveness Index Model

Sl. No	*Player*	*Log W*	*Strike rate index*	*Bowling average index*	*5 wickets/ innings index*	*10 wickets/ match index*	*Away wicket index*	*Bowler index*	*Overall effectiveness score*
1	S. K. Warne	2.85	2.08	2.04	0.86	0.82	0.49	6.30	2.21
2	A. Kumble	2.79	2.39	2.38	0.87	0.86	0.57	7.07	2.53
3	C. V. Grimmett	2.33	2.43	1.95	0.92	0.88	0.75	6.93	2.97
4	S. C. G. MacGill	2.32	1.96	2.33	0.96	0.96	0.74	6.95	3.00
5	R .Benaud	2.39	2.79	2.17	0.94	0.98	0.42	7.30	3.05
6	B. S. Chandrasekhar	2.38	2.39	2.39	0.94	0.96	0.78	7.46	3.13
7	Danish Kaneria	2.42	2.46	2.80	0.95	0.96	0.47	7.63	3.16
8	W. J. O'Reilly	2.16	2.52	1.81	0.96	0.95	0.63	6.87	3.18
9	Abdul Qadir	2.37	2.63	2.64	0.95	0.91	0.77	7.89	3.32
10	A. F. Vogler	1.81	1.56	1.83	0.98	0.98	0.70	6.05	3.35
11	Mushtaq Ahmed	2.27	2.45	2.65	0.96	0.95	0.71	7.72	3.41
12	G. A. Faulkner	1.91	1.87	2.14	0.99	1.00	0.57	6.56	3.43
13	S. P. Gupte	2.17	2.74	2.37	0.96	0.98	0.64	7.69	3.54
14	A. P. Freeman	1.82	2.05	2.08	0.98	0.95	0.67	6.72	3.69
15	Mushtaq Mohammad	1.90	2.41	2.35	0.99	1.00	0.35	7.10	3.74
16	A. A. Mailey	2.00	2.24	2.72	0.98	0.96	0.61	7.51	3.76
17	R. W. V. Robins	1.81	1.88	2.21	1.00	1.00	0.94	7.02	3.88
18	H. V. Hordern	1.66	1.69	1.88	0.98	0.96	1.00	6.51	3.92
19	Intikhab Alam	2.10	3.03	2.89	0.98	0.96	0.57	8.43	4.02

20	D. V. P. Wright	2.03	2.73	3.14	0.98	0.98	0.45	8.28	4.07
21	J. D. Higgs	1.82	2.61	2.50	0.99	1.00	0.56	7.66	4.08
22	N. D. Hirwani	1.82	2.36	2.42	0.99	0.98	0.68	7.43	4.21
23	I. A. R. Peebles	1.65	2.32	2.48	0.99	1.00	0.49	7.28	4.40
24	W. W. Armstrong	1.94	3.34	2.70	0.99	1.00	0.52	8.54	4.41
25	P. A. Strang	1.85	2.96	2.89	0.99	0.98	0.53	8.35	4.53
26	Shahid Afridi	1.68	2.41	2.86	1.00	1.00	0.54	7.81	4.64
27	D. A. J. Holford	1.71	3.42	3.16	1.00	1.00	0.55	9.13	4.76
28	D. Ramnarine	1.65	2.81	2.47	1.00	1.00	0.71	7.99	4.83
29	L. C. Braund	1.67	2.93	3.09	0.99	1.00	0.17	8.18	4.89
30	W. E. Hollies	1.64	2.92	2.43	0.98	1.00	0.77	8.11	4.93
31	J. C. Alabaster	1.69	2.95	3.05	1.00	1.00	0.39	8.39	4.96
32	R. B. Simpson	1.85	3.51	3.40	0.99	1.00	0.48	9.38	5.07
33	D. Bishoo	1.60	2.76	3.18	1.00	1.00	0.55	8.48	5.29
34	Wasim Raja	1.71	2.90	2.88	1.00	1.00	0.35	8.13	5.35
35	K. J. O'Keeffe	1.72	3.68	3.06	1.00	1.00	0.64	9.37	5.44
36	R. W. Barber	1.62	2.95	3.45	1.00	1.00	0.52	8.93	5.50
37	A. Mishra	1.63	2.94	3.48	1.00	1.00	0.58	9.00	5.51
38	C. G. Borde	1.72	3.97	3.73	1.00	1.00	0.81	10.50	6.12

Source: Data from espncricinfo.com. Analysis and tabular compilation by authors.

Qadir come below Stuart MacGill and Danish Kaneria. That only means that analytics can never tell the full story.

Our generation has seen Warne in full television glory, every minute movement and sleight of hand shown to us in finest detail. Just two steps, a pivot and an infinite variation of leg spin from the most prodigious to the most subtle, the drift causing every kind of doubt to the batter.

Never was this better demonstrated than by the slaughter of Mike Gatting in cold blood in the summer of 1993 (the ball of the century, remember) or by the way Basit Ali was bamboozled (between his legs) by the last ball of the day's play. The flipper, the top spinner, the slider, Warne had it all but to show that he too is human, Warne had an unremarkable googly. Clarrie Grimmett is the stuff of legends. We dwell upon him only briefly and know that is sacrilege. Undoubtedly the most accurate of leg spinners, he also worked tremendously hard. He kept adding variations continuously to his bowling to the extent that when batters started recognizing his flipper because they could hear the snap of his fingers, Grimmett, the wily fox, started bowling leg breaks with a snap of the fingers of his left hand! Some double bluff this! Grimmett's success in consistently dismissing Hammond for low scores was central to Australia's plan to win the Ashes against

Shane Warne in action.
Australia in India, 2004
Photo Courtesy: Kasturi & Sons

England in 1930. This leg spinner's book *Getting Wickets* is very difficult to lay one's hands on, but Cardus has written reams of rich description of Grimmett's wares. At no. 2, 6 and 8 on our overall Effectiveness Index list we have Anil Kumble, Chandrasekhar and O'Reilly, the three fast leg spinners bowling at brisk pace. Between these three and the Englishman, Doug Wright (the fourth leg spinner who bowled at brisk medium pace and is at no. 20) we have four leg spinners who bowled absolutely unbelievable leg spinners, googlies and top spinners at such speed that often the ball would take the bails away even as the batter was shaping to play. Our generation has been lucky to see Chandra in action and Kumble in all ferocious detail on television including that magical 10 in an innings at Delhi against Pakistan. But of O'Reilly we rely on what we have read. Nicknamed Tiger for his fierce temperament, reputed to have had a tumultuous equation with Bradman, the stories are replete with proof of how absolutely unplayable he was. So unplayable that when Len Hutton composed an All Time Best England XI to play Australia, he included Maurice Leyland in his dream team only because that left-handed batter had the best record against O'Reilly and that alone was enough in Hutton's book to earn him this honor! The Don, whatever may have been his fractious relationship with O'Reilly, was absolutely certain that he was the greatest bowler he had seen.

Five bowlers with less than 100 wickets make it to the top 20 in the list—Arthur Mailey of Australia, Albert Vogler of South Africa, Herbert 'Ranji' Hordern of Australia, Alfred 'Tich' Freeman the Englishman and George Faulkner the South African. Obviously their SR and match-winning abilities (5and 10-wicket hauls) are so powerful that they could overturn the disadvantage of having played fewer Tests and taken fewer wickets. We are simply thrilled that these four bowlers who have faded from memory have been brought sharply back to focus by this analysis. Vogler shone for a brief while as the most difficult bowler for a batter to face and cricket literature says that he had an exceptional googly that batters found impossible to pick. Ranji Hordern (named so for his dark complexion) played just seven Test matches and took 47 wickets but his SR shows how lethal he was. This googly bowler played much less cricket than others simply because his first calling was as a doctor and his Hippocratic Oath always took precedence over his cricket. Faulkner again, one of the earlier exponents of the googly, mixed that delivery with fast yorkers and the fact that he was a handful is evident because he too has a SR of a wicket in every 51 balls. However, he had a relatively longer career compared to Hordern, Vogler or Freeman and picked up 82 wickets in his 25 Tests.

Tich Freeman was someone very special. His county cricket record is mind boggling. Next only to Wilfred Rhodes in the number of first class wickets, he has an amazing record of being the only bowler in county cricket history to take over 300 wickets in a season and also the only bowler to take 10 wickets in an innings thrice. One simply cannot imagine an English leg spinner taking 300 wickets in a county season—even if 1928 was a dry summer. Given the typical English conditions, for Freeman to have taken over 200 wickets every season for eight consecutive years, is a staggering achievement. Could he have got some of his wickets through swerve and movement in typically English conditions rather than leg spin? The Wisden in its description of Freeman says no such thing—this short man was quite simply a remarkable leg spinner; classical slow leg spin with deceptive flight, tremendous control and the full repertoire of leg break, top spinner and googly. Historians say he was not as successful in Test cricket as in county cricket but we see no justification in that. Freeman ranks no. 14 on our list despite having played just 12 Tests (66 wickets) because his match-winning exploits are overwhelming—10-wicket hauls in three of his 12 matches simply mean that Freeman gave his side a winning chance by his very presence.

These four gems lie hidden and unnoticed in the treasure

trove of all-time great spinners. One now wonders why only Grimmett, Mailey and O'Reilly come to mind when we think of leg spinners of the pre-1940 era. Why do we forget the terrific exploits of Vogler, Faulkner, Hordern and Freeman?

Two bowlers who made Bradman seem mortal were Eric Hollies and Ian Peebles. Among cricket's most often told stories is that if Hollies had not dismissed Bradman for a zero in his final innings, Bradman would have finished with a batting average of more than 100 in Test cricket. Was the googly from Hollies that bowled him so foxy or did tears in his eyes prevent Bradman from seeing that particular ball? We will never know.

Here is a pearl of a story about the googly we have picked from Arthur Mailey's *10 for 66 and All That*, one of the most endearing books by a cricketer. In an unforgettable chapter on Mailey's first encounter with the 'immortal Victor Trumper', Mailey describes the anxiety and suspense as he gets a chance to bowl to his idol. A couple of perfectly good leg breaks were driven with absolute authority and disdain to the off-side ropes. Realizing that he might not get another over, Mailey decided to try his then newly invented googly. He tossed it up and saw Trumper coming down the wicket. The ball swerved out (unlike the leg break which would have drifted in). Trumper, uncertain, made the adjustment to play it away from his leg but the googly sneaked through between bat and pad. Trumper didn't attempt to regain his crease; he just smiled at Mailey, shook his head and said 'that was too good for me, son' and walked away. Mailey says he felt no triumph—he felt like a boy who had killed a dove.

Two Indian bowlers have a special place in our hearts. For the elder of us, Subhash Gupte was nothing less than a sight for the Gods! Gupte had a lovely action and his right hand would do a kind of 'S' before delivering that was truly captivating. He had good control, fine flight and all the variety—including two different googlies. In fact, often, he would lull batters with the easier to spot Googly no. 1 and then fool them later with the difficult to pick Googly no. 2. It became well known that Subhash would often greet new batters with a googly first ball. When the Commonwealth team toured India in 1956, he did this to Sam Loxton (apparently forewarned) who calmly pushed the googly away to square leg for a single. As he strolled across for the run, he was supposed to have told Gupte, 'Don't bowl me that stuff, Subhash; I can pick it every time.' Loxton later claimed he didn't get any more googlies that innings. In the Test matches of those days in India, after a few perfunctory overs of medium pace from G. S. Ramchand, Phadkar or Umrigar, the captain would summon Gupte to bowl. Subhash would then loosen up by bowling a few balls away from the turf to the keeper. Immediately there would be a buzz around the ground and 'oohs and aahs' as the spectators watched these preparatory rites. If only Subhash had better close-in catchers (Indian fielders in those days, barring Umrigar, just about caught balls that came comfortably into their midriff!) to support him, he would have taken closer to 200 wickets than the 149 he ended up with. The three Ws of West Indies—Everton Weekes, Frank Worrell and Clyde Walcott—were absolutely certain that Gupte was the greatest spinner they had ever faced.

Subhash 'Fergie' Gupte
Credit: V. Balaji

The second leggie for whom we have a special place in our hearts is the one and only Bhagwat Chandrasekhar who won nearly a dozen matches for India with his bowling. Immortalized for his heroic role in India's triumph over England at the Oval in 1971, Chandra was a sight to behold when in full flow. Sleeves

B. S. Chandrasekhar in action
Photo Courtesy: Kasturi & Sons

buttoned down at the wrist, shirt tail flapping, unruly hair flying, a brisk bounding run, 100,000 spectators at the Eden Gardens in Calcutta chanting 'Chandra! Chandra!' and five predatory close catchers waiting like vultures around the bat… when Chandra bowled, cricket had electricity that has never since been matched. In the series against England at home in 1972, so overwhelming was Chandra's domination that he took 35 wickets while the rest of his bowling comrades put together had 40 wickets. He had the Englishmen in such a trance that he even got a batter caught at short leg of a bouncer, a delivery that Chandra did unleash once in a while. In 1975, at the Eden Gardens, when West Indies was coasting to victory needing about 150 runs with Clive Lloyd and Alvin Kallicharan in command, Chandra turned the match on its head in a couple of very special overs. He nailed Lloyd's off stump with a lethal googly, got Kallicharan with another and sealed the fate of the West Indians by immediately claiming a third victim too. His colleagues have often said that there was no other cricketer who was as humble and self-effacing as this absolutely thrilling match winner.

Our stories are not just about those in this select list of 38 leg spinners. One man who ought to have walked into list if he played to potential was the slim wiry Laxman Sivaramakrishnan.

A man with a lovely action and plenty of guile, to our eternal regret, Siva disappeared from the scene as suddenly as he appeared. None who watched the final of the World Series Tournament between India and Pakistan in 1985 at Melbourne can ever forget the 'Ball of the Tournament' (or the leg-break of the decade). As Siva flighted one to Javed Miandad, that great player of spin skipped out to meet the ball on the half volley. But it kept dipping and dipping as though Siva was pulling it by string! Miandad swished at thin air, the ball broke away and the keeper whipped off the bails.

We conclude this tribute to leg spinners with a story about Vaman Kumar, a fine leg spinner who only played two Tests for India in 1960. He was treated shabbily by selectors but tormented the best of India's batters in the Ranji Trophy and Duleep Trophy matches. This gem was narrated to me (Raghunath) after I had played a good knock against Kumar in a first division league match at Chennai. Rangan, the cricket crazy captain at Nungambakkam Sports Club, ran the nets for not only his club but for all enthusiastic cricketers in South Madras. Among the top Madras cricketers who would come to the nets was Kumar. It was during one such outing at the nets that Kumar bowling to Rangan—a good bat himself—impishly wagered that Rangan would not be able to even touch with his bat 10 successive legitimate deliveries of his. This mind you, was on matting where the ball does not skid through. Rangan thought he would win the bet easily since even an edge would do. Later Rangan, recounting the scene in his inimitable style, said that every ball from V. V. Kumar buzzed and sang; he could neither fathom the turn nor account for the fizz; even trying to gain some extra time by playing back could not help Rangan put bat to ball. To his utter dismay Kumar won the bet. Kumar in his heyday was that good.

The stories can go on, for leg spin is timeless and infinitely romantic. The fact is that on a placid wicket on the morning of the first day of a Test match, if the opening bowlers have failed to make a breakthrough, the captain of the fielding side depends on his leg spinner to turn on the magic. As the leg spinner and his captain discuss the field placements, as the leg spinner spins the ball from hand to hand, as he licks his fingers and approaches the bowling crease, every person watching the drama waits with bated breath. With a leg spinner as we only too well know, the possibilities are simply endless.

7

BISHAN SINGH BEDI: OF LARGE HEART AND LARGE STORIES

Some months after *Mid-wicket Tales* had been published, Gideon Haigh, the cricket historian from Australia, wrote a generous review. He also sent it to his good friend in Delhi, the legendary cricketer, Bishan Singh Bedi. Gideon asked me to send Bedi a copy, which I (Giridhar) did with alacrity. Two days later, my phone rang. It was Bedi, exuberant and in his characteristic drawl, telling me he loved the book. I asked him, have you read it already? To which he replied he had only read a few chapters but liked what he had read so much that he had to immediately compliment us. I introduced him to Raghunath over email. Raghu was visiting his daughter in Delhi at that time and even before one could whip the bails off to a Bedi delivery, Raghu was having dinner at Bedi's farm house!

When Raghu met Bedi that first time, we had just begun work on our second book, *From Mumbai to Durban*, which would narrate the history of Indian Test cricket through the stories of India's greatest Test matches. As part of our research at that time, we were reaching out to cricketers and journalists to get their first-hand views, anecdotes and interesting snippets that would embellish the narration. That evening with Bedi was the first of our meetings with him. We did not have to persuade him because he had already made up his mind to help us. If you have browsed through the book, you will realize how much the great left-arm spinner contributed to it. He simply gave. I don't think he even remembers how much he told us.

In November 2015, Chennai was devastated by floods, rendering many people homeless. Lives were lost, houses ravaged. Bedi, living in Delhi, was getting desperately worried about his friends in Chennai. Not getting through to these people in Chennai, he called me to ask if his cricketer friends—W. V. Raman, Srikkanth and a few others—and his new friend, Raghu, were safe. I had to admit that I did not know about the cricketers but assured him that Raghu was safe. Bedi was distraught and rang off to check with some other friends. That's how Bedi is wired, genuinely concerned about his people.

Under happier circumstances some months later, I got a call one evening at 9 p.m. 'Bishan here. I am in your town, at the Leela. Want to come over for dinner?' Since I live very close to The Leela, I was ringing his door bell within minutes. Bedi welcomed me with a hug. And then mischievously he pointed me towards the shadowy corner of the room. Leaning against the wall was Sunil Joshi, former India left-arm spinner and in some ways, Bedi's protégé. I told Bedi that like a good South Indian, I had finished dinner much before his call came. So he said, 'Ok have a beer.' Then rubbing his hands and leaning in his luxurious chair he said, 'When Sunil dropped in to see me, I thought I will call you over so that you can press him for some stories too.' Sunil of course is a lovely raconteur with an impish sense of humor. We set up a meeting for a later day where he shared some lovely stories, which you will also find in the book.

That evening at The Leela, Bedi was in form. He told of his love for players like Pataudi and Jaisimha; of the spirit in which sport must be played. He narrated stories from the Indian tours to West Indies and Pakistan; told us about a crazy helicopter ride in Guyana; and about a nervous Jaisimha always smoking like a chimney before his turn to bat. Then, with loud guffaws, he told us wicked stories about Lala Amarnath and his endless bragging. In the middle of all that he also chided me (and Raghunath in his absence) of not being forthright and critical enough about dubious bowling actions in our earlier book. He said we were being unnecessarily politically correct while talking of Muralitharan in our chapter on great off spinners. Time flew as I soaked in the stories, and it was well past midnight when I reached home.

As the manuscript of our book *From Mumbai to Durban* reached its final stages, I emailed Bedi to reconfirm some of the stories and facts that he had told us. Raghu and I wanted to be sure we would not be misquoting him. One of those really tall tales was about Lala Amarnath's boast of doing 10,000 skips with the skipping rope in 30 minutes. We feared we might not have got the number right. Bishan is not so prompt on email and it was easier to speak to him over phone. As we repeated our query, he interjected to say, 'Nah, it's 30,000 that Lala claimed not 10,000 skips.' So what we thought was an already tall tale only became taller when we went back to Bedi to reconfirm.

That's the fun of being acquainted with Bedi. We are pretty sure he is the same with almost everyone, friendly within minutes of shaking hands. That heart, it is large, it is generous, it overflows.

8

FIRST-CLASS CRICKET: LIFEBLOOD OF THE GAME

Sixty years ago, hockey was certainly our national game, the one sport where we were champions, where the whole world marveled at our wizardry. But make no mistake, even in those days cricket had a huge hold on the ordinary Indian. It was of course a middle-class urban game, unlike hockey whose nursery was the villages of Punjab and Coorg.

Back then, and certainly till the mid-1970s, India would play just five Test matches at home during our winter (and not every winter) and went on tours either in the summer or the odd winter to play a series in England, Australia and West Indies. That was all—our international cricket calendar was just that. One remembers that after the Australians visited us in 1956, we waited a long while before West Indies visited us in the winter of 1958–1959. After we played against New Zealand at home in February 1965 our next Test series was in December 1966 against West Indies, also at home. Similarly, after our tour to West Indies in 1962, our next overseas visit was to England in the summer of 1967. If this was the frequency of our cricket Test matches, how did cricket have such a following? How did we ensure cricket was alive, kicking, thriving in those days when Test cricket was sparse, when India had not yet won the World Cup and when Tendulkar was not a name that carried a billion hopes?

The answer is simple. We had an interesting and competitive first-class cricket structure. We also had an immensely engaging league cricket structure in our metros apart from some excellent premier tournaments. Those were the days, when over 25,000 people would pack into the make shift stands of the Central College ground in Bangalore (Chinnaswamy Stadium did not exist then) to watch Mysore (it was not Karnataka then) play Madras (yes, not Tamil Nadu then)* in a match that would decide which state team from the South would qualify for the quarter finals of the Ranji Trophy. So, we would have E. A. S. Prasanna, B. S. Chandrasekhar and G. R. Viswanath on one side, and S. Venkataraghavan, A. G. Kripal Singh and Vaman Kumar on the other. Being three-day affairs, quite often the first innings lead would decide the outcome. The matches were fiercely competitive. If Mysore and Madras met in Bangalore in 1969, they would square up the next year in Madras. Every player knew that his performance in these tournaments would decide his place in the Indian team. Every match therefore was a step toward selection in the national side.

As important as the Ranji Trophy was the Duleep Trophy. In some ways even more so because the first step toward Test cricket was to get selected to the Zonal team. That was possible only if one did well in the Ranji Trophy. And thus a tight evenly matched set of games would take place between South, North, East, West and Central Zones. There was not a player worth his salt who would for any reason miss these two tournaments.

---

* The names of a number of Indian cities have been modified or changed in the last 20 years. Thus Madras, Bombay, Bangalore and Calcutta are now Chennai, Mumbai, Bengaluru and Kolkata respectively. Similarly, the state of Madras was officially renamed Tamil Nadu in 1968 while the state of Mysore was renamed Karnataka in 1973. In this book, while describing the cricketing events or narrating anecdotes that occurred before the names of these cities and states were changed, we have mostly referred to them by their older names although not on every occasion.

How important were these tournaments? A good performance in the Duleep Trophy on the back of consistent Ranji Trophy performances would mean that you could not be ignored by selectors. Here is a vignette from 1964 to 1965. North Zone was playing South Zone at the Kotla. And the Kotla was packed. M. L. Jaisimha's South Zone, playing Tiger Pataudi's North Zone (Pataudi played for North Zone before later shifting to Hyderabad and South Zone), was staring down the barrel at defeat and elimination from the tournament. Nine wickets down and just V. Subramanya, the Mysore skipper and middle-order batter, at the crease. What happened for the next two hours was incandescent magic. Shielding his no. 11 partner Habib Khan, Subramanya scored a resplendent century with strokes all around the wicket. Shirt sticking to his back, as he walked back to the pavilion, having got the vital lead for South Zone, he was given a standing ovation. The story does not end here. Subbu did this again for Mysore against Madras when with no. 11 Chandrasekhar, he moved from 100 to 200 playing an innings of brilliance and daring, dispatching the bowlers to all corners of the ground. Subbu, already nearing 30 years of age, must have given up hopes of ever playing for the country. But those centuries simply catapulted him into the Test team a year later. Such was the importance attached to our first-class fixtures. In the winter of 1970, Vijay Merchant was chairman of Selectors. Already winds of change were upon us and the word was that Pataudi would lose the captaincy to Ajit Wadekar for the forthcoming tour to West Indies. Merchant was also itching to do away with the seniors and bring in a number of youngsters into the touring party. And so the seniors—Dilip Sardesai, Jaisimha, Salim Durani, Chandu Borde, Hanumant Singh, Pataudi and others—were all primed up. Youngsters like Eknath Solkar and Ashok Mankad knew that they could grab seats on the flight to the West Indies if they did well. Venkataraghavan already elevated as the South Zone captain knew that he could be the vice-captain if he showed spark in leading South Zone.

For cricket lovers in India, remember, this was the only cricket they got to watch those days. Every player was on edge. And the games began. South Zone beat Central Zone and then they also beat West Zone. While Borde, Hanumant Singh and Pataudi did not do well, Jaisimha hit consecutive centuries; Durani showed that he was India's best all-rounder. Venkat became vice-captain; Jaisimha and Durani thus claimed back their places in India's Test team while the other stalwarts lost out. Apparently Jaisimha, talented as few others have been but also notorious for his party strewn evening life, was never more serious than those few weeks when he was determined to win back his place on the team to tour West Indies. The Irani Trophy (named after Zal Irani, one of India's cricket administrators) of course was the third major event in India's cricket calendar. It was just one match—the Ranji Trophy champions against the 'Rest of India'. Those days it would invariably mean that the best of Bombay's batters—Sardesai, Sunil Gavaskar, Wadekar, Vijay Bhosle, Manohar Hardikar, Vijay Manjrekar and so on—played the best spinners in the world—Prasanna, Chandrasekhar and Venkataraghavan. Even in the mid-1970s, the Irani Trophy made and unmade careers.

Dilip Vengsarkar
Credit: V. Balaji

Dilip Vengsarkar, not yet 20 years old, hit a magnificent century for Bombay against Prasanna and Bedi in 1975 to simply leapfrog over many players into the Indian team. Two years later, in 1977, T. E. Srinivasan and Yashpal Sharma were just a boarding pass away from a flight to

Australia but failed in the crucial Irani tie. They did not make it while Brijesh Patel and Ashok Mankad—both with mediocre Test records—retained their places for that tour. A few years later, in 1980, T. E. Srinivasan hit centuries to at last clinch a place in the touring party to Australia and New Zealand. Acknowledged as the most stylish batter those days, and unlucky to have missed selection earlier, this time he timed his luminescent performances to perfection.

Make no mistake; it was for urban India still a common man's game. One could watch an entire day's game for Rs 2 or an entire Test match at Chepauk from the popular D Stand opposite the pavilion for just Rs 15. One could play street and local maidan cricket with just a tennis ball, a bat and anything for stumps. All India Radio would bring all these first-class matches live into our homes. Walking back from school you could stop at the grocery store be it Mylapore in Madras or Ulsoor in Bangalore—one quickly knew which shopkeeper was interested in cricket—and get to know the latest score.

But what enabled such a rich supply of good cricketers into our first-class system was the very good and vibrant league system. Bombay, Madras, Bangalore, Hyderabad and Delhi, each city had a sound league system. Calcutta too made space for cricket though it was the football capital of the country. The humble weekend cricketer could enjoy his game playing the fourth division while the cricketer aspiring to make it to the state team would invest all his energies doing his best in the first division league. Coupled to this, India had premier tournaments that attracted the top teams. The Moin ud Dowla Cup was the jewel of the Hyderabad cricket season as was the Buchi Babu tournament for Madras. Delhi's Goswami Memorial Hot Weather tournament was unique as it challenged the cricketer to play in blazing summer and indeed the tireless Rajinder Goel would endlessly wheel away his left-arm spin with the sun beating harshly down his back. The Rohinton Baria tournament for Universities was a major event in our cricket season. It was something that everyone eagerly looked forward to and newspapers covered this tournament extensively. A certain Sunil Gavaskar brought himself to national notice by scoring tons of runs for Bombay University in the tournament. Not just Gavaskar, every state team had a number of cricketers who earned their call through performances in the Varsity tournament. Dilip Sardesai, Anshuman Gaekwad, Mumtaz Husain, Hari Gidwani, Michael Dalvi, V. Sivaramakrishnan, Brijesh Patel, Vengsarkar...many future Test stars and some splendid first-class cricketers were launched through this tournament.

All things considered, as far as league cricket was concerned, Madras and Bombay were spectacular but Jaisimha's Hyderabad and Prasanna's Bangalore were not far behind. Bombay's maidans were famous for fierce contests, for the Kanga league, Purshottam and Times Shield. Famous also because on the same large maidan, multiple matches would be in progress. One could be fielding at deep point for Indian Gymkhana against Mafatlal and a yard away could be Sardesai fielding at square leg for Hindu Gymkhana against Dadar Union. And somehow in Bombay, word would spread whenever a great contest was in progress. And magically a 1,000 strong crowd would swell to 5,000 to see Wadekar, Durani and Sardesai bat. People say that the Kanga League—cricket played entirely in the monsoon season—was one of the reasons Bombay produced batters. Bangalore was remarkable for its culture of tennis ball cricket tournaments. All the top cricketers took part and Subramanya of whom we have spoken earlier was uncanny in spotting talent and picked many talented cricketers literally from tennis ball cricket; famous among such inspired talent spotting being Viswanath and Chandrasekhar for example.

Back then, Madras produced the only sports magazine in India. *Sports & Pastime* from *The Hindu* group covered cricket, hockey, football, athletics and tennis, giving space to all the games. In addition, they sponsored a limited overs tournament for corporate houses from the mid-1950s. These matches were the first taste of one-day cricket we had; 30 overs each side and the final alone a full-day affair of 50 overs. Those days, the finals would often feature Parry against State Bank and that meant Kripal Singh batting against the wizardry of Vaman Kumar. Kripal was the immensely popular local hero of Triplicane, where the final was played at the Presidency college grounds adjoining the Marina beach. More than 5,000 people would watch the match and the atmosphere would be tense and riveting.

Professionalism and discipline in Bombay cricket was paramount. You could be India's leading Test cricketer or the most precociously talented but the rules applied. Raghunath playing for Indian Gymkhana has seen Ashok Mankad and Hanumant Singh as captains castigate and drop Test cricketers who were even a minute late reporting for the game. The captain could merely be a respected cricketer and not necessarily a highly ranked state cricketer, but his writ would run. If Vasu Paranjpe decided to sit out a Test bowler for coming late, then that was it and the Test bowler would carry drinks for the day. In that respect alone Bombay was head and shoulders over Madras. Madras had a superbly organized cricket league, but their cricketers somehow never had the focus and discipline of the Bombay cricketer. Venkat was the exception and for his stern discipline alone was he greatly resented by the easy going Madras cricketer. One incident remains etched in Giridhar's memory. It was January 1972 and the second morning of the match between Madras and Mysore at the Central College grounds in Bangalore. 9 a.m. and an hour more for play to begin, I (Giridhar) walk into the ground to chat with Venkat. He is already in full cricket gear, taking his customary practice catches. He is surrounded by only four fellow cricketers and as he takes his catches he keeps calling for the rest of his teammates to join him for practice. They all come in dribs and drabs, some still not in gear. He talks patiently and cheerfully to me but turns and lets out a fusillade at a fellow player who comes running, tucking his shirt in, and with his spiked cricket shoes in the other hand. Ask Venkat and he will tell you that no Bombay cricketer would ever take his cricket so lightly. Cricket was and is God to the middle-class Maharashtrian. The other idiosyncrasy of Madras cricket is that the crowd erupts into applause when a batter crosses 25. Apparently this is because when a batter crosses 25, his score will appear in the papers next day. Giridhar playing in Chennai for the first time in the 1980s experienced with a shock that when he crossed 25 in a minor match, the handful of spectators shouted 'Newspaper score'. Madras perhaps was the only city to celebrate mini milestones such as the crossing of 25 runs, and this may even be one reason why the immensely talented Madras batter invariably threw his wicket away after an attractive 40 or 50. Even in Test matches, knowledgeable Madras crowds would cheer when a player crossed 25 runs.

We can go on, but we hope we have been able to bring to you some pictures of what cricket was in the 1960s and 1970s. It was first-class cricket, supported by genuine cricket lovers. Today, as our first-class cricketers play to empty stands in huge stadiums the heart bleeds. We must somehow get the crowds back; our top cricketers must play Ranji and Duleep Trophy regularly. The lifeblood of Indian cricket is actually in its first-class cricket.

THEY TOO PLAYED FOR INDIA

In October 2008, a news item on ESPNcricinfo.com informed readers that T. E. Srinivasan, the elegant Tamil Nadu batter who played a solitary Test match for India in 1981, was battling cancer with great courage. Moved greatly by memories of the many fine innings that T. E. Srinivasan played and how cruelly unlucky he was not to have played more than just that one Test, Giridhar wrote this tribute to India's finest first-class cricketers who were not destined to play for India (http://www.espncricinfo.com/ blogs/content/story /613343. html).

My mind today is thinking of all those cricketers who played only the odd Test or two for India. How unlucky were they? Surely T. E. Srinivasan deserved more than just the one chance he got against New Zealand in 1981? Ask anyone who saw him hit dazzling centuries for Tamil Nadu in Ranji Trophy, for South Zone in the Duleep Trophy and against visiting countries and for Rest of India in Irani Trophy matches and they will nod most vehemently. An earlier generation will similarly vouch for how unlucky Ramesh Saxena the sty list with a very high back lift was to have play ed just a solitary Test for India against England in 1967. Search some more and you will discover more such solitary Test hard luck stories.

But then I pause and ask myself, won't they feel happy that at least they played a Test while many of their colleagues were not even that lucky? Would not those dozen other players have given their right arm to have played just once for India? Who do you think is more unlucky? Whom do you think did fate treat more cavalierly? Whose was the greater chagrin? Who is the more unrequited player? Is it the 'one Test' player for whom the door to Shangri-La was opened tantalizingly briefly only to be shut in his face? Or is it the player who waited 10, 15 even 20 years in vain for the door to open so that he could just have a glimpse of Shangri-La?

I start listing in my mind cricketers who ended their careers never having played for India but were perhaps just a selector's vote away from eternal glory. Rajinder Goel, Padmakar Shivalkar, Amarjit Kaypee, Bhaskar Pillai, Hari Gidwani, Michael Dalvi, V. Sivaramakrishnan, Satwender Singh, Kanwaljit Singh, Pandurang Salgaoncar...the list seems endless. Their records and their performances were no less than that of their contemporaries who played for India. Was it just destiny that they did not wear India colors? It takes us just a couple of players' stories to understand that it is often just a hair' s breadth between fame and obscurity.

It is the winter of 1974 and West Indies have come to India to play five Tests. India has just received the drubbing of their lifetime in England (remember we were shot out for 42 at Lords) and the team is in complete disarray. Things worsen as Lloyd's men pulverize India in the first two Tests. 0–2 down and three Tests to go; Indian selectors' patience with the regular players is running out. Batting places are up for grabs and the selectors are ready to take risks. And so it is in this scenario that Hari Gidwani play s for Combined Universities against the touring West Indians. Gidwani had already done so much in Varsity cricket that everyone knew that if he scored runs in this game he would walk into the Test team for the third Test. By a quirk of fate, Gidwani scores only a couple of thirties while a dour, bespectacled batter from M. S. University Baroda, less gifted than Gidwani, scores a century and grabs that batting spot in the Indian team. He proceeds to play for India with some if not remarkable distinction over the next 10 years. That stodgy batter was Anshuman Gaekwad. Gidwani never got a look-in again. He kept playing for Delhi and scoring runs; he went to Bihar and piled up tons of runs for them; he scored almost every time he went to bat. But he never played for India. Can one game, one ball, one error decide your fate so irrevocably. For Hari Gidwani it did.

My next story is about Padmakar Shivalkar and Rajinder Goel. Between 1960 and 1980 India had four left-arm spinners, any of whom would have walked into any Test side in the world except India. Except India, because this was the period when

Bishan Bedi played for India. All four were Test match material but there was only place in the Indian team for a left-arm spinner. Padmakar Shivalkar plugged away relentlessly and remorselessly for Mumbai in Ranji Trophy and was the most crucial cog in their bowling wheel. And Rajinder Goel did identical duty for Delhi and Haryana.

Over after over, season after season, from their teens, into their prime, and then into their late thirties, age catching up, shoulders getting sore, they toiled on. How strong must their will have been? How much must they have loved this game? How stoic and accepting must they have been? Knowing that the peerless Bedi could never be toppled from his perch they plugged away. Devastating and lethal on turning wickets, brave and skillful on heartless wickets they epitomized what cricket and team games are all about. What these two remarkable cricketers demonstrated over decades was a rare equilibrium and tranquility combined with limitless self confidence in their abilities. If we could create the Best XI from among players who did not play for India and set them up against an Indian XI they will make a real good fist of it. Of that I am sure.

9

WORRELL, BREARLEY AND OTHER GREAT CAPTAINS

'On Friday, I watched J. M. Brearley directing his fieldsmen very carefully. He then looked up at the sun and made a gesture which seemed to indicate that it should move a little squarer. Who is this man?' wrote *The Guardian* correspondent after Mike Brearley had conjured another impossible win against Australia in the famous Ashes series of 1981.

Cricket discourse in India is always strident. Within a year, a 'great captain' becomes a 'terrible captain' when the fact is that the team is playing poorly. Suddenly the terrible captain becomes great again after a couple of wins. Reasoned discourse is always the first casualty and something as enjoyable as sport becomes a cause for breast beating or the wildest of celebrations and hyperbole.

Both of us decided to step away from this din and simply look back with pleasure at some of the greatest captains of all time. We read about them all; we pulled out nuggets of brilliant prose by some of the greatest writers and we savored them. We realized that whether it was England, Australia, Pakistan or India, the national cricket captain's job is somehow treated as the second most important job in the country. It is clear that cricket captaincy, at least among the cricket playing nations, is something very special.

We cannot think of a better beginning than Frank Worrell of West Indies. Worrell symbolized for the Caribbeans and the world, the breaking of colonial hegemony. After years of sub-standard white cricketers leading a motley group of cricketers from the Caribbean Islands, when at last Worrell was given the captaincy in 1960, he welded his players of great talent into a team that became the world champions. The West Indies–Australia series of 1960–1961 is indisputably among the finest in cricket history. In the famous tied Test of Brisbane, after five days of see-saw cricket, Australia needed just eight runs with four wickets remaining. With Worrell calm and poised, his teammates found the passion and reserves of energy to tie the match with three run-outs. Such was Worrell's statesman-like leadership of the West Indians that the entire population of Melbourne came out to give Worrell a ticker tape farewell after that series, on a scale that is usually only given to visiting heads of state. Indians can never forget when their own captain Nari Contractor was grievously injured by a bouncer in West Indies in 1962, Worrell was first in the line to donate blood for his surgery. Barely a few years later, Worrell died succumbing to leukemia.

Obviously, cricket captaincy is more than just imaginative, inspired decision making in batting, bowling and field placements. When a team brings out its fullest potential on the ground, much thought and preparation has probably been done outside the ground. The captain has literally forged his troops into a team where roles, responsibilities and expectations have been understood. Motivation, individual and collective pride, a sense of destiny, the feeling of being blessed to perform and participate, all these are an essential part of the team culture and environment. One of us—Raghunath—played a lot of first-division league cricket in Chennai and Mumbai during the 1960s and 1970s. And one saw some great captaincy first hand. Here is one such example. In order to get promoted, your team had to finish in the top two among 12 teams in the Chennai league.

A win carried four points but a draw only carried a point. So our captain, Rangan would try and go for wins with early declarations and attacking fields. There were hardly any drawn matches for who wanted that measly one point for a draw. It was attacking captaincy and the courage to go for all or bust. The strategy was so sound that though we lost a few games, we won enough to always finish among the top teams. But strategy works only with committed execution. The attacking field meant we had to hold our catches and half chances. Our captain made sure we worked hard and practiced our catching strenuously. It paid off because we were able to take blinders at gully and short leg. Test cricket too has stories of captains who bet on top-class fielding as their main weapon. Jack Cheetham took a young unfancied South African team to Australia in 1951–1952 and drew the series against superior opponents with the most breath-taking fielding seen in Australia. All the experts agreed that team spirit and fielding was what made Cheetham's men heroes.

Another reminiscence: Our team Indian Gymkhana had bundled out a strong Cricket Club of India (CCI) team on a shockingly bad wicket at the Brabourne stadium. Since we were chasing a small target we were asked not to play cautiously and instead go all out with attacking batting, because it was only a matter of time before an unplayable ball got you. Our captain opened to show the way and the rest of us followed his lead and we, the underdogs, had pulled off a coup. The relevance of all this will strike those of us who recall that India, when set just a target of around just 120 at Barbados in 1997 on a wearing wicket where the ball was keeping low, played too cautiously and lost.

Talk to people who followed cricket in the 1960s and 1970s and they will speak with enormous admiration about Vasu Paranjpe's leadership at Dadar Union and that master strategist M. L. Jaisimha, captain of Hyderabad and South Zone, in those days easily the best captain in Indian cricket.

In the days of uncovered pitches, captains often declared when their side was collapsing so that they could quickly put the other side in and catch them before the wicket became better. And in response to such maneuvers, smart captains reacted by changing the batting order and sending in all their bowlers first. Two examples come to mind: Late one evening, with the conditions tailor made for a lot of seam movement, Don Bradman sent in his tail enders Bill O'Reilly and Chuck Fleetwood Smith to open Australia's batting, saying they were not good enough to put bat to ball on that wicket; his premise was that better batters would be good enough to get a touch and get out. He was proved right as O'Reilly and Fleetwood Smith lasted a crucial eight overs and gave the batters who followed a better chance. The other famous story is from 1977. Middlesex needed an outright win against Surrey and one day's play had been washed out. After bundling out Surrey for 42, Mike Brearley stunningly declared Middlesex's first innings after just one ball so that his bowlers could again run through Surrey a second time when the pitch was at its worst. Surrey collapsed for 89. Now, in better batting conditions and with sufficient time in hand, Middlesex knocked off the required runs.

Never say die! How clichéd this sounds, but it is this attitude that makes the difference between defeat and victory. One of the most romantic of such tales is the Test match between Australia and England at Manchester in 1961. England requiring 255 to win on the last day was cruising to victory at 150 for 1. Richie Benaud, Aussie captain, turned around to Wally Grout the wicketkeeper and said loudly enough for all to hear, 'we have to win this one.' He himself went around the wicket, bowled his leg spinners in one unbroken spell of six wickets for 70, and spun Australia to victory. *The Wisden Illustrated History of Cricket* (1989) says, 'Benaud had affected one of the most astounding escapes in Test history.' Talking of Benaud's captaincy, one must add that Worrell and Benaud in cricket history can never be separated. It is not that two of the finest captains played at the same time. It is simply that these two wonderful leaders actually assumed the mantle of statesmen, to make the Australia–West Indies series of 1961 the kind of beacon that Test cricket will always look up to whenever it questions its existence. Benaud had a sense of occasion that was uncanny and was one of the first cricket captains who understood the importance of communicating positively with the media. He brought charisma, strategic risk taking and flair to the captaincy. He brought a buzz and a zing to captaincy. Talking of flair, Benaud best demonstrated this by his relatively higher success rate in sending the opposition in to bat after winning the toss. It was, however, style with substance too. What appeared to be a sheer flair was actually backed up by forethought and meticulous advance planning. When Australia toured India under Benaud in 1959–1960, there was more excitement and keener anticipation of an Australian series than ever before or after. It seemed as though a cricket carnival was about to unfold. To a large part it had to do with the way Benaud approached the series and the manner in which he interacted with the media. It was not just India. Even Wisden, careful about going over the top, said that Benaud was 'the most popular captain of any overseas team to come to Great Britain.' Johnnie Moyes, Australian cricket commentator and journalist, and one of the best ever, said this of Benaud: 'Often in life and in cricket we see the man who has true substance in him burst forth into stardom when his walk-on part is changed for one demanding personality and a degree of leadership. I believe that this is what happened to Benaud.' Benaud like many Australian cricketers of those years retired from the Test cricket fairly early, when he was hardly 32 years old.

Australians if they were to be polled to nominate their best cricket captains ever would probably vote for Richie Benaud, Ian Chappell and Mark Taylor. Perhaps Allan Border too, for how he rallied his country when they were at possibly the lowest ebb in their cricket history. This does not discount Bradman's leadership but the Don, however, led strong Australian teams. Border on the other hand literally pulled up Australia from the floor. Ian Chappell, to an extent also did something similar in the early 1970s. He was given the captaincy after a poor run for Bill Lawry. First, the Australians came home from South Africa in 1970, licking their wounds after a terrible 4–0 hiding and then immediately in the Ashes series at home in 70–71, Ray Illingworth, the wily old fox, also wrested the Ashes from the Aussies. A fresh new team with a new captain was what the country needed. Chappell's first tour as captain was the 1972 Ashes series in England. Old hands were dropped and a young new team was forged under Chappell. There was bonding, barriers between seniors and juniors was broken, and the evenings over drinks were not beer sessions but building a fierce common resolve to fight to the end and do their best on the ground. Chappell also adapted and adopted good methods that he had observed and learnt from Benaud, Simpson and Lawry. That was combined with his own personal stamp of what was needed to forge a commando unit that would fight to the death. Those of us who had seen the neatly turned out, clean cut, clean shaven dapper Australians—Neil Harvey, Norman O'Neill and others—suddenly saw visibly combative, scruffy Australians, given to much swearing and sledging on the ground. It was almost as if they were whipping themselves into a growling fighting mood. For the best insight into Ian Chappell the captain, we must go to one of his mates, Ashley Mallett, the off spinner who played much of his cricket under his captaincy. This is a memorable extract from Mallett's writing on Chappell and we quote:

> South Australia were playing at the Gabba against Queensland once. As we were walking out onto the field, Chappelli brushed past one of our opening bowlers, Andrew Sincock, who was blowdrying his hair in front of the mirror near the dressing-room door. Chappelli sidled up to me and said: 'Mate, I want you to open the bowling. Come into the wind after Fang's

> [Wayne Prior] first over.' 'Why?' 'No bastard who blow-dries his hair just as we are about to take the field is going to open the bowling in any team I lead.' Mallett wrote, 'To those of us lucky enough to have played under his captaincy, he is very much the 'captain for life.' He could be hard as nails, but whenever an old team mate is in any way in trouble, Chappelli is the first man to his side.' Obviously Chappell built huge loyalties that translated into his players giving more than their best on the field for him.

Mark Taylor while being acknowledged as among the finest captains would himself pass on a lot of credit to Allan Border for having resuscitated Australia and handing over a side that was infinitely better than what Border himself inherited. When Australia sank to its lowest ebb and a weeping Kim Hughes threw in the towel, they turned to Border. The tough, no nonsense cricketer delivered one of the greatest recoveries. Within two years, he had wrapped his hands around the World Cup. Taylor's job thus was to ensure that what Border had started, he must finish. Taylor did that and much more. He was a natural leader; the confidence and assertiveness from the first day came naturally to him. He was inspirational; he made things happen; he tried out things with a sureness of hand be it field placing or bowling change. Taylor had a bustling 'I am in control' air that not only transmitted to his team but also communicated to the opposing team that it was Taylor who was calling the shots. He was no control freak and in fact allowed his players full expression. The way Shane Warne bloomed to full potential under his captaincy or the manner in which Mark Waugh could bat as freely as his soul commanded, was in large measure due to the way Taylor led them. He was a superb tactician and Warne will be able to recount many a victim as a result of the ploys that he concocted with Taylor. How would Taylor have led Australia if he had a lesser team? That is pure conjecture but on the evidence of what one saw, Taylor would have ensured that his team punched well above their weight.

Taylor somehow always conveyed that he held far superior cards even if he only had some ordinary ones in his hand. After Benaud, it was Taylor who brought a buzz into captaincy.

Mark Taylor also showed that great captains have a fine sense of occasion and history. He had the wisdom to embrace such moments. Against Pakistan, he declared the innings closed when his personal score came level with Bradman's 334 the highest by any Australian. Taylor was clear that no way would he ever cross the incomparable Bradman! Could there have been a better way of remembering and saluting their greatest batter? Closer home, and more recently, Mahendra Singh Dhoni, leading India in a Test against Australia, gave the reins of the final session to Sourav Ganguly, who was retiring from international cricket after that Test match. It was Dhoni's way of paying genuine tribute to one of India's finest captains.

Each nation has faced its own crisis at various times in its cricket. If it emerged stronger, cleaner and happier from each such crisis, the reason was that it chose its captain wisely. Just a few examples: When India was torn by the betting scandals and the earnest cricket lover was shattered, Ganguly forged a committed and honorable band of cricketers who wore their country's colors with pride. He was extraordinarily blessed that he had Kumble, Dravid, Tendulkar and Laxman with him to help rebuild the Indian team. Many years earlier, Indian cricket used regional intrigues, selection quotas and a 'walk all over me' attitude found in Tiger Pataudi, a leader who told his team, we are not playing for Bombay or Delhi or Madras, we are playing for India. He also told his men that he wanted to see a lot of mud on his players' trousers and grubby knees—for the first time an Indian captain was turning on the heat for better fielding.

During Pataudi's time we still carried the burden of the feudal shadow, of respect and reverence for age. It was a time when India had emerged from a painful war with China; it was a time when India's economy was hurting, a time when we were acutely conscious that we were struggling. Pataudi was just 21

An iconic fielding set-up by Tiger Pataudi's Indian team against New Zealand, March, 1965
Photo Courtesy: Kasturi & Sons

but thrust into the leader's role—after Contractor's near fatal injury—over the heads of Borde and some others. Those days the Indian team had clear regional cleavages and to compound that team selection was often whimsical. Ganguly on the other hand took over at a time when all of India felt deeply betrayed and saddened by the match fixing controversy. A sport that we all cherished had become sullied; the very foundations of our faith in clean sport as an integral part of society had been shaken. But Ganguly's India was also a young India with new self-belief; winds of change had swept through India, its economy, its culture; there was brashness and confidence that seemed to communicate that we can hold our own anywhere in the world; there were less visible and insincere respect for age; while Pataudi's Indian team comprised amateurs Ganguly's team had players who were well paid professionals and beginning to make a lot of money through endorsements in the liberalized global economy that India had embraced. While Pataudi's India had players drawn essentially from the metros, Ganguly's team now had members from smaller towns like Ranchi and Hubli.

Although we won a series overseas for the first time—New Zealand 1968—under Pataudi, it was under Ganguly that we began winning abroad regularly. We were no longer bad tourists, we were in fact in a mood to wrest the initiative on foreign soil; we recorded a series of wins. Pataudi has the halo—especially when time dulls the memory—of being an attacking captain but that was not really true. He did not have a great team and he would switch to defensive fields quickly. To his credit, when he saw that he had a fantastic spin quartet, he used that to the hilt. Pataudi's best captaincy actually came in his last series as player and captain in 1974–1975. By then his reflexes had gone, he was batting from memory and he knew his time was up. And that is when he led India like Zorro. He brought India back from 0–2 down to level the series. Audaciously and with a gambler's instinct, he kept Chandra on for an extra over when everything pointed otherwise. That 'extra over' from Chandra was a magical over and India went on to beat West Indies at Eden Gardens.

Pakistan skipper Imran Khan during a match against England at the 1987 World Cup
Photo Courtesy: Kasturi & Sons

Imran Khan of Pakistan was a leader of such stature and charisma that he was able to unerringly spot talent and draft unknown players straight into the national team. It was at his insistence that the concept of neutral umpires was first tried out in Pakistan in the series against India in 1989. Today, Sri Lanka is a major cricketing power, but till Arjuna Ranatunga became its captain the country seemed to be happy being bridesmaid. Ranatunga changed all that once and for ever. Sri Lankans have much to remember of Ranatunga's captaincy with pride: for how he combatively stood up for Muralitharan in Australia; for creating the World Cup winning opening combination of Jayasuriya and Kaluwitharana and forcing everyone to treat the Sri Lankan team seriously. There are many more such turning points in every cricketing nation's history where captains played the pivotal role.

Amid all this, the good captains confront 'under performance' squarely, brutally with some players, gently with others. An oft told anecdote is of the time when with few runs to defend, Mike Brearley motivated Bob Willis to bowl flat out at the Australians. On the other hand, seeing Ian Botham bowl just medium pace, Brearley, hand on hip and jaw out thrust, goaded and taunted Botham into a fury. He achieved what he wanted—an inspired Willis supported by a fired up Botham in red heat tore through Australia. As Rodney Hogg the Australian bowler once famously said, 'Brearley has a degree in people!' Everyone knows that Brearley the player could barely qualify for a place in the side for his batting. In fact, but for England's tradition of selecting its captain first and then the rest of the team, Brearley may not have played much for England at all. In contrast, Australia selects its best players and chooses the captain from that pool. England got it right with Brearley for without doubt he is among the best captains cricket has ever known. To be able to captain with such command, for players to look up to him and do his bidding, when he was himself a mediocre contributor must imply that Brearley must have been a magician of a leader. He was quite simply outstanding. Unruffled, technically very sound, able to move swiftly between attack and defense and above all the ability to get everyone together as a team to perform to their potential. He of course had a potent pace attack in the form of Willis and Botham who delivered the 1981 Ashes for him but the way he got the best out of them was what was so amazing. He wore very lightly, his educational qualifications, his scholarship and his superior intellectual abilities and could therefore connect with everyone at all times without being overwhelming. His book *The Art of Captaincy* is referred to as much as Don Bradman's *The Art of Cricket*.

Finally, captaincy is something that can be experienced and felt, for the more one tries to describe it the harder it gets. Brearley tries to simplify it by saying that cricket captaincy is a combination of good man management and technical competence. Surely within those few words there is the wisdom of a lifetime. Worrell, Benaud, Brearley and those other great captains, they had all this in great measure. Somewhere ultimately we would like to believe that above all, the really great captains are also good human beings. In this hardnosed business of leading the country's cricket teams we sometimes forget that.

10

A SPLENDID VIEW FROM THE TOP: WHEN VIRAT KOHLI LED INDIA FROM NO. 7 TO NO. 1 IN ICC TEST RANKINGS

This essay was written in January 2017

It is a great time for Test cricket in India. After spending a difficult period rebuilding the team from 2011 to 2014, the Indian cricket team now has 18 undefeated Tests in their bag, among them, 14 wins. Perhaps, the turning point was the come-from-behind series win in Sri Lanka in 2015. And now, routing New Zealand and England in the 2016-17 home season, without any debate on pitches or the luck of the coin. As 2017 begins, India is no. 1 in ICC Test ranking, ahead by some distance from the no. 2 team, Australia.

The best thing, however, is not that Indian cricket is savoring a view from the summit. Rather, it is the fiercely ambitious skipper saying, 'It's just the beginning. It's nothing compared to what we want to achieve.' In the past—in April 2004 after the win in Pakistan, or in December 2010 after retaining the no. 1 ranking at Durban—we felt a growing sense of complacence. This time, it feels that India is not merely at the top but committed to scale the new peaks that Virat Kohli has set his sights on. This new confidence comes from the fact that

India has a strong supply line of cricketers, toughened and well prepared by a combination of high-quality domestic structure and a tough baptism through the India 'A' teams.

Back in the 1970s, cricketers knew that a ton or a fiver in needle-sharp Ranji, Duleep and Irani Trophy games would provide a ticket for an Australia or England tour. Today, aspiring Indian cricketers not only have to prove themselves in the tough grind of domestic cricket, but also go through an additional rung—a stint with the India 'A' team. The extremely well-planned calendar for the India 'A' team provides players the opportunity—away from the pressure and demands of a billion people—to hone their technique, talent and temperament. Players who have proved themselves in domestic cricket—the long form of cricket and IPL—form a pool of talent that gets tempered in games for India 'A'. And these new players are incredibly fortunate to be pupils of a master like Rahul Dravid, who mentors them and helps them develop in equal measure the confidence, humility and the nous to learn quickly. The current bench strength that we see in the Indian team is not an accident, but the result of the rigor of domestic cricket.

After the 2016-17 England series, K. L. Rahul, Karun Nair and Jayant Yadav are on everyone's minds; we must acknowledge they are products of our domestic system and the India 'A' preparations. Go back further, and one will remember that others too—Ajinkya Rahane and Cheteshwar Pujara, for example—made it to the senior team because of the mountain of runs they scored in domestic cricket.

Waiting in the wings, again with runs and wickets behind them are batters like Manish Pandey and Abhinav Mukund and bowlers like Shardul Thakur, to name a few. When Wriddhiman Saha was injured in the Test match against England in Visakhapatnam, Parthiv Patel stepped in as replacement for the Mohali Test after being away from the senior team for over eight years. But such is the intensity of domestic cricket that when Patel came back into the team, he clearly belonged. Similarly, though our bowlers take turns at breaking down, the worries are lesser as India is able to put out different combinations. If Shami is not fit, let's get in Ishant. If the conditions help swing, bring in Bhuvneshwar. Back up? We have Thakur and Hardik Pandya waiting in the wings. A very different situation from five years ago, when Zaheer Khan broke down in the first session of a four-Test series in England. India had no bench strength and whimsically drafted in an unfit R. P. Singh. It was the first step to the thrashing that summer. Today, there is a choice of fast bowlers from an assembly-line situation.

As selectors recognize performances in domestic cricket and the India 'A' games, collateral benefits will follow. Rishabh Pant, the darling of the IPL circuit, knows that only performances in the longer format will hasten his entry into the Test team. Shreyas Iyer can put aside his poor IPL record to focus on scoring runs for Mumbai in the Ranji. Karun Nair has thrown the gauntlet to the selectors with his triple. Do they select him even when other established batters are available? Rahul has made the opener's spot his own even as Vijay is secure. Will Shikhar Dhawan make a comeback, or will Abhinav break through? Even as we write this, Gujarat opener, Samit Gohel, has shattered a 117-year-old record by carrying his bat through the innings for a triple century in the Ranji semifinal. Among the spinners, Jayant Yadav has moved ahead of Amit Mishra, but Kuldeep Yadav is already knocking at the door and so is left-arm spinner, Nadeem of Jharkand.

Every spot in the Indian Test team is now fiercely contested. This is a fine position to be in. Kohli and Kumble will have a gleam in their eye and a spring in their stride when they next step on to the Wanderers or the MCG. As connoisseurs of the game, we can only rejoice at this wonderful juncture in Indian cricket history.

Note: India remained no. 1 till May 2020 and enjoyed another long spell at the top from December 2021 to May 2023. As of August 2023, India is no. 1 in the ICC Test ranking.

11

BIG HITTING IS NOT NEW: ASK TRUMPER AND JESSOP

> Biggest hit at Lords—The only known instance of a batsman hitting a ball over the present pavilion at Lord's occurred when A. E. Trott appearing for MCC against Australia on July 31, August 1, 2, 1899, drove M. A. Noble so far and high that the ball struck a chimney pot and fell behind the building.
>
> —*Wisden Cricketers' Almanack 2010*

Ever since the Indian Premier League (IPL) began, we have often been asked to write about at least some aspect of this slam—biff—whoosh version of the game. There is such a crescendo of noise over the number of sixes hit in the IPL that we decided to dig into the big hitting exploits of great Test players of olden days and place big hitting in its proper perspective.

We grew up, learning and reading our cricket at a time when Test cricket and first-class cricket was all there was; ODIs and T20 were not even in anyone's faintest imagination. We read about the exploits of great attacking batters like Victor Trumper, Gilbert Jessop, Charlie Macartney, J. H. Sinclair and our own C. K. Nayudu with awe and admiration. Those were days when strike rate was not described as runs per balls faced, rather, in runs per minutes at the crease.

Cricket has kept changing so much that the best way to appreciate it is to look at each era independently. Comparing players from different eras is as unfair to them as changing the game itself. Rules have changed dramatically—what was leg before wicket (LBW) once is no more LBW and vice versa; uncovered pitches those days made batting a special skill while today we have well-manicured turf; protective gear was minimal in those days. Why, even just 40 years ago, a tail-ender like Chandrasekhar faced Jeff Thomson and Andy Roberts bareheaded. If Trumper or Ranjitsinhji came to a cricket ground today, they would think Martians are batting. A bat was a slim piece of 'English Willow' with a thin handle and a couple of rubber sleeves to absorb the shock of ball hitting against bat. The blade required 'seasoning'; it was regularly and lovingly massaged with linseed oil and preciously maintained to last many seasons. The bat's edge was truly an edge and if the batter did not 'middle' the ball it would only travel some yards. Today's bats are made using the finest technology; wood is highly compressed, handles are provided numerous sleeves and the bat has a lethal solid bow to it. The bat's edge is no longer an edge but actually provides the third side to the bat. So, the mishit flies 65 yards and the bowler, who induced that false shot, clutches his head at the unfairness of it all.

Given all this, we examined big hitting through the lens of strike rate, the percentage of runs scored through sixes and the number of sixes and see how things have panned out over the years. We restricted ourselves to batters with an average of over 30 and at least 1,000 Test runs (we lowered the bar on batting average for the early era batters). No surprises at all that modern batters have the highest strike rates, the highest number of sixes and the highest percentage of runs through sixes. We put these numbers in Tables 11.1 and 11.2 as a quick snap shot but having done that we will get back to reminiscing about the exploits of the oldies whose figures may not compare with the modern greats but who were in their times and circumstances perhaps as devastating as the modern big hitters.

TABLE 11.1: The Batters with Highest Strike Rates and Percentage of Runs in Sixes

Strike rate		*Percentage of runs on sixes*	
Modern era (Post-1990)			
Shahid Afridi (Pakistan)	87.0	Shahid Afridi (Pakistan)	18.2
V. Sehwag (India)	82.0	C. L. Cairns (New Zealand)	15.7
A. C. Gilchrist (Australia)	82.0	A. Flintoff (England)	12.8
Umar Akmal (Pakistan)	66.0	A. Symonds (Australia)	11.5
T. M. Dilshan (Sri Lanka)	65.9	A. C. Gilchrist (Australia)	10.8
Middle era (1945–1990)			
N. Kapil Dev (India)	80.9	Haroon Rasheed (Pakistan)	9.4
B. E. Congdon (New Zealand)	74.9	Imran Khan (Pakistan)	8.7
I. V. A. Richards (west Indies)	69.3	I. T. Botham (England)	7.7
D. T. Lindsay (South Africa)	64.3	K. L. T. Arthurton (West Indies)	7.4
R. A. McLean (South Africa)	63.7	K. C. Bland (South Africa)	7.2
Early era (Before 1939)			
M. W. Tate (England)	71.6	J. H. Sinclair (South Africa)	9
V. T. Trumper (Australia)	69.5	M. W. Tate (England)	7
C. G. Macartney (Australia)	69.2	H. B. Cameron (South Africa)	5.3
H. W. Taylor (South Africa)	66.7	F. E. Woolley (England)	2.7
J. H. Sinclair (South Africa)	65.9	W. R. Hammond (England)	2.2

Source: Data from espncricinfo.com. Analysis and tabular compilation by authors.

TABLE 11.2: Batters with Highest Number of Sixes

Player	*Match*	*Innings*	*Runs*	*Sixes*
A. C. Gilchrist (Australia)	96	137	5,570	100
J. H. Kallis (South Africa)	152	257	12,379	90
V. Sehwag (India)	96	167	8,178	88
B. C. Lara (West Indies)	131	232	11,953	88
C. L. Cairns (New Zealand)	62	104	3,320	87
I. V. A. Richards (West Indies)	121	182	8,540	84
A. Flintoff (England)	79	130	3,845	82
M. L. Hayden (Australia)	103	184	8,625	82
C. H. Gayle (West Indies)	91	159	6,373	75
R. T. Ponting (Australia)	165	282	13,346	73

Source: Data from espncricinfo.com. Analysis and tabular compilation by authors.

Clearly modern cricket is in a league of its own. The sixes and fours, and the strike rates in Test cricket have zoomed. The number of runs scored per day (or per over) and the much higher percentage of decisive Test matches is something that is to be greatly welcomed.

Why were so few sixes hit in the olden days? The answer is provided by two very compelling reasons. One is that in the first 33 years of Test cricket, the ball had to be literally hit out of the ground to be counted as a six. Many of modern cricket's sixes would have only counted for a four in those days. The second reason is that before one-day cricket took firm root, the distance from the pitch to the boundary ropes was much higher and in many of the established cricket grounds around the world, the distance would be 80 meters or more. For the IPL, we have much shorter boundaries so that commentators can frequently scream 'DLF Maximum'.

All this places in proper perspective the path-breaking attacking batsmanship of the early greats. For 100 years of Test cricket, there have been only four occasions when a century has been scored before lunch on opening day. Three of these four feats were from the bats of the golden oldies—Trumper, Macartney and Bradman.

Among the golden oldies, Victor Trumper was peerless. Acknowledged as the greatest Australian batter till Bradman made his entry, many of his shots (like Ranji's leg glance) were seen for the first time only when he played them. Each of his Test centuries came in quick time; for instance his 159 in 171 minutes and 185 not out in 230 minutes and so on. However, as Neville Cardus said, 'We can no more get an idea of Trumper's (winged) batmanship by looking at the averages and statistics than we can find the essential quality of a composition by Mozart by adding up the notes.' To get some idea of a genius who lived a century ago, one could read Arthur Mailey, the fantastic Australian leg spinner who played with Trumper and of course Neville Cardus, high priest of romantic cricket journalism,

Victor Trumper
Credit: V. Balaji

who saw Trumper bat in England and Australia. There is a picture of Trumper jumping out to drive that every cricket magazine has always used. It was the picture that Mailey had pinned to the wall as he grew up dreaming that one day he would play alongside Trumper for Australia!

Jessop from England was a big hitter on a different scale. His legend is all about one afternoon in 1902, when he hit a century in 75 minutes to take England to the most unlikely victory over Australia (see Table 11.3). He was known to be a fearsome hitter and that innings made him immortal. Many of his 'fours' cleared the ropes on the full and in fact one of his boundary hits was caught in the players' balcony. But those days, as we have mentioned earlier, the ball had to clear the stadium to count as a six. Perhaps many of the fours by Jessop that day would actually count as a six by today's rules. Jessop had a tremendous first-class career and scored over 20,000 runs

TABLE 11.3: Fastest Test Centuries (in Minutes)

Minutes	*Batsman*	*Match*	*Location*	*Year*
70	J. M. Gregory	Australia vs. South Africa	Johannesburg	1921–1922
77	G. L. Jessop	England vs. Australia	The Oval	1902
78	R. Benaud	Australia vs. West Indies	Kingston	1954–1955
80	J. H. Sinclair	South Africa vs. Australia	Cape Town	1902–1903
81	I. V. A. Richards	West Indies vs. England	St. John's	1985–1986

Source: Data from espncricinfo.com. Analysis and tabular compilation by authors.

at a mind boggling rate of over 80 runs an hour. Richie Benaud summed up Jessop for us in one pithy sentence: 'Perhaps the best one-day player to have ever lived and never played that form of cricket.'

There were others of that era too who would have walked into any one-day side. Charlie Macartney of Australia was one. Nicknamed Governor-General, he played not one, not two but many attacking innings. Those who saw him bat, pick his 151 in 172 minutes, against England on a sticky wicket at Headingley in 1926 as one of his best. It was apparently a violent innings, but it also had some of the deftest shots. Robertson-Glasgow memorably described Macartney's cuts being 'so late they are almost posthumous.'

Jimmy Sinclair of South Africa believed that belting the ball was the sole purpose of batting. It is no surprise that he features among those with the highest strike rates or sixes from batters of his time. Another batter of course was Frank Woolley, easily the best left hander ever before Neil Harvey made his appearance.

J. M. Gregory has the distinction of scoring the fastest century in terms of time, taking just 70 minutes to belt a ton against South Africa. Luckily, there are records to also show that his century took 67 balls. And in the years since he performed that feat, only Brendon McCullum (54 balls), Viv Richards (57 balls) and Adam Gilchrist (58 balls) have bettered him.

The years immediately after World War II and till the advent of one-day cricket was in a sense the most boring period in Test cricket and much of the blame for that would have to go to England and its pernicious pad play. If it had not been for the wonderful spirit of Richie Benaud, Neil Harvey, Frank Worrell, Clyde Walcott, Everton Weekes, Garry Sobers, Rohan Kanhai, Ted Dexter and others, that period would have been unbearable. This was also a period when India's own Salim Durani would respond with a six when the crowd clamored for one and M. L. Jaisimha clouted sixes between periods of self-imposed denial.

Viv Richards plays a shot, World Cup, 1987
Photo Courtesy: Kasturi & Sons

The 1970s and 1980s, however, were by great fortune, the periods of renaissance. Perhaps when one looks back, one would recognize that this was the period when cricket took a grip on itself and reinvented and saved itself. This era belonged to swashbuckling knights such as Viv Richards, Kapil Dev, Gordon Greenidge, Roy Fredericks, Majid Khan, Ian Botham, Clive Lloyd, Imran Khan and others even as there was space for the artistry and elegance of G. R. Viswanath, Dilip Vengsarkar, Zaheer Abbas, David Gower, Greg Chappell, Mohammad Azharuddin and other stylists. People remember Sobers and Ravi Shastri for their exploit of six sixes in an over in first-class cricket but strangely one forgets Kapil Dev hitting Hemmings for four sixes of four successive balls of an over to help India avoid a follow on in a Test match in England in 1990.

One is almost certain that great batters of yonder years would have reveled and gloried in our modern times. But we should also try and imagine what the modern greats would have done had they played 100 years ago. Virender Sehwag's blithe spirit would have found the same expression; Trumper and Macartney would have rejoiced playing alongside him. We would like to conclude this essay by listing the fastest double centuries in Table 11.4 and the fastest triple centuries in Table 11.5, both of which encapsulate Sehwag's uniqueness. The irony of using figures to describe the genius of Sehwag will escape none, for after Trumper, has there ever been someone who batted with a disdain for numbers as Sehwag has!

TABLE 11.4: Fastest Double Centuries in Test Match Cricket

Batsman (Country)	*Balls*	*Versus*	*Venue*	*Year*
Nathan Astle (New Zealand)	153	England	Christchurch	2001
Virendra Sehwag (India)	168	Sri Lanka	Mumbai	2009
Virendra Sehwag (India)	182	Pakistan	Lahore	2005
Virendra Sehwag (India)	194	South Africa	Chennai	2008

Source: Data from espncricinfo.com. Analysis and tabular compilation by authors.

TABLE 11.5: Fastest Triple Centuries in Test Match Cricket

Batsman (Country)	*Balls*	*Versus*	*Venue*	*Year*
Virendra Sehwag (India)	278	South Africa	Chennai	2007
Mathew Hayden (Australia)	362	Zimbabwe	Perth	2003
Virendra Sehwag (India)	364	Pakistan	Multan	2004

Source: Data from espncricinfo.com. Analysis and tabular compilation by authors.

12

THE SEVENTEENTH MAN

By all accounts, including his own autobiography, Gandhiji kept more than a fair distance between himself and sports. A reluctant participant at school in the compulsory games, he never was convinced that sports should occupy much of school curriculum. As for adults, he could never understand the time and effort they invested in this pastime and believed it occupied an unnecessarily large space in their lives.

And therefore, it is perhaps a most delicious piece of our history that the Mahatma signed an autograph book, which had the signatures of the 16 cricketers of the Marylebone Cricket Club (MCC) team touring India in 1933, nominating himself as the seventeenth player of an Englishman's party. Apparently, Laxmi Merchant, sister of India's legendary opening batter Vijay Merchant, had gone to him with the book, a page of which contained the Englishmen's autographs. Gandhiji, instead of signing on another leaf, stays with the page that has 16 English cricketers' autographs and writes, 'No. 17' and then signs it 'MK Gandhi'.

What does one make of that? We believe this was Gandhiji's impish humor at its best. A child-like prank on the one hand and a superb political signal on the other—he was against British rule and not against the British people. Humor and wit was a precious strand that Gandhiji always clasped, never letting go.

He had after all said in all seriousness, 'I would commit suicide if I did not have sense of humour.' As cricket lovers, we might wish Gandhiji had demonstrated a little more affection for that game but as lovers of wit we believe he more than made up.

When people speak of Gandhi and cricket, the story of the pernicious cricket tournament called the Quadrangular, established by the British, often comes up. The tournament, as fans know, had four teams based on their religious affiliations, contesting for a trophy. The Hindus, Parsis, Muslims and Europeans were pitted against each other. It later also became the Pentangular upon the inclusion of a fifth team called 'the rest', comprising players belonging to other religions. Despicable as the tournament was in its conception, for the cricket-loving Maharashtrians, Parsis and Gujaratis, it was a wrenching compromise to watch these games, because they loved cricket.

It is in this context that we describe the two serious 'cricket' interventions that Gandhi made. He might have not been a player, or even a fan, but such was his leadership and the sweep of his views on nation and society that the game in India listened to him. Gandhi's crusade for communal harmony and amity started almost as soon as he arrived in India. His was a constant battle cry (admittedly an odd phrase to go with the apostle of non-violence) imploring the two major communities to embrace the spirit of living together. Though the Ranji Trophy came into being in 1934 as a result of a rising demand for a state-based tournament, the Quadrangular and later the Pentangular continued to be played. In 1940, the socio-political tensions were so heightened that people questioned the wisdom of holding such inter-community tournaments. While some teams wanted to play, the Hindus were definitely uncomfortable. The management of PJ Hindu Gymkhana, home to the Hindus' team, went to the Mahatma for advice—should the Hindus' team participate in such a tournament? Gandhiji said that he found it totally unacceptable that any competition could pit religion against religion. PJ Hindu Gymkhana listened to the Mahatma and withdrew from the tournament that year. The tournament without them went limp, had little public interest, and the All India Radio also withdrew their running commentary.

The other major influence that Gandhi had on cricket was in the context of his crusade against untouchability, which began within a few years of his arriving from South Africa. On every occasion and at every forum, Gandhiji hammered away, and his speech at Nagpur in December 1920, asking people to banish this most sinful, inhuman practice, was a watershed moment. In 1920, the Hindus' team had a trio of the finest cricketers—all three brothers—from the Dalit community. Palwankar Baloo, the eldest, had already made a name for himself as a spinner of great ability. He had gone with the All-India team to England in 1911 and was outstanding on that tour, taking over 100 wickets in the 23 matches that the team played. Even at his peak, because of his caste, Baloo was never made captain; lesser players from the upper caste were. And in 1920, he also found himself out of the team. His brothers, Vittal and Shivram, opted out in protest. Their team lost the first match. The PJ Hindu Gymkhana management, aware of the rising tide of public support for the Dalit cricketers, reinstated Baloo and his brothers. In what was a momentous decision at that time, Palwankar Vittal was made captain in 1923. When the Hindus won the tournament, he was jubilantly carried on their shoulders by the other members of the team.

After retirement from professional cricket, Frank Worrell, became a Jamaican senator

Photo Courtesy: Kasturi & Sons

Elsewhere in the world too, discrimination and prejudice has tarnished sports and cricket. In England, the upper-class amateur cricketers were called 'gentlemen' while the paid working-class cricketers were called 'players'. They had separate dressing rooms and an annual fixture called Gentlemen versus Players too. Seventy-five years after playing their first Test match, England in 1952, finally had a working-class professional as captain. The West Indies only had white captains till 1960, although the black cricketer George Headley captained them on one occasion in 1947-48. After decades of injustice, Frank Worrell, finest of cricketers, noblest of men, became the first black to captain them for an entire series when he took the team to Australia.

And what of South Africa, where Gandhi's lifelong fight began on the night of 7 June 1893 at the Pietermaritzburg Station? During the Apartheid Era, South Africa was banned from the Olympics in 1964, even as they continued playing rugby and cricket with white teams from Australia, England and New Zealand. Matters came to a head when MCC selected Basil D'Oliveira (a mixed-race South African who had become a UK citizen) for their 1968-69 tour to South Africa. John Vorster, the South African Premier, threatened to not allow the MCC to play if it included D'Oliveira. The MCC refused to budge and called off the tour. In 1970, South Africa was banished from international cricket. It was only after South Africa lifted the Apartheid and took steps towards racial integration and the formation of a democratic non-racial government that they re-entered international cricket. Fittingly, the first tour by the reinstated South African cricket team was to Gandhi's India in 1991. The two countries now play for a trophy that is called the Gandhi–Mandela Trophy.

India's first great cricketer, the man with magic wrists and the inventor of the leg glance, Ranji, was born in Gandhi's own Kathiawar, just three years after Gandhi. Vinoo Mankad, one of the world's greatest all-rounders ever, was also from these parts. As was Amar Singh, a fine swing bowler. Two of India's finest cricketers in the current team—Cheteshwar Pujara and Ravindra Jadeja—also belong to Saurashtra. We can compile a strong XI from Saurashtra but are certain that because his home team is strong, the Mahatma would align himself with the state that puts up the weakest team.

13

LEG BEFORE WICKET: THE CHANGING PARADIGM

This piece like earlier ones began as an animated discussion between the two of us. This time about umpiring in general and LBW in particular. The essence of the LBW Law has remained the same over time: (a) to be LBW the ball must hit the batter's pads in line with the stumps and is likely to hit the stumps beyond any reasonable doubt; (b) if the ball pitches outside the leg you cannot be leg before even if that delivery was likely to hit the stumps; (c) a batter can be LBW even if the batter is struck outside the off stump provided the batter is not offering a stroke in the opinion of the umpire (this rule was introduced around 1970).

But two significant changes in LBW rules have to be mentioned. One, that in the first 50 years of cricket, prior to the 1930s, the law stated that the ball had to pitch in line with the stumps and also go on to hit the stumps. Thus a batter, if hit on the pads in line with the stumps would not be out if the ball had pitched outside off stump. This rule was changed in 1937, to allow for this dismissal. The other significant change was introduced in 1970, where batters could be given out LBW even if they were struck outside the off stump, provided they offered no shot and in the umpire's opinion the ball was likely to hit the stumps. Both these rules were meant to curb excessive pad play which had made the game a real bore. Of course right through the history of the game, no batter could be given out LBW to a ball which pitched outside leg stump.

But it is not just the rules alone that have changed over time. In fact two of the most significant changes in the game's history that have occurred in the last 20 years are: (a) the introduction of neutral umpires since 1989 and (b) the use of technology for line decisions and referrals for clean catches. Given the above facts, it is interesting to study if there was an increase in LBW dismissals post 1937 and a further increase post 1970. To begin this discussion, we present in Table 13.1, LBW dismissals in absolute numbers and as a percentage of total dismissals since the Test cricket began. Now while the changed rule explains the increase in LBW dismissals since 1970, the increase since 1990 can possibly be attributed only to the use of neutral umpires and the increasing use and availability of technology. Can we say that since 1990, the rules are being interpreted differently? Are the umpires not applying benefit of doubt to batters as often as before? Are the decisions in favor of the home country and against the visiting nation—a huge bone of contention earlier—a thing of the past since the introduction of neutral umpires?

We decided to dig a little deeper. We examined the LBW dismissals for the period 1930–1989 and for the period since 1990. The summary is given in Table 13.2.

TABLE 13.1: The Increasing Trend of LBW Dismissals

Era	*Number of LBW dismissals*	*Total number of dismissals*	*% of LBW dismissals*
1877–1914	286	4,480	6.4
1920–1939	503	4,101	12.3
1946–1970	1,499	12,317	12.2
1971–2000	3,892	25,674	15.2
Since 2000	5,520	32,654	16.9

Source: Data from espncricinfo.com. Analysis and tabular compilation by authors.

TABLE 13.2: Host LBW Dismissals: The Clear Increase since 1990

	% LBW dismissals	
Host country	*Between 1930 and 1989*	*Since 1990*
Australia	11.3	15.6
England	13.7	16.3
India	13.9	15.2
New Zealand	10.6	17.6
Pakistan	16.3	17.7
South Africa	13.1	15.9
Sri Lanka	15.0	15.0
West Indies	13.0	19.8
Zimbabwe	13.0	20.3
All	13.0	16.8

Source: Data from espncricinfo.com. Analysis and tabular compilation by authors.

In the period since 1990, LBW dismissals as a percentage of total dismissals have risen to 16.7 per cent from 13 per cent in the period 1930–1989. That is a 30 per cent increase in the incidence of LBW dismissals in the last 20 years as compared to earlier years. When we looked for Test matches which had the maximum LBW dismissals, our search showed almost all the top entries are from post-1980 Tests.

Next we stacked up 20 batters each from the pre- and post-1989 period on the percentage of their LBW dismissals and found that 16 of the 20 pre-1989 era batters have the least percentage of LBW decisions. The only oldies with a higher percentage were Ken Barrington and Javed Miandad. Similarly among the 10 batters in this sample with the least percentage of LBW dismissals, all but Mahela Jayawardene belong to the pre-1990 era. Without burdening readers with the entire list of players and the percentage of LBW dismissals, we present in Table 13.3 a partial list of these 20 batters to underscore the point that there is a stark difference in the percentage of LBW dismissals for batters before and after 1990.

Back then in the pre-1990 era, batters enjoyed what is well known as a consistent and clear 'benefit of doubt' on LBW with umpires. It was an unwritten rule for umpires that when a batter played well forward, he would not be given out LBW. You wouldn't want to be the one who gave a Garry Sobers, Viv Richards, Sunil Gavaskar or Javed Miandad out wrongly and changed the course of the match.

TABLE 13.3: Percentage of LBW Dismissals: Batters from 1930 to 1989 and since 1990

Sl. no	*Player*	*Span*	*LBW dismissals*	*Total dismissals*	*% LBW*
1	D. G. Bradman (Australia)	1928–1948	6	70	8.6
2	S. M. Gavaskar (India)	1972–1987	17	198	8.6
3	L. Hutton (England)	1938–1953	12	123	9.8
4	D. P. M. D. Jayewardene (Sri Lanka)	1998–2008	16	153	10.5
5	G. S. Sobers (West Indies)	1955–1968	15	139	10.8
6	M. C. Cowdrey (England)	1956–1968	19	173	11
7	G. R. Viswanath (India)	1969–1982	16	145	11
8	Zaheer Abbas (Pakistan)	1975–1984	13	113	11.5
9	D. B. Vengsarkar (India)	1978–1990	19	163	11.7
10	D. C. S. Compton (England)	1938–1955	14	116	12.1
11	R. T. Ponting (Australia)	1995–2008	35	191	18.3
12	A. J. Stewart (England)	1990–2003	40	214	18.7
13	Inzamam-ul-Haq (Pakistan)	1994–2006	33	174	19
14	Javed Miandad (Pakistan)	1985–1993	33	168	19.6
15	S. R. Tendulkar (India)	1990–2008	47	234	20.1
16	K. F. Barrington (England)	1959–1968	24	116	20.7
17	S. Chanderpaul (West Indies)	1997–2009	35	166	21.1
18	N. Hussain (England)	1996–2003	34	155	21.9
19	Younis Khan (Pakistan)	2000–2006	21	89	23.6
20	G. C. Smith (South Africa)	2002–2008	31	126	24.6

Source: Data from espncricinfo.com. Analysis and tabular compilation by authors.

The batters of the 1960s with great reputations like Colin Cowdrey for instance, used this advantage well both in shot selection and risk taking. The old English adage 'when in doubt stretch forward' was employed by all great batters with little fear or uncertainty. Good batters made runs.

When they got a start, they made big scores—the crowds came to watch their favorites hit centuries.

The downside was that batters could get away with a lot of pad play. In the 1950s and 1960s, cricket was threatened by masters of pad play. Cowdrey and Peter May in their huge stand completely neutralized the magic of Sonny Ramadhin with such pad play. The barracker at Sydney became immortal when he angrily asked the English batter Peter Parfitt to tie his bat to his legs because he would score more runs that way! In 1967, at Chepauk, when Charlie Griffith joined Sobers (with only Hall and Gibbs to follow), there were more than 90 minutes left on the last day for India to seek victory. Sobers asked Griffith to stretch forward and take everything from Prasanna, Bishan Bedi and Chandrasekhar on his front pad—with complete confidence that Griffith would not be given out. It is probably to neutralize such pernicious pad play that the rules were changed around 1970 to penalize batters padding up outside off stump.

It is fascinating to note that for the period 1930–1989, the higher percentage of LBW against visiting teams as compared to home team is sharply evident in the case of the subcontinent. In contrast, there is hardly any difference in percentage of LBW decisions for the home team and opposition teams in England, Australia, South Africa and West Indies. In fact in New Zealand the percentage of home team LBW is greater than the guests. All this is summarized in Table 13.4.

The picture since 1990, that is, since the introduction of neutral umpires is equally illuminating. The difference in LBW for home team and opposition team has been greatly reduced in the subcontinent. On the other hand, the percentage of opposition LBW has risen above the percentage of home team

LBW dismissals in the case of Australia. While the overall increase in LBW since 1990 is evident, the numbers remain relatively lower in Australia and South Africa. One strong and logical reason for this is that the wickets are bouncier and so the ball would more often go over the stumps (Table 13.5).

TABLE 13.4: A Comparison of LBW against Hosts and Visitors (1930–1989)

Country	*Host LBW (%)*	*Opposition LBW (%)*
Australia	11.1	11.5
England	13.9	13.5
India	10.9	17.1
New Zealand	12.2	9.6
Pakistan	11.7	19.6
South Africa	12.9	13.1
Sri Lanka	7.7	23.9
West Indies	12.9	13.1
All	12.3	13.8

Source: Data from espncricinfo.com. Analysis and tabular compilation by authors.

TABLE 13.5: A Comparison of LBW against Hosts and Visitors (since 1990)

Country	*Host LBW (%)*	*Opposition LBW (%)*
Australia	11.9	16.0
England	16.5	16.1
India	16.9	22.2
New Zealand	15.7	15.9
Pakistan	18.1	26.1
South Africa	15.6	15.0
Sri Lanka	14.5	19.5
West Indies	21.3	15.5
Zimbabwe	15.8	13.9
All	16.0	17.3

Source: Data from espncricinfo.com. Analysis and tabular compilation by authors.

In essence, neutral umpires meant two things:

1. Only the best umpires in the world would form an elite panel.
2. It would serve to take away the long-nursed grudge that home umpires tilted the game in favor of the home team.

The one caveat is that neutral umpires—the best drawn from an elite pool of the best umpires in the world—may sometimes not be able to judge the bounce as well as a local umpire would, because they would be less familiar with the conditions in that country.

Top batters—Sachin Tendulkar, Ricky Ponting, Jacques Kallis, Younis Khan, Shiv Chanderpaul or Kevin Pietersen—unlike batters of the earlier era—were being given out LBW more often. The batter plays half forward defensively or is trying to work the ball to leg, is rapped on the front pad, apparently in line with the leg stump (remember the ball still has to travel 7–8 feet to the stumps). You are surprised to see the umpire raising the finger and stupefied to see Hawk eye showing the ball kissing the top of leg stump. The Hawk eye is positioned high up and has an inherent inability to extrapolate and predict the destination of the ball after pitching. Those who watched cricket before the 1970s will remember that umpires in those days crouched low so that their eyes were almost at stump level, precisely because that enabled them to judge the trajectory better.

Finally, it all boils down to good umpiring—which means consistency in decision making. It does not matter that Dickie Bird or Venkataraghavan would make instant judgments or that others needed to play it over and over in their minds before arriving at a decision. From Frank Chester to Sid Buller in the early days to Dickie Bird, David Shepherd, Venkat and Simon Taufel in later years, the best umpires understood the essence of umpiring and displayed consistency and predictability in their rulings. In that split second of time an umpire has to look at the bowler's landing foot, instantly look up and judge length, line, height, deviation, decide if there was an inside edge on to the pad or not, and decide LBW or not LBW. Umpires used their judgment and applied the unwritten code of benefit of doubt consistently. The best of umpires got most of their decisions right. Today, the pressure on modern-day umpires is becoming unbearable with every decision being cruelly dissected by Slo Mo, Hawk eye, Snickometer and Hot Spot. In all this discussion, we have deliberately not touched upon the Decision Review System or what is popularly known by its abbreviated name DRS. The DRS would ultimately be an application of these rules and the technology.

Having done our analysis, we took the opportunity to chat informally about umpiring with Venkat—the only International Cricket Council (ICC) Elite panel umpire to have played over 50 Tests and also captained his country in Tests and the World Cup; winner of the CEAT Award and one who earned the highest respect from all, both during his days as a player and later as an umpire. The essence of what Venkat said about umpiring and LBW decisions was: The good umpire, besides integrity needs concentration and competence to achieve consistency. The powers of concentration cannot be overemphasized when one remembers that the umpires are there for 90 overs a day for all five days without a break. The din and noise from the crowd can make it very difficult. This concentration and consistency is what a good umpire demonstrates in the LBW. He will make the same decision whether the batter is a no. 1 or 2 or whether he is 9, 10 or jack. Though himself a bowler, Venkat said that one must bear in mind that when a batter plays forward, even to a spinner, the ball is quite likely to bounce higher than stump height, unless it hits him below the shin. As an engineer, he says, he could appreciate the uncertainty of line and height over 8–10 feet of travel. This analysis and judgment of whether the ball would hit the stumps is the crux of competence in judging LBW.

14

AN EVENING WITH SALIM DURANI

It was 5 p.m. in the evening on a Friday in September 2008. My colleague and I (Giridhar) had checked in at the Delhi airport for our flight to Bengaluru. There was still an hour for our flight to be called and we gravitated to the airport restaurant for we could then have a glass of wine with the 'lounge card' that the airline provided its frequent flyers. About 15 minutes later—and we had already irrigated our throats—we were intensely discussing some office stuff when my colleague saw a tall, stooping man in blue blazer walk uncertainly into the restaurant and remarked, 'Must be an old actor of the sixties, looks familiar.' I turned around and instantly said, 'That's Salim Durani!' My voice was not pitched low enough and it carried to the old man who looked up and the joy of being recognized was evident. He gave me a big grin and a cheery wave. It was quite natural for me to walk up, shake his hand and ask him to join our table. After all, I was meeting a man who hit a sixer every time I clamored for one, when he was batting for India! *Chaliye*, he agrees and walks with me to our table.

He is sitting a yard across from me and when the waiter comes to ask him what he would like: I see a bemused look in his rheumy eyes. He is not a frequent flyer and will have to pay for his drink. Already fond of Durani the cricketer, my liking grew even more as he simply and with not a trace of self-consciousness asks for the card because he fears the drinks here are expensive. He goes up and down the list agonizing over the various drinks and their exorbitant prices. After much humming and hawing, he asks for a rum with a lot of soda to make it last longer. A few minutes later, he says he should not have ordered a drink, and then almost to himself says that we keep making mistakes in life. There was—or did I imagine it—a fleeting shadow of great sadness on that time-ravaged face. It still was a handsome visage.

But that somber moment was soon gone because I narrated a story that quite made his day. That story came to me from Raghunath who played cricket almost good enough to make the Ranji squad. I remembered every word of the story that Raghu narrated to me a good 24 years ago, as we walked off after a long and enjoyable session at the nets while preparing for a local tournament in Madras. Fielding for Indian Gymkhana, in 1969, Raghu had the privilege of watching Salim Durani at his imperious best from his position on the ground. The captain set a field of deep third man, deep point, deep cover point, deep cover...every fielder just yards from the other and yet Durani kept uncorking a series of cuts, square drives and cover drives that left them standing. Word spread that Durani was in gorgeous form—*Durani mood mein hai* was the message—and within 30 minutes more than a thousand enthusiasts had come all agog to watch the magician at work! And as I narrated this episode to Durani, I had my first glimpse of this man's generous nature. Rather than, as would be natural, talk about his own batting, when given such a cue, he was more curious about the man who narrated the story. When did Raghunath play, was he a left hander too, where is he nowadays...nothing about his own batting but all curious about the person who had such a nice story on him!

Over the next 45 minutes, we covered a variety of topics and cricketers. And each time one saw Durani, generous with praise, large hearted, never a sour word about any player.

Sample these: 'Venkat...*bahut intelligent cricketer, engineer tha* (and you could see in that hushed tone great respect for that educational qualification).' 'Prasanna...much greater than all his contemporaries, I could wait the whole day just to see him beat the batter with his floater.' 'Gavaskar...the finest among all our batters, he hated getting out even after making 150.' 'Sachin... God created him and said, go play cricket.' And on went Durani, about cricketers past and present; a good word for everyone.

I then ask him to tell me about his own game. And I realize that he has greater pride in his left-arm spin than in his batting. It was the only time during the entire conversation that I saw Durani assertive. He became animated; the drink was forgotten as he said: I could spin the ball anywhere; I used a lot of change of pace; I used to release the ball in a variety of ways; my arm ball would hustle off the pitch...Do you know that on the first day of a Test match in 1964 on the dead Madras Corporation wicket, I reduced Australia from 99 for no loss to 211 all out? Two years earlier I had Dexter's England in a whole lot of trouble with my bowling...nine wickets here, six wickets there... Durani during those moments simply loved recounting to me his bowling exploits.

But he was strangely modest about his batting. I think that even to this day Durani is torn inside by the realization that he did not use his enormous batting skills sensibly. The mood had shifted subtly.

I decide to change the topic. I ask him, how did our tailenders, back in those days when there were no helmets, manage to play the fearsome fast bowlers without getting hit. These days even the best batter keep getting hit on the helmet. Durani's explanation is all arms and gestures as he explains that those days even the fastest bowlers used swing more than bounce. And then, he adds, these days, actions are also more suspect. (And I said to myself, aha! at last one disparaging word.) He pauses, looks up at the roof, almost in contemplation and then says, but don't think people did not get hurt. I finished with cricket in 1974 after being felled by a bouncer in a Ranji match. I was batting on 94 when a bouncer from Gunwant Desai struck me down. They had to operate on me. And he parts his black hair (dyed or natural?) to show me where the surgeon had to do his stuff.

I tell him that when we played cricket in school, and gave ourselves names of Indian cricketers, I was Chandu Borde while my closest friend was Salim Durani. We never won many matches but we loved our cricketers. Durani smiles indulgently. I tell Durani that I can never ever forget his two wickets at Trinidad in 1971 that opened the gates for our win against West Indies. Durani laughs happily.

An hour has flown. Our flight has been called. His rum is still half full and he has managed to spend an hour in the company of a fan who cherishes his exploits. As we are getting up in walks, Saba Karim, the former India keeper, and they greet each other. Salim in fact gets up to clasp a fellow cricketer's hands in a gesture that is so gracious that it cannot be described. I think Salim has some good company till his flight is called.

15

WOMEN'S CRICKET: A DELIGHT FOR THE TRUE CRICKET LOVER

Ten days before the start of the 2013 ICC Women's Cricket World Cup in India, matches, including the opening fixture and the final, were shifted out of the Wankhede and into Brabourne Stadium. The Mumbai Cricket Association had wanted the Wankhede for the men's Ranji Trophy final and the BCCI had agreed to shunt out the women.

As if that indignation wasn't enough, the event was marked by an abysmal lack of effort put into marketing. You could be outside the stadium and barely realize a World Cup was on. An underprepared, underpaid, unsupported Indian team finished seventh out of eight nations. 'I don't think they had as much support going into this tournament as they would need,' Clare Connor, the ICC women's committee chairperson then, didn't mince her words. Diana Edulji, former India captain and administrator, saw this as another 'insult' to women's cricket from the administrators.

In the final, Ellyse Perry hobbled on an injured ankle to take three wickets in her first three overs as Australia marched to the title. The Brabourne stands were near empty to witness one of the most heroic efforts in any final.

Ten years later, those same stands are heaving. Chants of 'Perry! Perry!' greet one of the greatest all-rounders as she throws

Australian all-rounder Ellyse Perry during the 2017-18 Women's Ashes Test at the Oval. Perry went on to score a marathon 213 not out

Photo Courtesy: Wikimedia Commons

herself to stop the boundary or smacks sixes down the ground. It's the first Women's Premier League, and the RCB faithful are in love. Even the Mumbai Indians patlan have embraced her genius on their stomping grounds. Her face, along with the more familiar ones of Indian captain, Harmanpreet Kaur, and vice-captain, Smriti Mandhana, dots billboards across the city and greets you in the day's newspaper. The best female cricketers occupy internet streams and prime time television every evening for three weeks.

In the nearby Oval Maidan, a girl in whites dreams of being as good as them. The boys she plays alongside have found new heroes in these women too. That girl, dragging her cricket kit along, isn't a rare sight on cricket grounds anymore. A few years ago, Shafali Verma, India's Women's Under-19 World Cup-winning captain, had to pretend to be a boy to play and train because there were no academies for girls near where she was. But now, in a country that cheers on her big-hitting ability at the top of the order for India and Delhi Capitals, fewer girls and young women have to hide who they are as they take to cricket.

In the spring of 2023, women's cricket in India has blossomed into something special. And it looks nothing like it did a decade ago.

The seeds for the women's game in the country were planted five decades ago. Women in India played cricket recreationally before that, of course, but for the first time, they organized themselves. In the early '70s, across the country, young women formed cricket clubs and state teams. They were brought together by little more than happenstance, a youthful sense of adventure and a stubborn love for the sport. The first women's nationals in 1973 featured two-and-a-half teams: Mumbai, Maharashtra, and Uttar Pradesh, who needed players from Mumbai and Maharashtra to make an XI. Many players were barely out of school, if even that. Later that year, the second edition saw more teams participate in the event at Varanasi. The sport only grew from there.

Ask any of the pioneering women about those early years, and they'll reminisce about the long, unpredictable train journeys, the makeshift sleeping quarters in community halls, a single shared bathroom, shared cricket kits and the poor conditions they played in. This, they will say, was both the fun and the pain of playing cricket in those days. Funds were always scarce, skepticism in their ability aplenty. Administration veered between the apathetic and the inspired. The Indian team won a few matches, and lost many more. But the persistence and passion of this early group, even as they moved from playing into coaching and administration, kept women's cricket in the country going through even its deepest challenges.

Today, the Indian Women internationals team travel in business class. Even state teams stay in good hotels. At a domestic tournament before the WPL, the teams spilled out onto the corridors, poring over their phones and laptops, watching as they and their colleagues earned lakhs and crores and had their lives changed over minutes during the first WPL auction. That they are in a position to do so was because the generations before them persisted.

For instance, in 1976, Diana applied for a job in Western Railway and became the first female cricketer to be employed by them under the sports quota. Eight years later, the left-arm-spinning all-rounder convinced the then railway minister, Madhavrao Scindia, to open jobs to more female cricketers and field a team. Until national contracts were introduced in 2016, a Railways job was the main source of financial stability for women playing cricket. It was the difference in them giving up or sticking to cricket at a crucial time in their lives. As a result, the Railways attracted—and more significantly, retained—generations of the best talent; they are still the undisputed champions of domestic cricket. In another corner of Mumbai, Radha Yadav's father, a vegetable seller, agreed to her pursuing cricket because of the lure of a steady job with the Railways. But, in a sign of how things have changed for this generation, a government job is no longer the deciding factor in whether a woman stays in cricket. Radha, a left-arm spinner like Diana, and a regular with the Indian T20 side, has been able to support her family since she was just a teenager, without a Railway job, because of her national contract, match fees, and now, the WPL money that she earns.

Indian left-arm spinner Radha Yadav

Photo Courtesy: Wikimedia Commons

Shantha Rangaswamy earned the ire of administrators and lost her place in the side while fighting for better facilities; before the BCCI took over, Shubhangi Kulkarni considered breaking her own FDs to keep the Women's Cricket Association of India going, and give India the best preparation for the 2005 World Cup; Mithali Raj played through knee injury to take the nation to the final then and become the leading run-getter in women's ODIs—they all fought the battles that made it just a little bit easier for the generation to follow.

But how did we get from their time, and the disaster of 2013, to women's cricket in India, particularly the WPL, becoming the second-most expensive women's sports property after the WNBA?

Mithali Raj batting for India against England in 2012. She is currently the player with the most runs in women's international cricket
Photo Courtesy: Wikimedia Commons

Changing social mores have helped. Women are claiming more spaces and more visibility in society. More people (although not nearly enough still) are recognizing these claims, and sports, like so many other sectors, has benefitted from the greater participation of and attention given to women.

The tipping point, though, perhaps came in 2017. The biggest catalyst for the growth of women's cricket in India was Harmanpreet Kaur's 171 not out in the semi-final of the 2017 World Cup. That rainy day in Derby, Harman, with an injured shoulder and heavily strapped left hand, swung for the fences, and into the nation's hearts and consciousness. Circumstances meant she had barely eaten all day, but there was a fire in her belly to beat a formidable Australian side full of winners. From 41 in 60 balls at one stage, she unleashed a batting beast to finish unbeaten on 171 in just 115 balls. India stormed into the final. They lost the trophy, but came back to a country whose view of women's cricket had changed. There have been great knocks before, and iconic performances since. But that moment was the perfect confluence of occasion, performance and circumstance; it coincided with the growth of social media, found a space

Indian skipper Harmanpreet Kaur during her iconic knock at the 2017 Women's World Cup semifinals
Photo Courtesy: Wikimedia Commons

on prime-time television, caught the attention of marketers who were keen to reposition their brands in support of women, and made heroes for a whole new generation of boys and girls. No chauvinist who said that women's cricket was boring or that women couldn't play cricket would be taken seriously again.

Despite the leap taken that day, we'd still have to wait another six years for the women's IPL to begin, a dismal 15 years after the men's edition kicked off. But when the Women's Premier League finally came—benefitting from sudden and uncharacteristic alacrity from the BCCI—it marked another tipping point in the story of women's cricket in India. It seemed as if the promise of what could be, which had been building up over five decades, was finally being realized.

The battles are still being fought—for equality, for equal pay, for respect, for recognition, for not having to be grateful for getting things they deserve or due to them by right. Domestic cricketers still face financial and social challenges when they play the game. The idea of a girl playing outside, be it for pleasure or profession, is one that needs reinforcing.

When there was no money in cricket, the women played for the love of the game, for the pride in wearing national colors, for the thrill of being part of something special. Now when there is money in the game—and a lot of it—does that take away the passion and the pride? Not at all! Those motivations are reinforced by the privilege of professionalism. The joy today comes in being the best cricketer they can be. The thrill of raising standards on and off the field. These women are part of a revolution that has helped normalize a girl playing cricket—and that is a point of pride and sets the stage for more thrills.

—Karunya Keshav is an independent journalist who writes on cricket, gender and media. She is co-author of The Fire Burns Blue: A History of Women's Cricket in India. *The book was written with the late Sidhanta Patnaik, who was one of the biggest cheerleaders for the underdog in sport.*

16

A SPECIAL PLACE IN OUR HEARTS: THE RIGHT-HAND STYLISTS

Some years ago, after a spellbinding music concert by the maestro T. V. Sankaranarayanan, we went on stage to tell him that he had given individually autographed goosebumps to his mesmerized audience. What was in his music that transported each of his rapturous listeners to their own personal nirvana? To which, Sankaranarayanan, an avid follower of cricket and also the most modest among the maestros, asked us in return, whether he had done even a fraction of what G. R. Viswanath did for him?

What is it about the stylists that they make for themselves such a special place in our hearts? Why is G. R. Viswanath the most loved cricketer for people of our generation who grew up watching him bat? Why is V. V. S. Laxman so special? Obviously all fine batters play excellent shots; many play with such technical excellence that they are a joy to behold. Be it the imperious on drive of a Viv Richards or a copy book straight drive by Sachin Tendulkar, they are superb examples of the best of batsmanship. But those whom we are attempting to classify as stylists in this essay come with a unique appeal that tugs at our hearts. Perhaps the allure of this special band of cricketers is that they more than anyone else lend themselves to our imagination. Be it the modesty that comes so naturally to most of them or the aura of vulnerability, for we know that in attempting the absolutely silken late cut they may be felled when in full flight.

If cricket is a game that has great romance then at the core of it are the stylists. To the good length leg cutter pitched outside off, Mohammad Azharuddin will conjure a flick that sends the ball to mid-wicket. Perhaps nothing more delectable than the leg glance has ever been created. For that invention alone is Ranjitsinhji revered as the ultimate wizard. When he first demonstrated that you can turn your bat with such precision to send the ball to fine leg, people rubbed their eyes in disbelief. Today, everyone in the world plays this shot with aplomb but this was the shot when one first heard the phrase 'oriental magic'.

If that heart tugging vulnerability is too 'namby-pamby' a reason then there is cricketing aesthetics that sets this breed apart. Almost all of them use light bats and yet with their wrists, their timing and their bat speed, impart such velocity to the ball that it leaves most fielders standing. But then, many powerful blows from a Kevin Pietersen or Virender Sehwag also leave fielders standing. The difference is that even hard-boiled fielders instinctively clap when the stylist unfurls his shots. That is because none of us is immune to magic. When the bat turns into a wizard's wand—a front foot cover drive on the rise for instance—the fielder, who is above all a cricketer himself, can only applaud something the other person possesses and which is beyond him. And the shots they play, these are the epitome of nonviolence. When the ball goes to the cover fence, it seems to have been caressed. When the ball is sent scurrying to the square leg fence, it seems to go in unbounded joy; commentators would never ever use the phrase, 'whipped off his legs,' 'thumped of the back foot,' 'drilled through the covers' to describe the stylists.

We began this piece with music because we believe that silken batsmanship produces the same effect on our souls that great music does. It is not mere coincidence that Neville Cardus was moved by just two passions—music and great cricket. People who watched cricket during those times said that Cardus often wrote what he imagined in his mind's eye than what he actually observed. But was it Cardus' fault? On the contrary, if Ranji or Archie MacLaren played such divine cricket, it was natural for a sensitive soul to transport himself into his own world of joy. Simply put stylish batsmanship is a part of the fine arts, just as much as sculpture, painting or music.

So who in our opinion are right-handed batters who qualify for the 'stylist' tag? (A clarification needed here: later in this book we have written an article exclusively on the stylish left handers, so this essay is devoted only to right handers.) This has necessarily got to be subjective. Readers may unanimously agree on many, while they may also be aghast at some of our choices. So take a look at our list in Table 16.1.

One can see that even within this band of stylish batters there are actually two subgroups. One group for instance consists of Viswanath, Laxman, Frank Worrell, Laurence Rowe, Azharuddin, Mahela Jayawardene, Victor Trumper and Mark Waugh, the ultimate in elegance and style. The other group consists of the tall, elegant, upright and more careful batters. Stylists yes, but cavalier, no. These are of course Peter May, Greg Chappell, M. L. Jaisimha, Martin Crowe and Tom Graveney. In this second category, we could make a serious case for Dilip Vengsarkar of India and Walter Hammond of England. Both were splendid drivers, for we have read of Hammond's cover driving and seen Vengsarkar's on-driving to know they were elegance personified. But Vengsarkar was awkward with his half cock forward defensive, and Hammond approached his batting with such solidity and seriousness.

We cannot do justice to all the batters on our list, so perhaps we will touch upon just some of them. We begin with Laxman. So much has been written about him in such eloquent prose that anything we write would merely be gilding the lily. You name a shot and Laxman played that; what is more, he played it more prettily than anybody else. Often compared to his Hyderabadi predecessor Azharuddin for his wristy artistry, there was a defining difference.

TABLE 16.1: The Authors' Shortlist of Right-hand Stylists

	Player	*Country*	*Span*	*Matches*	*Runs*
1	Greg Chappell	Australia	1970–1984	87	7,110
2	Mark Waugh		1991–2002	128	8,029
3	Victor Trumper		1899–1912	48	3,163
4	Alan Kippax		1925–1934	22	1,192
5	K. S. Duleepsinhji	England	1929–1931	12	995
7	Peter May		1951–1961	66	4,537
8	K. S. Ranjitsinghji		1896–1902	15	989
9	Tom Graveney		1951–1969	79	4,882
10	Reg Spooner		1905–1912	10	481
11	V. V. S. Laxman	India	1996–2012	134	8,781
12	Mohammad Azharuddin		1984–2000	99	6,215
14	G. R. Viswanath		1969–1983	91	6,080
15	M. L. Jaisimha		1959–1971	39	2,056
16	Martin Crowe	New Zealand	1982–1995	77	5,444
17	Mohammad Yousuf	Pakistan	1998–2010	90	7,530
18	Zaheer Abbas		1969–1985	78	5,062
19	Mahela Jayawardene	Sri Lanka	1997–2012	132	10,517
20	Roy Dias		1982–1987	20	1,285
21	Frank Worrell	West Indies	1948–1963	51	3,860
22	Seymour Nurse		1960–1969	29	2,523
23	Lawrence Rowe		1972–1980	30	2,047
24	Carl Hooper		1987–2002	102	5,762

Source: Data from espncricinfo.com. Analysis and tabular compilation by authors.

Unlike Azhar, Laxman played the fast stuff superbly and nothing exemplified it better than the pull that he played to such perfection. And he was as good of the front foot as of the back. But the best thing about Laxman is that he was India's greatest third/ fourth innings match winner. Yes, the 281 against

Kolkata, rated among the greatest of all time knocks; but also the fact that of his 27 knocks above 50 in the third or fourth innings, India won 13 of those matches and only lost seven. So, behind that gentle smile and almost apologetic boundary scoring persona, was a man with steel and determination. So for those who think style comes at the expense of dependability, Laxman is the biggest proof that they are wrong. To us the essence of Laxman is that nice guys finish first. Among our heroes, whom we have not seen, Trumper will always stand first. So whether we write about great openers or about fast-scoring batters or stylists, Trumper will be there. Cardus doted on him. Mailey, the legendary leg spinner, worshipped him and played Test cricket only because he went to bed every day, genuflecting in front of a poster of Trumper, promising himself that one day he will play alongside his idol. But even people born many years after Trumper died write movingly on him. Reading Ashley Mallett write about Trumper—as an example—is to simply experience the affection that generations of cricketers will always have for one who was in every sense the noblest of batters.

From one favorite to another: Frank Worrell was obviously much more than cricket. To his beloved West Indies, he was the culmination of a socio-political revolution, described better than anywhere else by C. L. R. James in *Beyond a Boundary*. In terms of universal affection, Worrell is by any yardstick the most beloved. Of the three Ws of West Indies cricket—Worrell, Walcott and Weekes—Worrell was the stylist. Precociously talented, he scored at will, always elegant, and everything about his batting was sheer poetry. His batting moved opposing captains to open admiration while his demeanor and spirit of sportsmanship remains one of the greatest advertisements for nobility in sport. Trumper died very young, so did Worrell. In faraway Chennai and Delhi, we mourned his passing as deeply as did his beloved countrymen.

Another stylist nonpareil who is idolized for the spirit with which he played the game is Gundappa Viswanath. You could place 20 fielders between cover and third man but Viswanath's cuts and square drives would still find the boundary. And bad wickets seemed to bring the best out of him. On placid wickets when the other batters made merry, Viswanath seemed somehow bored; what he needed was the challenge of a green top, a turning track or a battery of fast bowlers to face. The greatest, non-century innings ever played by an Indian is certainly the 97 not out by him against Lloyd's team in January 1975. The next highest score by a batter was 19. Another example, this time from Melbourne in 1981 against Dennis Lillee and company: 114 out of a total of 237 where the next highest score was 25. Adversity stirred this gentle soul. Perhaps that is what was required for this artist to paint the ground with vivid colors. Living by the cut he often died by it; on such occasions even before the bowler could appeal, Viswanath would tuck his bat under his arm and walk away. He was clearly the fairest of sportsmen to have ever graced a cricket field. There was time in the early 1970s when the immensely gifted Viswanath would get out invariably in the thirties when he looked good for a century. And yet prosaic writers were moved to poetry, by such paltry contributions. For within that 30, Viswanath had compressed four of the best shots of the day!

Gundappa Viswanath executing a square drive
Credit: V. Balaji

Zaheer Abbas, contemporary of Viswanath, was the most stylish batter to have come from Pakistan. His speciality was his back foot play and he used his bat like Zorro. Staid Englishmen in 1971 were thrilled out of their skins as they saw the bespectacled Zaheer combine supreme artistry with a monumental hunger for runs not often associated with batters of his ilk. He remained stylish to the end; even as form deserted him and age slowed his reflexes we could still see glimpses of why he was among the most sublime batters of all time.

If we had to pick a batter from the Englishmen in our list, it would be Tom Graveney. Everything about Graveney was grace and style. Tall and upright, he had a nice back lift and his cover driving and on driving was unsurpassed. Whimsical selection was the sole reason that Graveney played a lot less than he deserved. Recalled at the age of 40 in 1966 to save England against the rampaging West Indies, Graveney showed what class is all about. Against Weslie Hall, Charlie Griffith, Garry Sobers and Lance Gibbs, he reeled off scores of 96, 109 and 165. He met fire and brimstone with classical batsmanship. Raghunath had once asked Venkat, the Indian off spinner freshly returned from a tour of England, who the best player of spin was. Venkat without hesitation said Graveney for he had timing, footwork and the gift to find gaps in the field where none existed!

We could go on. Honestly we are tempted to pay tribute to Rowe and Jayawardene, to Duleepsinhji and Mark Waugh, but we must stop somewhere. Perhaps the best way to sign off is to remember some of India's most stylish first-class batters. For every Jaisimha who made it, there was a Vijay Bhosle or a Ramesh Saxena or a T. E. Srinivasan who did not make it. In the 1970s, there was no finer sight in India's maidans than the classical back foot square drives of Srinivasan. Playing for South Zone against Imran Khan and the touring Pakistanis, Srinivasan hit a century of such dazzling beauty that it is recalled even today, with stars in the eyes, by those who witnessed that radiant batting display. Sadly he played just one Test for India; the loss was not his as much as that of the country and the spectators in other parts of the world. This essay is as much a tribute to the memory of great stylists like Srinivasan and Saxena as it is to their more famous brethren like Trumper and Worrell.

Note: Two modern-day batters who would walk into the exclusive club of supreme stylists would be India's Rohit Sharma and Pakistan's Babar Azam. Rohit makes batting a thing of beauty with his arc of drives, pulls and hooks. Babar is incredibly easy on the eye with his sublime timing and classical footwork. To Laxman, Viswanath and Jayawardene, they would be kindred spirits.

17

LEFT-ARM SPIN: ITS PLACE IN CRICKET HISTORY

The authors are separated in age by about 11 years. Therefore, it is not surprising that while for the elder of us, the first glimpse of a great left-arm spinner was Vinoo Mankad casting a spell at Chepauk; for the younger, growing up in faraway Delhi, the first sight of a wonderful left-arm spinner was a blue-turbaned Bishan Singh Bedi bowling for the first time in his life to an international side, the West Indians led by Garry Sobers. How far back that is can be gauged from the fact that the *patka* was unknown on a cricket ground and it was a full-fledged turban that Bedi wore on the field.

Cricket literature has always romanticized leg spin because the allure of wrist spin and its infinite potential for subtlety and trickery perhaps has no equal. The left-arm spinner has somehow got typecast as the honest, dependable craftsman, essential but not the star. Seen in that context, the left-arm spinner is much like the 9 to 5 office goers, punctual and correct; round the wicket, a bit of drift, on a good length, break away and with the heart for a long battle.

Add to this the fact that when one scans the best bowling figures in an innings, one finds no left-arm spinner in the top 15 performances. No left-arm spinner has taken more than eight in an innings. In contrast, both off spin and leg spin have pride of place in this hall of fame because of the immortal 10 wickets hauls by Laker and Kumble. While there are five off and leg spin bowlers with over 300 wickets, there is just one left-arm spinner with over 300 wickets.

Left-arm spinners are represented in the list of top bowling performances in a match, but what is telling is the fact that three of these four great performances belong to the 19th century and early 20th century (Johnny Briggs, Colin Blythe, and Wilfred Rhodes). The fourth is ancient too, Hedley Verity in the 1930s. There have been numerous occasions in the last 30 years that off- and leg-spin bowlers have 'run through the opposition' and 'bowled their sides to victory.' It will be hard for us to find an example for left-arm spin and we will be forced to dig further back into the days of Underwood and Bedi.

Bishan Singh Bedi's bowling—sheer poetry
Photo Courtesy: Kasturi & Sons

The great purveyors of left-arm spin have been every bit as artistic as their leg-spinning friends. Watching Bedi bowl was like seeing a classical ballet. A few steps and that absolutely divine pivot at the point of delivery. Every ball was a searching examination for the batter acutely aware that he was being lured into quicksand by deception in drift, flight and turn. Add the variety of arm balls and the picture of a spider's web is complete.

Left-arm spin has its quota of characters too. Bobby Peel, one of the early heroes of left-arm spin was apparently so colorful a character that he was once banished from a Test match for turning up inebriated on the morning of the match. Phil Edmonds of England was as much an intellectual as his famous captain Brearley but was temperamental to the point of being freaky. Phil Tufnell was a heady combination of talent and unmanageable maverick. But pause a while; left-arm spin is not just the orthodox tweaking of ball between thumb and fingers. There is the small matter of left-arm Chinaman bowlers, the unorthodox left-arm wrist spinners. The funny thing (and by that one is not alluding to the sight of Brad Hogg bowling Chinaman with his tongue hanging out) is that for a country as impoverished as Australia has been in left-arm finger spin, it contributes half the names of Chinaman bowlers. Starting with Fleetwood Smith, Australia has regularly thrown up Chinaman bowlers, from Lindsay Kline to Johnny Martin right down to Brad Hogg. Even their change bowlers Bevan and Katich, were Chinaman bowlers. In fact Arthur Mailey, the legendary leg spinner of the 1920s repeatedly described Fleetwood Smith as a wondrously gifted bowler in his book, *10 for 66 and All That.*

Left-arm spin has cast its charm on the novelist too. The delightful book, *Sherlock Holmes at the 1902 Fifth Test* is all about the mystery of a missing Wilfred Rhodes. Wilfred Rhodes incidentally began as a no. 11 batter but had moved to opening the batting in Tests. This fact will strike Indian readers for their own Ravi Shastri began as a no. 10 in his first Test and later opened the batting. It is another matter that Shastri's left-arm spin progressively deteriorated.

Rhodes, completely blind in his later years, was always present at Test matches at Headingley with his friend the great Sydney Barnes, who was fully deaf. Between the two of them, they 'heard and saw' Test matches, an eternally cherished piece of English cricket history. One of Rhodes' famous quotes went thus. When Hedley Verity in the 1930s was at his peak and the world's best left-arm spinner, Rhodes was asked, 'Is there any kind of ball Hedley bowls that you didn't bowl?' To which he impishly replied, 'Ay, the one the batter cuts for four.'

There is pathos too in this tale of left-arm spinners. Blythe took 100 Test wickets at breakneck speed but was killed in World War I. Verity, whom Bradman considered the best left-arm spinner he had ever faced, was killed in World War II. Briggs, whose 8 for 11 in 1898 are still the best figures ever in an innings, suffered and died of epilepsy in an asylum at a young age.

In the left-arm spin stakes, after England, it is India that has a strong and distinguished presence. Mankad in the period after World War II was the best among his contemporaries. And like Rhodes before him, Mankad was a genuinely great all-rounder who also opened the batting. We have had occasion to write about Gupte in the essay on leg spinners so we talk about Mankad here. Perhaps the greatest spinning all-rounder the game has ever produced (if you exclude Sobers who was part fast/medium bowler and therefore not purely a spin all-rounder) Mankad in our opinion will pip Wilfred Rhodes for the spot. He won India their first Test against MCC in 1952 and followed this up with their second Test win against Pakistan. He had 10 wicket hauls on both occasions. He remained the quickest to reach the double of 100 wickets and 1,000 runs for a long time and the highest wicket taker for India till the spin quartet overtook him. As an opener, he hit hundreds against Lindwall and Miller (Australia)

Vinoo Mankad at his guileful best
Photo Courtesy: Kasturi & Sons

and Bedser and Trueman (England) in their countries (not on subcontinent pitches). As a spinner he carried a huge workload with marathon spells and was often economical while retaining his wicket taking ability. Bedi came a decade after Mankad retired but the years between were not barren either. Nadkarni and Durani, fine spinners both, played a number of Tests. Between them they took nearly 200 wickets and had a hand in the few wins that came India's way in the early 1960s. They were contrasting men to say the least. While Durani was an absolutely exciting devil may care all-rounder, Nadkarni played even a club match as if his life depended on it. Nadkarni brought intense concentration to his trade and was known for his economy and maiden overs; his economy rate (1.67) is unsurpassed among all bowlers with over 30 Test wickets. But 'maiden Nadkarni' was also a wicket-taking bowler against attacking batters, especially the Australians, Neil Harvey, Norman O' Neill, Bob Simpson, and Brian Booth, who used their feet and tried to attack him. Durani on the other hand was simply gifted; he would bowl some unplayable stuff when the mood took him, come up with a clutch of wickets and the game would suddenly sizzle to life. Remember how he set up India's first victory against West Indies at Trinidad in 1971, gobbling up Sobers and Lloyd. He had a long run-up; he was a tall man with a high action and released the ball close to his left ear, unlike most left-arm spinners who were more round-armed.

How can the authors forget the memorable meeting with Durani one evening at an airport lounge as the aged old man went down memory lane to describe his bowling exploits in the few wins that came India's way in those parched days? Doshi, Shivalkar and Rajinder Goel were contemporaries of Bedi who would have walked into any other Test team. Doshi played his Test cricket only after Bedi retired and in the few cricketing years left, he quickly racked up over 100 wickets. Much later, in the 1980s India had two left-arm spinners playing in the same 11—Ravi Shastri and Maninder Singh. Maninder, a pure bowler, was a genuine talent who found the burden of being called 'the next Bedi' impossible to bear and never realized his potential. I (Giridhar) met him at Delhi just after he had announced his retirement and can never forget that ineffable look of sadness on his face, as he talked about his retirement.

Why do left-arm spinners have a more round-arm action than their right-arm off-spinning counterparts? For the left-arm spinner, usually bowling round the wicket most times to right-hand batter, perhaps the round-arm action is a necessity. Often watching Bedi we wondered how he released the ball at a variety of trajectories, some above his head, some in front of his eyes, but whatever the release, the flight was such that it was always coming to the batter from a height that was above the batter's eye level. The right-arm spinner has the googly and top spinner up his sleeve. The left-arm spinner relies mostly on the ball that hurries straight through to surprise the batter. Without a wickedly concealed arm ball, the left-arm spin bowler is only half the bowler one ought to be.

Note: Ravindra Jadeja made his debut in 2012. He is already fourth in the list of wicket takers among left-arm spinners and lethal in home conditions. He is easily among India's best fielders ever.

BARREN AUSTRALIA, DOMINANT ENGLAND

One striking aspect of Test cricket is that Australia has never had a great left-arm finger spinner ever in all its 134 y ears of cricket history. An immediate confirmation of this is the fact that the best figures for an Australian left-arm spinner are not provided by a bowler but by great Australian batters and part-time spinners—Allan Border (7 for 46, best bowling in an innings) and Charles Macartney 1 (1 for 85, best bowling in a match). If you ask this question of those who have been following this sport only for the past 15 y ears or so, their answer will again throw up a batter Michael Clarke (6 for 9 in 2004 at Mumbai). Clearly, therefore, Australia has a gaping hole in its left-arm spin history

We pulled in such an amount of rich data that we are spoilt for choice. We have tried to cull and present what we believe will be interesting slices of analysis. There are two caveats to our work. We decided to consider only those left-arm spinners who have at least 30 wickets against their name, and all our data and analysis is based on this cut-off. The second caveat is that we have collected and analyzed all data as of November 7, 2011. With Test cricket being played every day, this caveat is also important to bear in mind.

The strikingly key insights are:

- Of the 5,297 wickets captured by left-arm spin in Test cricket, only 4 per cent belong to Australia. While England and India account for over 56 per cent of these wickets, all the other major cricket-playing countries have a higher stake in this pie.
- Of the 3,122 wickets that Aussie spinners have taken, only 213 have been captured by the left-arm spinner. That is less than 7 per cent. In contrast, more than 51 per cent of wickets captured by England's spinners have gone to left-arm spinners.
- There is not a single Australian left-arm spinner with 100 wickets to his name. On the other hand, there are a

dozen Englishmen, four Indians and three South Africans who have achieved this milestone. Just to rub it in, every other cricket-play ing nation other than Zimbabwe has a name on this honors board and if Ray Price play s long enough even Zimbabwe may be on it leaving Australia all alone.

- Ray Bright is the highest wicket taker among Aussie left-arm spinners with 53 wickets. Of those who have taken 30 wickets, two are Chinaman purveyors (Fleetwood Smith and Kline), while the other two are batters who bowled part-time left-arm spin (Border and Macartney) with whom we started this story.

In contrast, England has always had a commanding presence in left-arm spin, from the day s when Test cricket was just between Australia and England right down to modern times.

- Of the 3,561 wickets credited to English spinners, their left-arm purveyors have more than 51 per cent to their name.
- More than 35 per cent of all wickets that have fallen to left-arm spinners in Test cricket have been captured by the Englishman.
- They have a dozen left-arm spinners on that honors board of those with 100 wickets and more. In fact, there are only 24 left-arm spinners in cricket history with such a qualification and if half of those are Englishmen, that tells the story of dominance in simple terms.
- English spinners have taken 10 wickets in a match almost as many times as Australia (36 times). The striking feature is that on 27 of these occasions (75 per cent of the occasions) it has been the left-arm spinner who has achieved this distinction.
- Unsurprisingly the best bowling figures in an innings or a match by any left-arm spinner belong to England. If Briggs had the almost impossible figures of 8 for 11 in 1898, Hedley Verity claimed 15 for 104 in a match in the years preceding World War II.

- From Peel, Briggs, Rhodes, Blythe in the early years to Verity and later Underwood England has had match-winning left-arm spinners. Even the temperamental Edmonds and the maverick Tufnell were match winners on their day. In fact Johnny Wardle was a superbly gifted orthodox spinner who could also run through sides with his Chinaman. Unfortunately, conservative English captains just did not have that zest to allow this hugely talented spirit the freedom to bowl such mesmerizing stuff. The straight and narrow (read finger spin) rather than the glorious and unpredictable (read Chinaman) for these staid men!
- England' s bowling average of 27.5 (runs/wicket) for left-arm spin is better than the bowling averages for any kind of spin by any country. We make this comment, by excluding Sri Lanka, because that colossus Muralitharan's achievement is so overwhelming that it is not truly representative of that country's off spin.

We felt that the striking contrast in one aspect of Test cricket between the two countries was worth a close look. We have marshaled facts to show how woefully weak Australia has always been in left-arm spin and how England has always been dominant in this department. Is it merely an inexplicable quirk of cricket history that a country that has been very strong in all forms of bowling including the Chinaman and mystery spinners has simply not been able to produce even one substantive left-arm spinner? It is a conundrum that we find fascinating. See Table 17.1.

TABLE 17.1: Enigma: Why Is Australia So Weak in Left-arm Spin?

Country	Player	Span	Match	Wickets	BBI*	BBM†	Average	Economy rate	Strike rate	5 Wickets in inning	10 Wickets in match
Australia	R. J. Bright	1977–1986	25	53	7 for 87	10 for 111	41.13	2.36	104.5	4	1
	C. G. Macartney	1907–1926	35	45	7 for 58	11 for 85	27.55	2.08	79.1	2	1
	L. O. Fleetwood-Smith	1935–1938	10	42	6 for 110	10 for 239	37.38	3.04	73.6	2	1
	A. R. Border	1978–1994	156	39	7 for 46	11 for 96	39.1	2.28	102.7	2	1
	L. F. Kline	1957–1961	13	34	7 for 75	8 for 90	22.82	1.96	69.7	1	
Bangladesh	Mohammad Rafique	2000–2008	33	100	6 for 77	9 for 160	40.76	2.79	87.4	7	0
	Shakib Al Hasan	2007–2011	24	89	7 for 36	9 for 115	31.02	2.84	65.4	8	0
	Enamul Haque Jr	2003–2009	14	41	7 for 95	12 for 200	39.24	3.02	77.7	3	1
England	D. L. Underwood	1966–1982	86	297	8 for 51	13 for 71	25.83	2.10	73.6	17	6
	G. A .R. Lock	1952–1968	49	174	7 for 35	11 for 48	25.58	2.03	75.5	9	3
	H. Verity	1931–1939	40	144	8 for 43	15 for 104	24.37	1.88	77.5	5	2
	A. F. Giles	1998–2006	54	143	5 for 57	9 for 122	40.6	2.86	85.1	5	0
	W. Rhodes	1899–1930	58	127	8 for 68	15 for 124	26.96	2.49	64.7	6	1
	M. S. Panesar	2006–2009	39	126	6 for 37	10 for 187	34.37	2.87	71.7	8	1
	P. H. Edmonds	1975–1987	51	125	7 for 66	7 for 66	34.18	2.13	96.2	2	0
	P. C. R. Tufnell	1990–2001	42	121	7 for 47	11 for 93	37.68	2.42	93.2	5	2
	J. Briggs	1884–1899	33	118	8 for 11	15 for 28	17.75	2.35	45.1	9	4
	J. H. Wardle	1948–1957	28	102	7 for 36	12 for 89	20.39	1.89	64.6	5	1
	R. Peel	1884–1896	20	101	7 for 31	11 for 68	16.98	1.97	51.6	5	1

	C. Blythe	1901–1910	19	100	8 for 59	15 for 99	18.63	2.45	45.4	9	4
	N. G. B. Cook	1983–1989	15	52	6 for 65	11 for 83	32.48	2.42	80.2	4	1
	J. C. White	1921–1931	15	49	8 for 126	13 for 256	32.26	1.97	97.9	3	1
	N. Gifford	1964–1973	15	33	5 for 55	8 for 127	31.09	1.99	93.4	1	0
	E. Peate	1881–1886	9	31	6 for 85	8 for 58	22.03	1.95	67.6	2	0
India	B. S. Bedi	1966–1979	67	266	7 for 98	10 for 194	28.71	2.14	80.3	14	1
	M. H. Mankad	1946–1959	44	162	8 for 52	13 for 131	32.32	2.13	90.6	8	2
	R. J. Shastri	1981–1992	80	151	5 for 75	8 for 179	40.96	2.35	104.3	2	0
	D. R. Doshi	1979–1983	33	114	6 for 102	8 for 103	30.71	2.25	81.7	6	0
	S. L. V. Raju	1990–2001	28	93	6 for 12	11 for 125	30.72	2.25	81.7	5	1
	R. G. Nadkarni	1955–1968	41	88	6 for 43	11 for 122	29.07	1.67	104.1	4	1
	Maninder Singh	1982–1993	35	88	7 for 27	10 for 107	37.36	2.4	93.3	3	2
	S. A. Durani	1960–1973	29	75	6 for 73	10 for 177	35.42	2.47	85.9	3	1
	P. P. Ojha	2009–2011	12	48	6 for 72	7 for 204	36.85	2.83	78	1	0
	S. B. Joshi	1996–2000	15	41	5 for 142	8 for 169	35.85	2.55	84.1	1	0
New Zealand	D. L. Vettori	1997–2011	106	353	7 for 87	12 for 149	33.61	2.6	77.4	20	3
	H. J. Howarth	1969–1977	30	86	5 for 34	9 for 100	36.95	2.15	102.7	2	0
	S. L. Boock	1978–1989	30	74	7 for 87	8 for 156	34.64	2.33	89.1	4	0
	B. W. Yuile	1963–1969	17	34	4 for 43	6 for 112	35.67	2.51	85.2	0	0
	T. B. Burtt	1947-1953	10	33	6 for 162	7 for 106	35.45	2.7	78.5	3	0

(Table 13.1 Contd)

(Table 13.1 Contd)

Country	Player	Span	Match	Wickets	BBI*	BBM†	Average	Economy rate	Strike rate	5 Wickets in inning	10 Wickets in match
Pakistan	Iqbal Qasim	1976–1988	50	171	7 for 49	11 for 118	28.11	2.21	76.1	8	2
	Pervez Sajjad	1964–1973	19	59	7 for 74	9 for 112	23.89	2.04	70.2	3	0
	Abdur Rehman	2007–2011	10	45	4 for 65	8 for 210	33.8	2.55	79.2	0	0
South Africa	P. R. Adams	1995–2004	45	134	7 for 128	10 for 106	32.87	2.98	66	4	1
	P. L. Harris	2007–2011	37	103	6 for 127	9 for 161	37.87	2.65	85.5	3	0
	N. Boje	2000–2006	43	100	5 for 62	8 for 134	42.65	2.96	86.2	3	0
	C. L. Vincent	1927–1935	25	84	6 for 51	8 for 149	31.32	2.69	69.6	3	0
	N. B. F. Mann	1947–1951	19	58	6 for 59	7 for 72	33.1	1.98	99.9	1	0
Sri Lanka	H. M. R. K. B Herath	1999–2011	32	109	7 for 157	8 for 133	35.08	2.89	72.5	6	0
	S. T. Jayasuriya	1991–2007	110	98	5 for 34	9 for 74	34.34	2.46	83.5	2	0
	S. D. Anurasiri	1986–1998	18	41	4 for 71	5 for 149	37.75	2.33	96.9	0	0
West Indies	A. L. Valentine	1950–1962	36	139	8 for 104	11 for 204	30.32	1.95	93.1	8	2
	S. J. Benn	2008–2010	17	51	6 for 81	8 for 108	41.41	2.89	85.9	3	0
	Inshan Ali	1971–1977	12	34	5 for 59	7 for 158	47.67	2.61	109.3	1	0
Zimbabwe	R. W. Price	1999–2011	21	79	6 for 73	10 for 161	35.92	2.82	76.2	5	1

Source: Data from espncricinfo.com. Analysis and tabular compilation by authors.
Notes: *Best bowling in innings. †Best bowling in match.

18

NURTURING NEW BATTERS: LOOK FOR EARLY SIGNS OF GREATNESS

Truly great and enduring Test teams like Lloyd's West Indies of the 1980s and Steve Waugh's Aussies of the 1990s were a unique combination of great batters and great bowlers. India climbed to the top largely because of its legendary batters. After a decade of stirring exploits that helped India reach the top, all of them have ended their illustrious careers. We need to begin all over again. It means India will need replacements for four of their top six batters. We are probably going the right way if the promise of Cheteshwar Pujara and Virat Kohli is any indication. We will need more. It is going to be arduous and painful; we will face sterner Tests before we can climb again. And the Indian fan, impatient and mercurial, will add more pressure and heat than anywhere else.

In the 80 years since India started playing cricket, we have only 14 batters with an average of over 40 and at least 2,000 Test runs. Six of these 14 batters—Tendulkar, Dravid, Sehwag, Laxman, Gambhir and Ganguly—as though by some divine benediction, came together at the same time in the last decade.*

* In the last 10 years, five more batters have joined this club: Shikhar Dhawan, Virat Kohli, Rishabh Pant, Cheteshwar Pujara and Rohit Sharma.

Interestingly, today's situation has a parallel with the late 1960s. As Pataudi, Borde, Sardesai, Jaisimha and Durani (all fine batters but none with an average of over 40) were ebbing away, Vijay Merchant—as bold a selector as he was conservative as a batter—threw in a slew of youngsters into the team for the home series against New Zealand and Australia in 1969 and later for the tour to West Indies. G. R. Viswanath, Eknath Solkar, Chetan Chauhan, Ambar Roy, Ashok Gandotra, Ashok Mankad, Mohinder Amaranth, Sunil Gavaskar and many more were tried out in a frenetic hurry. In that stampede, some got washed away after a couple of chances; others like Viswanath, Amarnath and Gavaskar, clicked and stayed on to be counted among India's and the world's finest.

Obviously, one need not go down that path of Russian roulette, where Ambar Roy was always just one bad shot away from being catapulted out of Brabourne Stadium to the oblivion of Ballygunge. We must be able to identify a set of batters and give them a decent run. Give them the assurance and security and hope they vindicate that trust. Yet, how long is fair enough? How short a run is unfair? We have many instances of giving a batter one or two Tests and then forgetting his very existence (Deepak Shodhan and T. E. Srinivasan come to mind). On the other hand, one remembers how frustrating it was when the selectors provided too long a rope to players who simply were not consistently good at Test level (Ashok Mankad and Brijesh Patel come to mind). We decided to massage and interpret data on Test batters to see if we can answer the questions: How long a run should we give the newcomers? By when should we simply cut our losses?

Whom should we give a longer run? When should we move on to give others a chance? Our analysis showed:

- There are just 34 batters in Test history with an average of over 50 among those with over 2,000 Test runs. Out of these 34 batters, 29 showed early signs of greatness—

within their first five or at best 10 Tests they were averaging above 40. Of the five batters whose initial 10 Tests were not so productive, three had at least a century to show.

- Those five batters who did not set cricket grounds on fire with their batting in their first 10 Tests were Garry Sobers, Jacques Kallis, Kumara Sangakkara, Steve Waugh and Matthew Hayden. Of these, remember, Sobers, started as a bowling all-rounder and Sangakkara as a wicket-keeper batter. Therefore, only Kallis and Steve Waugh truly are the exceptions. Hayden, as cricket followers may remember was dropped for a few years after an unsuccessful start and his career only took off from his massive scores in India in 2001.
- If a batting average of 50 is too steep a cut-off, let us bring the bar down to 45. That allows 47 more batters to join the fun and games with this analysis. But here again, these fine batters did not need a prolonged series of chances to prove their worth. Of these batters, 24 had an average of over 50 in their first five or first 10 Tests and 38 (80 per cent) had an average of over 35 in their first 10 Tests.
- Admittedly, the list of nine batters who had relatively modest starts contains some stunning names: Inzamam ul Haq, Rohan Kanhai, V. V. S. Laxman, Hashim Amla, Bobby Simpson, Lindsay Hassett, Martin Crowe, Justin Langer and Gary Kirsten. Of these nine batters who had relatively slower starts (less than an average of 35), four had a century to show that they had promise. The truly slow starters among them with averages in the 20s and no century to show were Kanhai, Simpson and Laxman. Indian readers with justification will point out that Laxman was a middle-order batter forced to play many of his early Tests as an opener; after he reverted to middle order, success came his way.

- Let us take this analysis to the next plane—to look more closely and specifically at India's batters. There are just 28 Indian batters who have over 2,000 runs and an average of over 30. Of these 28, 14 have an average of over 40—the six modern batters Virender Sehwag, Gautam Gambhir, Rahul Dravid, Sachin Tendulkar, Laxman and Sourav Ganguly and the others—Polly Umrigar, Vijay Hazare, Gavaskar, Viswanath, Vengsarkar, Mohinder Amarnath, Azharuddin and Sidhu.
- Only 3 of these 14 batters had slow starts. Like Laxman whom we have discussed earlier, Vengsarkar too was a middle-order batter who failed when he was forced to open in his initial Tests. Reinstated to the middle order, he blossomed to be a fine success. Umrigar is the one stunning exception and we were taken aback to realize that this stalwart had such a slow start to his Test batting career.
- Everyone would agree that 30 is a modest average. If we had batters with that average in our line-up there is no way we will go anywhere near the top of Test rankings. Proof? When the great spin quartet of Bedi, Chandra, Prasanna and Venkat created winning opportunities for India we just did not have enough batting to muscle our way to victories. Our batting began with Gavaskar and ended with Viswanath. By the time Mohinder Amarnath and Dilip Vengsarkar strengthened the batting, the spin quartet had faded away.
- Our analysis shows that batters who end up with an average below 40 are also not likely to show much promise in their first five Tests or 10 Tests. In other words, if they are not scorching the scoreboard early, it seems unlikely they will do it when given a longer rope. Of the 14 Indian batters with an average below 40, only three batters began well. Jaisimha had an average of 50 in his first 10 Tests but was whimsically treated

for the rest of career. Sanjay Manjrekar, technically the finest batter before Dravid arrived, had an average of 52 with double centuries against fearsome attacks overseas. The third batter who showed early promise was, well, Kapil Dev the all-rounder. Now that says something—an all-rounder rather than another batter is all we can throw up as an exception. Search some more and you will find Dhoni (an all-rounder again) as the next nearest example.

- So summing up this section, one can be reasonably certain that if Indian batters are not averaging in the range of 40 plus in their early Tests, they will end up as only moderately successful batters. Greatness will evade them (Ajit Wadekar, Ashok Mankad, Brijesh Patel, Krish Srikkant come to mind—more than a hundred Tests between them for modest returns).
- The scenario need not have been so grim or barren. India had a number of batters who began well, averaging over 40 but just did not get enough chances. Let us examine and learn from these 'missed chances.' The most bizarre case is that of Deepak Shodhan, a left hander who played just three Test matches, averaged 60 plus, had a century on debut and yet was ignored for ever after. In a country where we were desperate for good openers we found Madhav Apte and yet Apte played just seven Tests. He averaged almost 50 with a century to boot but never played for India again. Abbas Ali Baig, century on debut, average of 44 in his first five Tests was dropped after he failed in a couple of Tests against Pakistan. Hanumant Singh, averaged 40 in his first 10 Tests and Kripal Singh, averaged 36 after 10 Tests. Both of them like Shodhan and Baig hit centuries on debut. But Hanumant was dropped summarily and Kripal played 14 Tests over a nine-year period when he should have played 20 Tests in his prime. Sadagopan

> Ramesh averaged 56 in his first five Tests and 47 in his first 10 Tests and had two centuries. We ignored these numbers, pontificated that his feet do not move properly and lost a potential 'plus 40' opener for ever. Pravin Amre (again century on debut) and Sandeep Patil were also potential 'plus 40' batters that India never tapped into fully. Incidentally, two of our finest batters, Rusi Modi and Vijay Merchant, played just 10 Tests each but averaged over 46. The cupboard therefore was not barren; just a combination of giving too long a rope to some, none at all to some, short sightedness in the case of others and cussedness too in the case of a few.

We are saying that most batters who end up successful show signs of success early within their first 10 Tests. If one gives too long a rope to batters who have not been successful, we may be wasting time and robbing others of their chances. On the other hand, if someone strikes early stick with him, chances are that he will make good. India has had a number of batters who started well but were not given chances. Don't do that mistake. Perhaps over the next two years, a Merchant-type formula, but more carefully calibrated is required where as many batters as feasible are given a continuous run of five to seven Tests on the trot. When you want to bet on genuine class like Viswanath or Hanumant Singh, tell them you believe in them and give them 10 Tests. If they make the grade fine, or else cut your losses and move on to newer players. This is the path—fair and firm—that we need to take with Suresh Raina, Rohit Sharma, Murali Vijay, Manoj Tiwary, Ajinkya Rahane and other promising youngsters. Virat Kohli and Cheteshwar Pujara have already passed the kind of cut that we have described in this essay. Both have centuries and batting averages in their first 10 Tests to show that they will have very fine careers. As India tries to rebuild its batting over the next two years, they will need to experiment and try out quite a few youngsters and at such a time, this kind of a yardstick might well be useful.

19

THE WHOLE NEW WORLD OF ANALYTICS AND CRICKET

The Kolkata Test and the series win against Australia in 2001 was the most significant turning point in India's Test history. Ganguly and Wright, captain and coach, plotted and executed a memorable coup. Laxman and Dravid's immortal partnership became the stuff of legend but the torpedo against Steve Waugh's men was young Harbhajan Singh. In those days, the use of data or video analysis was not even on the horizon. Strategy and tactics boiled down to a deep understanding of the game, memory and instinct. Ganguly's instincts said Harbhajan; Wright backed his captain. What followed was meticulous planning and relentless practice. On a good-length area outside off stump, Wright and Ganguly drew a box 20 cm wide and 60 cm long and asked Harbhajan to bowl there. The lad had spin and terrific bounce and every time he bowled in that box, he would hit the top of off stump.

The present-day TV viewer, used to a plethora of visuals and statistics on TV, would realize there was nothing called a pitch map those days. Today, every ball in every game is in the video bank and at the hit of a button one is provided the most sophisticated analysis. You have pitch maps of the finest grids, a cluster of bowling areas called the 'beehive' showing the height at which the ball reaches a batter's crease with all the minute dissections of speed, spin and bounce. Batters' scoring areas, their strengths off front or back foot, the 'wagon-wheel' are now a part of drawing room conversations as info-graphics allies with action to holds cricket crazy viewers in a thrall.

Javagal Srinath, arguably India's finest pacer after Kapil Dev, ended up with fewer Test wickets than he ought to have got. His colleague Venkatesh Prasad told us, 'Sri was the best Indian fast bowler I have seen. He bowled back of length, so even if the batters were beaten, the ball would go over the stumps. It was only with experience that he bowled a little fuller.' What Prasad implied was that had professional coaching along with video-analytics existed then, Srinath would have perfected his length a lot earlier. Prasad's own story is telling. When we asked him about his magical spell of five wickets for no runs in the 1999 Test against Pakistan at Chennai, Prasad, who is now a bowling coach, said, 'There was no computer or video analysis during my time. Everything depended on the bowler memorizing what he observed. I literally drew images of field placements in my notebook and tried to remember and execute on the ground.'

India may have been slow in accepting the necessity of a professional coach but when analytics arrived, India was quick to embrace it, as early as 2003. Money was pouring into the BCCI coffers and the team could afford the best of resources to strengthen its preparations. And that is where S. Ramakrishnan (Ramky), one of the world's foremost specialists in cricket analytics, enters this story.

For Ramky, it was a journey that started more than 30 years ago when he began video-graphing games using a Handycam gifted by his father. His first experiment was on himself. A first-division cricketer, Ramky was shocked by the video evidence of his faults as a batter. His big breakthrough came at the MRF Pace Foundation in Chennai where the legendary Dennis Lillee was head coach and T. A. Sekhar, a fine pace bowler was assisting him. Around that time, a fiery fast bowler had come into the reckoning, but there were murmurs that his action was doubtful. How Ramky's video analysis of the bowler changed the entire story must be told in Ramky's words: 'A promising fast bowler was suspected of throwing and would have not got into the MRF camp. But my video-camera analysis cleared him. It showed that the pacer obtained his special bowling ability not with a bent arm but with a perfectly legitimate wrist action. That fast bowler was Sreesanth.' This cleared the decks for Ramky to engage deeply with MRF. Lillee and Sekhar helped Ramky improve his analysis so that he could dissect the bowling action into loading, delivery stride, release and follow-through. Ramky added his own insights on run-up, elbow action and rhythm to break-down the bowling action frame by frame!

Sekhar says there was no data analysis when he played for India in the 1980s. Pre-match meetings were limited to the captain and manager exhorting players to give off their best. This was true even under fiercely competitive and thinking captains. When Sekhar became a selector, the committee never went beyond scorecards and averages. It was his stint at the MRF Pace Academy and his association with Ramky that exposed him to the power of analysis. The initial VHS technology was cumbersome and one couldn't easily retrieve what one wanted. When Sekhar visited the Perth Academy in 2001, he obtained a new tool called the 'Silicon coach' that had been developed in New Zealand. Using this tool, Sekhar and Ramky were able to film and replay frame by frame, to analyze a bowler's action threadbare. Sekhar talks of this journey of video-analytics like an exhilarating adventure.

In 2002, Ramky attended a meeting of international cricket coaches in Sri Lanka at the invitation of Bob Woolmer. 'Thanks to Sekhar, I could make a presentation. Buchanan and Wright were also there. It was a hit.' Following this, Wright invited him to talk to the Indian team. It was meant to be a 30-minute session on how video-analysis worked but the entranced Wright asked him to continue. He asked Ramky to share some clips with the Indian players for he wanted to Test the waters before asking the analyst to join his think tank. And that Ramky says, is how, 'we were catapulted into the Indian team in 2003. We became the performance analysts of the Indian cricket team and got the opportunity to play a small but significant role in the success story of the Indian team.'

Once Wright and Ganguly had the support of senior cricketers like Dravid, Tendulkar and Kumble, they began using analytics to provide feedback to each player on his technique and performance. On the 2004 tour to Australia, at Ramky's behest, Ganguly got 25 VHS tapes of the Australian players from the previous Ashes series from ESPN. Ramky digitized these to provide inputs on every opposition player. Team meetings thereafter were more focused and strategies to counter each Aussie batter and bowler were discussed. Along with Wright and Ganguly, Ramky credits Dravid for introducing analysis into the game at the national level. He says, 'Dravid was a great influence in this change of culture and attitude towards adopting new technology.' Srinath, almost at the end of his career but much respected in the team, was a strong advocate of the use of technology. With Tendulkar, Kumble and Sehwag also endorsing this, computer-aided analysis became an integral part of India's coaching, team preparation and strategy.

This was only the beginning. The revolutionary impact of analytics on the way the game was played and the manner it would be presented to television audiences as spectacular entertainment was still some years away.

* * *

When Andy Flower took over from Peter Moores as England coach in 2009, he also took forward his predecessor's conviction that analytics would add crucial value to his coaching inputs. He hired a strong analyst who used pitch maps and Hawk eye to dissect bowlers. Numbers were crunched and players told in great detail, things that a coach could not have otherwise provided. Was it a coincidence that England went to the top of ICC ranking in Tests, ODI and T20 cricket during this period? But a few years later, it seemed England had taken analytics to its extreme. Outspoken players like Pietersen and Swann talked about the claustrophobic presence of video-analytics and endless spreadsheets. On the other hand, South Africa, who roped in Prasanna Agoram, a gold medallist engineer from Chennai, as their performance analyst in 2010, were clearly delighted with what he contributed to their game. India too seemed to have achieved the fine balance between use of technology and the natural expression of talent that cricketers possessed at the highest level.

Even as coaches and cricketers were trying to find the best use of performance analytics, the commercial demands for providing TV audiences compelling viewing were making visual analytics leap to a different orbit. The World Cup in 2015 was a major inflection point as ICC used analytics to create spectacular TV entertainment out of the world's premier cricket tournament. The benchmark for analytics got higher with IPL. R. Mohan, veteran cricket journalist, suggests that any discussion on cricket analytics must draw the distinction between red-ball and white-ball cricket. The innovations and developments in analytics are driven by white-ball cricket; by the demands of IPL Franchises and sponsorships, advertisements and TV revenue. Video-analytics has become a major element in keeping television audiences glued to a high-voltage entertainment where excellent camerawork combines with surreal analytics. Commentators now have a rich variety of statistical information to have lively conversations that include the audience. 'The kind of fantastic data being mined is a very natural development. Technology, big data and analytics are coming together to drive the way the game is played and watched,' says Mohan.

All teams at IPL are completely invested in analytics. There is a video analyst and a performance analyst—often a certified cricket coach—who provide feedback on technique to individual players. The franchise also has a strategic analyst who works with the owners and chief coach right from the time of player auctions. Does the franchise need an attacking opener, death-overs bowler or a wrist spinner? How does a franchise pick a squad of 25 players, each with role-specific requirements and with bench strength to cover for injuries? Kolkata Knight Riders—much like Oakland Athletics broke ground in the NBL in 2002 to select players using sabermetrics—used player analytics in 2014 to create a winning combination within their purse.

Analytics is making limited-overs strategy unfold in radically different ways; batters no longer think slog overs—any over in an innings can be targeted as a 20 run over. Innovations are tested and tried for every kind of delivery—the yorker, knuckle ball or whatever. The corridor outside the off-stump is not sacred anymore. Strategies are built on inputs like individual player's scoring areas—where boundaries are being hit, how many dot balls are being played, predicting pressure points in the game when a dismissal is likely. Every opposing batter's dismissal patterns are dissected to strategize bowling options against him. Sunil Narine's pitch-map of carom balls will be studied by opposing teams to decide which batter would best counter him. Game strategy and playing eleven against a particular opponent are chosen depending on the venue. At practice sessions, batters are asked to hit deliveries in their problem areas through a field set in an open ground; bowlers have to bowl a specific line, length and pace. It is a very busy time before the game begins!

The longer format is still a game of attrition but analytics throws up different strategies for every batter and bowler in Test cricket too. Line, length and field placements to contain batters and frustrate them are still in vogue. Sekhar says that in the period between 2000 and 2008, Ramky and he were always in touch when India was touring, since most fast bowlers in the Indian team had trained at the MRF Pace Foundation. On one such tour to West Indies in 2006, Sreesanth had lost his outswinger. Ramky and Sekhar held a video conference to analyze Sreesanth's bowling videos and helped the pacer revert to his old action to produce those effective out-swingers again. 'Sreesanth got five wickets in the next Test at Kingston to bowl India to a win,' concluded Sekhar with relish. The batting machine still has a limited use to iron out technical faults that show up through analysis. On the other hand, the ramp shot to a bouncer or reverse sweep to the first ball faced are now common in Test cricket. Run rates in Tests are up and there are hardly any draws in recent times. The fear that Test Cricket will lose its primacy in the near future may be unfounded because the money is coming not through gate receipts but through advertising and sponsor revenues. The logic is that viewers, including smart phone viewers, will watch whenever time permits, be it ODI or Tests, so long as the game provides entertaining action accompanied by spectacular visuals and analysis.

The best of performance analysts have the ability to marry a lot of data with videos to help coaches plan strategy and enhance individual performances. They are no longer anonymous but much sought after. Shrinivas Chandrasekaran, who is Bangladesh's performance analyst, earned his spurs with Sunrisers Hyderabad by plotting dismissals of batters like Chis Gayle and Brendon McCullum in the IPL. Analytics is already an integral part of most other sports and Ramky who pioneered all this, says without a trace of hyperbole, 'India may not be winning all the medals, but in the future all medal winners are going to be helped by Indian Analytics.'

Cricket, like many field sports, is a game of great skill where mind and body, hand and eye, have to decide in a fraction of a second. Practice and instinct, memory and ability must coalesce in the athlete to create the magic. And analytics is taking player capabilities and team performance to a higher plane. However, one wonders whether the video-analytics and slow-motion replays for the millions of TV-glued audiences, lull viewers into thinking the game is easy. Ensconced in front of a TV, pakodas at the elbow, people who have never a caught a ball thrown at them, can play armchair expert. In the late-night sky, a steepling mishit that looks like a dolly is dropped. How the heck could he drop it? Mercifully, there appears on the screen a visual that shows two lines on the screen—one if the ball had dropped straight and the other showing the actual path of the ball wickedly swerving away. The armchair pundit is quietened for the moment.

20

LEFT-ARM FAST: JUST A FEW PEARLS

We did a dip stick survey with friends, who are knowledgeable followers of cricket, asking them to name five well-known left-arm fast bowlers, relying only on their memory and without giving them more than a few hours to respond. Of 27 friends, only 11 could name five left-arm fast bowlers. Almost everyone called out Wasim Akram's name. Many mentioned Zaheer Khan; quite a few remembered Chaminda Vaas and then they gave up. On the other hand, 23 of 27 friends easily named five right-arm fast bowlers and five right-handed batters and were also able to name five left-handed batters. The same people also struggled to recall the names of left-arm spinners and only 10 of them could name five left-arm spinners. That in itself tells a story—left-arm bowling has somehow not been able to etch itself in the mind in the way right-arm bowling or left-hand batting has. Everyone agrees that left-arm fast bowling is a key weapon in the bowling arsenal. Is not the sight of the left-arm fast bowler running smoothly up to the crease and delivering, as joyous a sight as any in cricket? And yet we struggle to recall even five left-arm fast bowlers. Surely there must be a reason?

We decided to go to our trusted friend, the databank of cricket statistics available to modern-day writers at the click of a button, on espncricinfo.com to check out the actual situation. And there is enough evidence to show that indeed, barring just a handful, there are not enough left-arm fast bowlers with huge numbers and feats. Here is a quick snapshot summary from Test cricket.

- In terms of wickets taken, the gulf between left-arm fast bowlers and the others—left-arm spin, right-arm spin and right-arm fast is huge. While left-arm fast bowlers have taken 5,224 wickets, right-arm fast bowlers have over 33,000 wickets, right-arm spinners over 13,000 wickets and even the left-arm spinners have taken 20 per cent more wickets than the left-arm fast bowlers (see Table 20.1).
- The two left-arm fast bowlers who have crossed the 300 wicket mark are Wasim Akram and Chaminda Vaas (when we wrote this piece Zaheer had not crossed 300). And those who have over 150 Test wickets can be counted on the fingers of one hand: Zaheer Khan, Garry Sobers, Mitchell Johnson, Alan Davidson and Bill Johnston.
- The difference kicks in when we look at the bowlers who have more than 100 wickets. There are nearly twice as many left-arm spinners as left-arm pace men with over 100 wickets.
- Interestingly this kind of chasm is not seen when one compares left-handed batters and right-handed batters. While 57 right-handed batters have over 5,000 runs, 27 left-handed batters too have crossed this great milestone. In fact, left handers constitute over 26 per cent of batters who have crossed the 1,000 run mark in Tests.

TABLE 20.1: Left-arm Fast: Just 9% of Wickets

Bowling type	*>300 wicket*	*>200 wicket*	*>100 wicket*	*>50 wicket*	*Total wicket*
Left-arm fast	6	7	16	36	6,054
Left-arm spin	2	6	30	50	8,709
Right-arm spin	7	17	41	83	16,983
Right-arm fast	22	51	104	223	40,511

Source: Data from espncricinfo.com. Analysis and tabular compilation by authors.

So let us move on to the best left-handed fast bowlers. Well there is Wasim Akram on a pedestal of his own, undisputedly the greatest left-arm fast bowler of all time. And this is just not on the basis of numbers (414 wickets, at an average of 23 runs per wicket and a strike rate of a wicket every nine overs) for to use that as the yardstick would be to trivialize his mastery of the art. Wasim had a relatively short run up and an unbelievably quick arm action that surprised the batter. The great man would then switch to round-the-wicket and cause fresh problems with a new angle. He could generate pace from a short run using his unique shoulder action and unbelievable arm speed and unsettle batters with clever change of pace. Add to that the ability to bowl excellent yorkers, and move the ball both ways and one had perhaps the most complete bowler. Every batter who played Wasim rates him as one of the most difficult bowlers to play.

Wasim Akram—The Sultan of Swing
Photo Courtesy: Kasturi & Sons

Perhaps only our older readers would have seen Alan Davidson of Australia bowl in a Test match. But one of your authors—Raghunath—has seen him bowl in pomp in the Madras Test of 1960. Those who have seen him will agree that before Akram, Davidson was clearly the greatest fast bowler. He played just 44 Tests (Akram played 104) and captured 186 wickets at an average of 20 runs per wicket and a strike rate that gave him a wicket every 10 overs. For someone as broad as Davo, his smooth action was amazing. He seemed to glide

Alan Davidson bowls Nari Contractor during the India-Australia Test series, 1959

Photo Courtesy: Kasturi & Sons

in and bowled with such control taking the ball away from the left-handed openers. He would suddenly bring it in to surprise the left hander moving across the crease and bowl him leg stump behind his back. There are photographs of Geoff Pullar, England's left-handed opener looking bamboozled playing the wrong line. Pullar, asked about these dismissals later, was quite emphatic that those deliveries would have also dismissed any other left hander. Davidson was often close to unplayable in the period '58 to '63. We had also heard this story—when a member of Steve Waugh's great Australian team was extolling Matt Hayden's batting, Neil Harvey (a golden oldie and teammate of Davidson) was heard to say that good as Hayden was, Davidson would have got him in one over. Such was the regard for Davidson's bowling. Clearly Davidson is the second greatest left-arm fast bowler of them all.

Indian left-arm fast bowler Zaheer Khan
Credit: V. Balaji

And then there is Zaheer Khan. In terms of wickets he may be behind Chaminda Vaas but over the last few years Zaheer has emerged as the foxiest, craftiest left-arm fast bowler. People talk of spinners sometimes bowling with a fast bowler's aggression (Kumble and O'Reilly) but Zaheer is the ultimate example of a fast bowler with the cunning scheming brain of a spin bowler. And of course, he has elevated the art of bowling round the wicket and the art of reverse swing to an all-time high.

Chaminda Vaas and Muralitharan carried Sri Lanka's bowling on their shoulders. Relatively small made, Vaas had a smooth action and movement that got him wickets. His control over line and length was immaculate and he bowled the fuller length to get swing.

We may strive to be objective but are as susceptible to bouts of favoritism as anyone else. But few will argue with our taste if we said that Garry Sobers is along with Kapil Dev our favorite cricketer. Sobers makes an appearance in this essay, because he has 235 Test wickets bowling left arm. It is almost impossible to estimate how many of his 235 Test wickets came from his left-arm fast, or left-arm orthodox or from his Chinaman bowling. Between the two of us, we have seen him take wickets with all three forms of left-arm bowling. When he bowled his fast stuff, he was very effective. He would often take the new ball with Hall. He did everything with a feline grace that nobody has ever remotely matched—his walk to the wicket, to toss the coin, to lead his men out or to take his turn at the crease—Sobers was magic. And then every so often he had the habit of throwing his head back and laughing while playing his cricket.

Sobers must be followed by Worrell, even if Worrell is 21st in the list of wicket takers (69 wickets with a best of seven for 70) simply because he had a huge part in the making of Sobers. Statesman, leader, one who elevated the game through his principles of fair play, Worrell was a better bat than bowler. But his left-arm fast was valuable and often timely for his team.

Talking of West Indians, is it not very ironic that they who gave the world its greatest and unending battery of right-arm fast bowlers from E. A. Martindale, Learie Constantine, Hall, Griffith, and Gilchrist to Roberts, Holding, Garner, Croft, Marshall, Ambrose and Walsh did not throw up a single left-arm fast bowler barring the brief and insipid appearance of Bernard Julien.

Think about it. During that same period, India despite being known for its paltry fast-bowling resources played a number of left-arm seamers. Surti and Solkar (Solkar was very slow, but terrorized Boycott out of the England team in 1971) were followed by Ghavri (109 wickets), Ashish Nehra (44 wickets), Zaheer Khan (288 wickets), Irfan Pathan (100 wickets) and R. P. Singh (40 wickets). In fact Irfan Pathan has a hat trick in Test cricket against Pakistan in 2005, one of the rarest feats possible.

Any cricket follower in India when asked about England's left-arm fast bowling will first mention John Lever, for how can one forget the furore over his alleged use of Vaseline against India in 1977. Strangely, in their land so conducive to swing, England has not produced a star performer in this category and none crossed the Rubicon of 100 wickets. They had right-arm fast bowlers such as Larwood, Gubby Allen, Bedser, Trueman, Statham, Tyson, Snow, Willis, Botham, Flintoff, Hoggard, Anderson and Stuart Broad but hardly a left-arm fast. Bill Voce (98 wickets) partnered Larwood in the 1932 Bodyline series; Ryan Sidebottom was promising during his 22 Test career, but they will have to go back 120 years to Geoff Hirst to locate another left-arm fast bowler with over 50 wickets.

The one country with a reasonably regular presence of left-arm fast is Australia, with over nine players (more than 50 wickets) representing the country. Apart from Davidson, three other bowlers who took over 100 wickets are Mitchell Johnson (we wrote this essay much before his astounding bowling in the Ashes series against England in 2013–14), Bill Johnston and the very tall Bruce Reid. Gary Gilmour is famous for his match-winning dream spell that demolished England in the World Cup semi-final in 1975. He swung the ball late and prodigiously to get batters LBW.

Talking of Gilmour and the World Cup reminds us that India's left armer Nehra also took a terrific six-wicket haul in the World Cup in 2003 to help India beat England.

So what is the difference and variety that the left-arm fast bowler brings to the attack? For one, the left armer bowls over the wicket introducing a new angle to the right-handed bat and the batter is forced to play balls pitching in line with the stumps. That is because the natural movement is the inswinger to the right hander who can be caught leg before and this makes it difficult for the batter to leave balls thinking they will continue on their course. Forced to play the ball, as it goes away with the angle, there is now a high possibility of inducing the edge to slips or the wicketkeeper. Going round the wicket, as the great Wasim and Zaheer both have shown, then poses fresh problems to batters. Batters grow up from school days playing right-arm fast bowlers and, therefore, when they encounter the left armer, they do so without adequate exposure. Batting is ultimately the reflex response in a fraction of a second and the left armer's line of attack induces some hesitancy in the mind and therefore the reflex too is affected. As the two of us discussed the subject, it dawned upon us that while in school cricket we had even encountered the Chinaman bowler, it was only in college cricket that we played the left-arm fast bowler. Of us, Raghunath who played the bowling of Ghavri in the 1970s felt that being a left-handed batter he probably was less discomfited than the right-handed batter. So we leave you with that thought: Is it easier for the left-handed batter to face the left-arm fast bowler? Before you say yes, one would do well to ask a certain Mr Graeme Smith of South Africa about his discomfiting encounters with Zaheer Khan of India.

Note: The recent years have been great for left-arm fast bowlers. Mitchell Starc (debut 2011, 333 wickets), Trent Boult (debut 2011, 317 wickets) and Neil Wagner (debut 2012, 258 wickets) have been outstanding. Shaheen Shah Afridi of Pakistan is the exciting new left-arm fast with more than a 100 wickets in just 27 games. All four proudly carry the banner for their tribe of bowlers.

21

600 SIT-UPS A DAY: THE WICKETKEEPERS

If leg spinners are a strange breed, what would you say about the tribe of wicketkeepers? Who in their right minds would keep slabs of meat inside their gloves all day long (as the keepers in the early years of cricket did) to stop or catch what passes the batters? Or squat and stand and throw themselves about all day long as they do even today? For that is what stumpers have chosen to do, to take on perhaps the most thankless of tasks on the cricket ground! Today's wicketkeepers don the best of gloves, inners and pads cut off at the knee. Back in the old days, keepers wore cumbersome, heavy leg guards, the abdomen guard and of course the aforementioned slab of meat to protect their palms. Over after over to be on your haunches, do innumerable sit-ups, gee up the fielders, pass on tips to the captain and also have the stout heart to accept the fact that people will more often only remember the missed chance than the brilliant catch on the leg side. All things considered, the keeper's job is perhaps the most demanding in cricket.

As we cast our mind back, almost the first image that comes to mind is the photograph from an Ashes Test of the 1930s—Bert Oldfield is still on his haunches behind the wicket while Hammond has completed his cover drive of a spinner. Nothing epitomizes better the truly great keeper. The best of keepers do not get up early because that is what enables them to make the adjustment to take the deflections that come off the bat. Oldfield of course was legendary. He combined beautifully with Grimmett and knew when that master would bowl the googly on leg stump for Oldfield to remove the bails even if only the heel was off the ground. Keeping well to spinners has always been accepted as the hallmark of great wicketkeepers. Among the best keepers in this aspect were, yes Oldfield again—incredibly 40 per cent of his dismissals were stumpings. *Wisden Cricketers' Almanack* says:

> Oldfield's *piece de resistance* was evidently the dismissal of Hobbs, when Ryder sent down an unexpectedly fast delivery that rose cap high: Hobbs, in avoiding the ball, moved momentarily out of his crease; Oldfield, meanwhile, in an amazing movement, had taken the ball and flicked a bail off.

In those days of uncovered wickets and wickets affected by rain, the best keepers stood up—remember no helmets then—to spinners and made leg-side catches and stumping a part of their everyday job. Who were the keepers who were great at their craft? In the early years of Test cricket before World War I there were J. J. Kelly, Dick Lilley, Jack Blackham and H. Carter.

Johnny Moyes, the highly respected Australian commentator writes of Blackham:

> With eyes like a hawk, he would stand right up to the stumps and take the fastest bowlers—and Spofforth was fast in 1878—doing away with the long-stop, and thus give his Captain another man to use in the field. In those days a long-stop was considered as essential as cover-point, so you can imagine how Blackham revolutionized Wicket-keeping…It is learnt that he scarcely had a sound finger on either hand; it was the price he paid for standing up to men of speed with his hands covered with gloves so skimpy that they would never be used nowadays for anything except pruning roses in the garden.

After the war, came Bert Strudwick, George Duckworth and Leslie Ames for England and Oldfield for Australia. Because these two countries played the most, they produced keepers with the best skill and technique. Don Tallon, Godfrey Evans and Gil Langley continued the tradition of good wicket keeping from these two countries while Cameron and John Waite of South Africa were worthy of being counted in the list. Moving on over the years we have Grout, Knott, Taylor, Syed Kirmani, Deryck Murray, Ken Wadsworth, Wasim Bari, Jeffrey Dujon, Rodney Marsh, Ian Healy, Jack Russell, Mark Boucher, Adam Gilchrist... This is just a 'top of the mind' scan of keepers over the years who distinguished themselves in the game. Prasanna Jayewardene of Sri Lanka also emerged as probably the best among keepers. His glove work is a throwback to the old days—dapper and very reliable keeping. And Matt Prior has shown how you can transform from mediocre to excellent by sheer hard work and intelligent honing of skills.

Pakistan can look back with pride at Wasim Bari (and Imtiaz Ahmed who was also a fine bat) while India can never forget Engineer and Kirmani. But for a horrendous series in West Indies in 1976 when he kept fluffing chances of Venkataraghavan, Kirmani sustained a high quality of keeping. Engineer was flamboyant and therefore both spectacular catches and missed chances are strewn in his wicket-keeping record. Kirmani kept superbly to the fast and unfathomable leg spin of Chandrasekhar, as litmus a Test as ever can be. Some swear that Kirmani once effected a stumping of such brilliance, taking a wickedly rising ball from Chandra over his left shoulder and flicking the bails off, that it has never had its equal ever again.

Wally Grout was easily the best keeper from Australia in the long period between Tallon (1950s) and Healy (1980s). He was unobtrusive, superbly efficient and would stand up to Davidson the peerless left-arm swing bowler. These days, we see keepers stand up to the medium pacers in limited overs cricket to prevent batters from jumping down the wicket. But for Grout it was an aggressive wicket creating option. At Madras in 1959, seeing Manmohan Sood, the Indian batter, dragging his back foot out of the crease in the process of playing inswingers to leg off the toes—Grout signaled to Davidson and stood up. Davidson beat Sood with a big swinger and Grout completed the leg-side stumping. It was wicket keeping at its best. Keepers in the earlier era stood up a lot more to medium pacers. Examples that come to mind are Duckworth to Tate and Evans to Alec Bedser. In fact, because of the nature of wickets and because many of the keepers stood up to the fast bowlers perhaps the byes conceded may be higher for the keepers of those days.

The authors recall Jeffrey Dujon do some acrobatic wicket keeping to Roberts, Marshall and Holding when the Windies came to India in the 1980s. But he never had an opportunity to keep to high-class spinners. In fact, except for Walcott (who had the opportunity to create dismissals with Ramadhin and Alf Valentine) all the West Indian keepers have a very low percentage of dismissals off spinners. This is true of New Zealand keepers as well. This also holds true for the South African keepers, especially after the departure of their great googly bowlers by 1930. South Africa of course would be pleased that Boucher holds the record for most dismissals having overtaken first Healy and then Gilchrist. Healy is probably the best modern day example of a wicketkeeper equally proficient in keeping to pace and spin. The great keepers are not flashy, they are unobtrusive. The biggest praise that such keepers expect would simply be: 'He doesn't miss anything.' That phrase brings us to talk of Alan Knott, the Kent and England keeper, about whom his teammates say they cannot remember him missing anything significant. Knott kept brilliantly to Derek Underwood even on bad wickets and unlike most others, never seemed to have had off days or a poor series. Knott's contemporary Bob Taylor was considered by many to be a superb keeper but Knott was good enough to keep Taylor out through his career. In fact after Knott retired, Taylor who was almost as old as Knott kept wickets for many years—and was easily the best among keepers of his time.

There have been quite a few instances where superior keepers have been kept out of the team by a less proficient keeper because that person was the better batter. Leslie Ames played for England between 1929 and 1939 and kept Duckworth out of the England team. In the 1960s, Jim Parks, a nondescript keeper, kept out more competent keepers. Keith Andrews of Northamptonshire was an outstanding wicketkeeper who played just twice for England because ebullient Evans—etched in our memory is the photograph of an airborne Evans breaking the wicket—and his bustling batting kept him out. More recently in Pakistan, Kamran Akmal retains the job on the basis of his batting. In India, Naren Tamhane of Bombay and P. Krishnamurthy of Hyderabad were two outstanding keepers who lost out to keepers who were not as good as them but who were preferred because they were better batters.

Which of the wicketkeepers were excellent batters? Gilchrist of course to begin with: the most destructive no. 7 in Test-cricket history, 17 tons, many of them helping Australia wrestle a win from difficult situations, he also won two World Cup finals for Australia. Kumara Sangakkara, a most cultured left hander is a pivotal batter for Sri Lanka. Who can forget this lion heart's near double century as he almost shepherded his country to an improbable fourth innings target against Australia? Clyde Walcott of West Indies, one of the three Ws, had a batting average of 56 and 15 centuries. Walcott would have walked into any World XI of his time on his batting alone. In fact he kept wickets in 15 Tests and was good enough to keep to spinners such as Ramadhin and Valentine, a task that must have surely called for some level of competence. Alec Stewart played with the certainty that he was worth his place in the England team as a pure batter but in 82 of the 133 Tests that he played in he also kept wickets—without inviting censure while never qualifying to be clubbed with the very good keepers. Andy Flower was

Zimbabwe's best ever batsman and gave them the bonus of a reasonably efficient keeper. There have also been examples of some who began as ordinary keepers but grew with the job. Rodney Marsh started his Test career being derisively labeled 'Mr Iron Gloves' for his clumsy wicket keeping, but improved so much over the years that 'caught Marsh bowled Lillee' became a part of cricket folklore. Dhoni started as an ordinary keeper who entered the team because of his destructive batting. Of course he is among the rarest instances of a keeper who is also a key batter and also the captain of the team. He has seen the highest of highs and the lowest of lows as captain. And now in February 2013, after a nightmarish sequence of Test losses, Dhoni has brought all of India to its feet with one of the finest double centuries at Chennai. Dhoni may never be bracketed with great keepers but will certainly be bracketed with the greatest all-rounders to have played the game.

An annoying feature in modern-day cricket is the way keepers keep up a constant verbal exhortation after every delivery. Chirpiness from keepers such as Evans and Engineer was to keep their sides positive but this ability to disturb the batter with chatter and sledging is unfortunately being seen as a part of modern-day wicketkeeping skills! However, one skill that wicketkeepers nowadays have added is the ability to convert mediocre or even poor throws from fielders into run outs—something vital in these days of third umpire camera verdicts.

Finally, however, there is perhaps something silently glorious about the wicketkeeper. It is the nature of sport that it is the swashbuckler who is in the limelight—be it center forward, swordsman, racehorse or batter. It takes a certain deep immersion in Test cricket to recognize that it is the keeper who is at once both the shepherd and the workhorse. The great glove men concentrate through every ball of the innings so that they do not miss the crucial snick or let that hated bye through. To do this over five days and then also chip in with the bat shows that the true warrior in cricket is the wicketkeeper.

22

THE DAY DHONI RESIGNED

This essay was written in January 2017

A niece in Mumbai is in tears; the techie in Hyderabad is shocked; our temple priest is distraught; in Lucknow, a rickshaw-puller's heart is unbearably heavy; and countless Chennaites are unable to accept that 'Namma Dhoni' has given up captaincy. Strange, because they ought to be familiar with Dhoni's style—goodbye without notice or fanfare. Dhoni, one of a kind.

Mahendra Singh Dhoni relinquishes the captaincy with a cupboard overflowing with numerous awards and an adulation that the public has only showered on Kapil Dev and Sachin Tendulkar. The 2007 T20 World Cup, the 2011 ODI World Cup, the 2013 Champions Trophy, the ICC no. 1 ranking in Tests—they all came to India when Dhoni was captain. Even at 26, when Dhoni won his first T20 World Cup, he was not at the forefront of celebrations, but busy peeling off his jersey and giving it to a young boy. Few remember him stepping up to receive any of these trophies, but everyone recalls as though it were yesterday, that towering six to long on, the twirl of the bat, and an unhurried plucking of one stump as a souvenir. Dhoni walked off the Wankhede pitch that night in 2011 as though it were just another day in office. As though he was completely unaware that he was bathed in glory. No surprise that as he grew older, he featured even less in the photo ops. That placidity and almost contemptuous disregard for whether the team had won or lost—that was no façade.

Everyone agrees he was an outstanding ODI and T20 captain, but some accuse him of being less interested as a Test captain. For us, that's an unfair summary. As the editor of Wisden India told us, one must view Dhoni's Test captaincy in two phases—before 2011 and after 2011. Before 2011, he had the fabulous batting line-up of Sehwag, Dravid, Tendulkar, Ganguly and Laxman along with bowlers, Zaheer and Harbhajan, at their peak. But post-2011, these players were on the wane; the fab four exited and Zaheer, Harbhajan and Sehwag were spent forces. Dhoni had to bide his time while India licked its wounds and rebuilt their team.

That is why the 2013 Champions Trophy in England must be considered one of his finest victories. It came after India had taken a series of knocks in Test cricket and a most unsavoury betting scandal in the IPL. No one believed that India, a team in transition and its governance in turmoil, was a serious contender. But Dhoni and his team created magic, won every game, and India was almost perfection personified.

We close with something very dear to Dhoni—his respect and admiration for India's armed forces. After all, when India retained their no. 1 Test ranking at Kolkata in February 2010, Dhoni gave his jersey to an officer of the Indian Army, a Shaurya Chakra winner. In that photo, you can see the Indian captain is prouder than the Army officer as the jersey exchanges hands. Perhaps his proudest moment was the investiture ceremony when he was given the rank of Lieutenant Colonel in the Indian Territorial Army.

'Cricketers like Dhoni come once in a century,' says Gavaskar. That is no hyperbole.

A fortnight later

For writing our cricket books, Raghu and I have met quite a few cricketers, especially the older players like Bedi, Prasanna, Venkataraghavan, Srikkanth, Srinath, Kirmani and others. Among the younger players, though also retired, we have met and spoken at length to Venkatesh Prasad, Rahul Dravid and V. V. S. Laxman. But we had not met any of the current superstars.

However, a month after our second book, *From Mumbai to Durban* was released and just a fortnight after M. S. Dhoni had announced that he was giving up white-ball captaincy, we had an unexpected meeting with him. For the first and only time. It was well past 8 p.m. on the 30th of January, 2017 when Col Shankar (a decorated army officer, now retired), a close friend of MSD called me and said he would like me to meet him. 'Dhoni is in Bengaluru to play an ODI against England tomorrow, so just come over. I have told him that you both must meet.' It had been a long day at the university and I had just reached home. Short notice be damned, I wolfed down my dinner and in 30 minutes was there at the Ritz Carlton Hotel where the Indian cricket team was put up. Col Shankar met me at the foyer and steered me through all the security and into Dhoni's room. MSD was expecting us and greeted us with a broad grin, rather than words of welcome. Kedar Jadhav was also in the room, a quiet guy who smiled and went back to pottering with the coffee kettle.

Introductions done, Dhoni and I spent around half an hour with Shankar, taking great pleasure in seeing his two friends talking to each other. Once we were plonked on the sofa, Shankar said, 'Giri, show him your book.' MSD looked at our book, flipping the pages, pausing a minute here and a minute there before going straight to the photographs. There are enough of them in the book and Dhoni spent time looking at them, sometimes smiling, sometimes pointing at them with flashes of reminiscences.

M. S. Dhoni turns nostalgic with Giridhar while browsing old photographs
Photo Credit: Colonel Shankar

Dhoni signed copies of *From Mumbai to Durban* for Giridhar and Raghunath
Photo Credit: Colonel Shankar

And as he was going through them, he paused and asked, 'Do you have a picture of the Mohali victory against Australia, that one wicket victory?' I said, yes and pointed to the photo of Raina, Laxman and Ojha in a threesome bear hug of elation. Delighted, Dhoni looked at it for at least a few minutes, savoring the memory. It is, I think, his favorite Test. Then with that famous grin, he told me, 'You know, I don't read much but I love looking at photographs.'

Kedar Jadhav brought us some coffee and a short while later, Dhoni told me that rather than take a copy of a book that he won't read, would I mind if he signed the copy and returned it to me as a memento. I said, 'Yes, but on the condition that you must also sign a second copy of the book for my co-author Raghunath who lives in Chennai.' Colonel Shankar—he seemed to have thought of everything—produced a big black felt pen, and with a flourish M. S. D. signed, 'Mahi'. The idea of bringing two books when I went to meet Dhoni, of course had also come from Shankar. Making sure we had some great photographs of the meeting? Shankar again. And Kedar Jadhav, playing perfect foil, ensured we had a second cup of coffee before we left.

23

ALL ABOUT OPENING BATTERS

Indian cricket's best years have been 2001–2010 and with good reason too. Everyone knows that during this period we had the finest batting in the world, the 'fab four' as they were called. And we had a decent bowling combination of pace and spin that could deliver 20 wickets on the back of the strong totals our batters regularly posted. But one reason our fabulously gifted middle order was able to deliver so regularly was that they were provided a terrific platform by our openers, Virender Sehwag and Aakash Chopra for a brief while at the start of our climb and later by Sehwag and Gautam Gambhir. In fact even the short-term opening combinations consistently delivered during this period. Conversely, our worst period in Test cricket—from the summer of 2011 to the winter of 2012 when we were blanked out 0–4 in England and Australia and then lost a home series to England—not only coincides with the fading away of the middle order greats but also with the complete failure of Sehwag and Gambhir to provide solid opening partnerships.

Clearly, therefore, the foundation of a successful team is its opening pair and cricket history provides consistent evidence for this assertion. Let us look at recent events. England in the last two years briefly rose to premier position in Test cricket and they had in Andrew Strauss and Alastair Cook, a truly successful opening pair. Australia who strode the cricket world like a colossus for 15 years from the mid-1990s to 2008 had Mark Taylor and Michael Slater to open for them and this was followed by the formidable combination of Justin Langer and Matthew Hayden for many years. Without this opening pair, could Ricky Ponting and others in the middle order succeeded so often? Would McGrath and Warne have bowled so confidently if they did not have the fantastic totals that Australia put up on the foundations of their opening partnerships?

Who before Australia ruled the cricket world from 1976 to 1992? West Indies and immediately one thinks of their fearsome fast bowling—from Roberts and Holding to Ambrose and Walsh—and the imperial batting of Richards. But we must remember that it was the success of Gordon Greenidge and Desmond Haynes, their opening pair that provided them the foundations of an invincible team.

Australia's formidable opening pair, Bobby Simpson and Bill Lawry going out to bat, 1964
Photo Courtesy: Kasturi & Sons

Bill Lawry and Bobby Simpson in the 1960s for Australia; Len Hutton and Cyril Washbrook for England in the 1950s; Jack Hobbs and Herbert Sutcliffe for England in the 1920s and Hobbs and Wilfred Rhodes in the early years of the 20th century—each of these greatly successful pairs was the reason for their teams to be successful. Stable opening pairs provided a solidity and sense of comfort that cannot often be expressed in runs.

Why was India never consistently at the top? In the 1970s, we had an all-time great spin bowling attack that was so good that they could fight even if their batters only gave them around 250 runs to bowl with. They were that good; not just in India but in Australia, West Indies and England. But you cannot win matches when your batters don't give you enough runs. For India, it was not that it did not have good batters. They did. Who can fault a lineup that during the 1960s had Vijay Manjrekar, Tiger Pataudi, Hanumant Singh, M. L. Jaisimha and Dilip Sardesai or in the 1970s had G. R. Viswanath, Dilip Vengsarkar, Ajit Wadekar and Mohinder Amarnath? The problem was that these batters would often be exposed early to the new ball as we never seemed to get a good opening pair going. Gavaskar was simply majestic and easily among the greatest three opening batters of all time. But he never had a great partner. Workmanlike, honest, diligent Chetan Chauhan who tried his best at all times was the one partner he had for some consistent period of time. His other partner of some duration, thrilled him one minute and infuriated him the next, and that of course was Krishnamachari Srikkanth. Countless times, Srikkanth would swish airily and miss, Gavaskar would go down the pitch to talk sense into Srikkanth. The pupil would nod his head again and again earnestly and vigorously, as though he had learned a lesson for a lifetime, but the next ball would play another outrageous stroke, that might either be six over cover or spooned into mid-off. Gavaskar would endure that and soldier on. That is how Gavaskar collected his 10,000 runs in Test cricket alone most times; holding up his end and wishing somebody equally resolute could share the burden at the other end. If people at times saw a petulant side of Gavaskar, a churlish side to him, it must be because his frustrations at the lack of support at the other end must have frayed his nerves no end.

In Test history, of the 22 opening pairs that have batted together in a minimum of 35 innings and whose overall average for the opening stand is at least 40 runs, there are eight from

England, five from Australia, two each from India, South Africa, Sri Lanka and West Indies and one from Pakistan. Here are these 22 opening pairs in Table 23.1.

Greenidge and Haynes were together for over 75 Tests, spanning 13 years and there has not been a more durable opening pair in cricket history. Greenidge was attacking and when the mood took him as in that double hundred against England in 1984, totally destructive. There seemed to be a suppressed anger in him, and we get an insight into this in the movie *Fire in Babylon* where Greenidge is one of the players who talks fairly extensively and intimately about the emotions coursing through West Indians of that period. Haynes, in stark contrast, was clearly sunny and his happy nature was never far from the surface.

If there is one defining feature of a partnership, it is chemistry. The evidence of this chemistry between openers is their running between wickets.

History tells us that Hobbs and Sutcliffe ran superbly and had a great understanding. It was obviously the genius of Hobbs for judging a run because his earlier partnership with Rhodes too was remarkable in this aspect. In our times, there can be no finer example for this than Lawry and Simpson. Their mutual understanding was simply uncanny; there seemed to be such a telepathic understanding between them, that both could set off without even the customary call. We saw it in 1964 in India; our fielding was no great shakes and except when the ball went to Surti or Pataudi, these two would steal singles and convert the ones into twos. One look and off they went. The immense benefit was that the pair could rotate strike at will. Even without any domination of the bowling, they would tidily collect a few singles every over. Ask any bowler what exasperates him the most. It is not being hit for a boundary of a bad ball but being milked for singles of decent balls. No other opening pair can come remotely near Lawry and Simpson for running between wickets.

TABLE 23.1: The Most Durable Opening Pairs in Test History

Opening pair	*Country*	*Career*	*Innings*	*Runs*	*Average*
W. Rhodes and J. B. Hobbs	England	1910–1921	36	2,146	61.3
J. B. Hobbs and H. Sutcliffe	England	1924–1930	38	3,249	87.8
L. Hutton and C. Washbrook	England	1946–1951	51	2,880	60.0
R. B. Simpson and W. M. Lawry	Australia	1961–1967	62	3,596	59.9
J. H. Edrich and G. Boycott	England	1964–1972	35	1,672	50.7
C. P. S. Chauhan and S. M. Gavaskar	India	1973–1981	59	3,010	52.8
C. G. Greenidge and D. L. Haynes	West Indies	1978–1991	148	6,482	46.6
D. C. Boon and G. R. Marsh	Australia	1985–1988	41	1,871	46.8
G. R. Marsh and M. A. Taylor	Australia	1989–1992	47	1,980	44.0
G. A. Gooch and M. A. Atherton	England	1990–1995	44	2,501	56.8
M. A. Taylor and M. J. Slater	Australia	1993–1999	78	3,887	51.1
Saeed Anwar and Aamir Sohail	Pakistan	1994–2000	37	1,563	43.4
M. S. Atapattu and S. T. Jayasuriya	Sri Lanka	1997–2007	118	4,469	40.3
G. Kirsten and H. H. Gibbs	South Africa	1998–2002	52	2,283	44.8
J. L. Langer and M. L. Hayden	Australia	2001–2007	113	5,655	51.4
D. Ganga and C. H. Gayle	West Indies	2001–2008	49	1,954	40.7
M. P. Vaughan and M. E. Trescothick	England	2002–2005	54	2,487	48.8
H. H. Gibbs and G. C. Smith	South Africa	2002–2008	56	2,983	55.2
M. E. Trescothick and A. J. Strauss	England	2004–2006	52	2,670	52.4
V. Sehwag and G. Gambhir	India	2004–2012	87	4,350	51.8
A. J. Strauss and A. N. Cook	England	2006–2012	117	4,711	41.0
T. M. Dilshan and N. T. Paranavitana	Sri Lanka	2009–2012	38	1,506	40.7

Source: Data from espncricinfo.com. Analysis and tabular compilation by authors.

Australia's fortunes took an upward swing from the mid-1980s and by the time they conquered West Indies in the Caribbean Islands in the mid-1990s, they had been helped by three very good and solid opening pairs. Australia's rejuvenation began with David Boon and Geoff Marsh in the period 1985–1988. Everyone will remember that Australia's World Cup triumph in 1987 was in great part due to their terrific opening stands. This duo was followed by Mark Taylor and Marsh and then during their complete ascendancy in the mid and late 1990s, Australia had skipper Taylor and Slater as their openers. The Australians' vice-like grip on cricket supremacy continued till 2008 because Langer and Hayden then formed a fantastic opening pair in what was inarguably one of the greatest Test teams.

Sri Lanka's best period in its cricket history began with its World Cup triumph in 1996. For the next 10 years they more than held their own in Test cricket. Sure, Muttiah Muralitharan alone was enough to spin them to many victories but for runs in their bank they had a marvelous opening pair. The technically sober Marvan Atapattu with his phenomenal appetite for long innings was the ideal foil for the aggressive and destructive Sanath Jayasuriya.

Another interesting insight is that in the last 10 years, every leading cricketing nation has had a successful opening pair. In the last four years, the no. 1 spot has been held in turns by Australia, India, England and South Africa. And the opening pairs for these countries: Hayden and Langer; Sehwag and Gambhir; Strauss and Cook; and Graeme Smith and Herschelle Gibbs. This is perhaps a key indicator that in the coming years, as long as each country has a strong opening pair, no one country will dominate Test cricket and that much like one-day cricket, any of the top six countries can easily aspire to become no. 1 among Test-playing nations. And it is likely that the hold on the perch will be tenuous because any of the others could quickly topple them.

Openers are a different breed. They are wired differently. They take up perhaps the hardest job in cricket—of facing the fast bowlers, absorbing the attacks, wearing the attackers down and creating the ground for the batters to follow. While the admirable few like Sehwag and Jayasuriya, turned the tenets of opening upside down, with the motto, 'attack is the best form of defense,' the others trusted their technique and concentration to see off the new ball. Thus watchfulness, mental fitness and a sturdy temperament alloyed to a sound technique are the essential ingredients. That technique has to be honed endlessly; to judge line and length, assess the bounce and to use the depth of the crease to play fast bowling off both front and back foot. How often have we seen openers who are so handsome on the front foot, flounder and seem inadequate when they play off the back foot? Opening in the subcontinent is different from opening in the seaming conditions in England and very different from tackling the bouncy and pacy pitches of Australia and South Africa. And yet the opener is the same; he has to adapt. More than other batters, it is the opener on whom the burden falls. For the more time he is able to weather the new ball attack, the more the chances that the stroke players who follow him will succeed.

Courage is quite simply the prerequisite. And little wonder that many of the stories of courage on the cricket field feature opening batters. In the days when protective gear such as helmet and chest guard were not known, to bat against fiery pace must have required indescribable courage in addition to technical skill. Modern-day television has spoilt us because sitting in our drawing room we look at the slow motion replays and fail to fathom how incredibly skillful a batter must be to see a ball coming at 90 miles an hour and move hands and feet instinctively to defend, attack or leave the ball. Batting against really fast bowling, the response time is so short that the reaction is pure reflex action. The first decision is to play or leave the ball and most classical openers leave more deliveries than they play—and to gain that extra fraction of a second, they need to be good back foot players with a steady head and good balance. Therefore, even as we dissect opening batsmanship and try and identify the best openers, we must bear in mind that anybody who opened for their country or even at first-class level had to be a courageous athlete.

There are 90 openers with more than 1,500 Test-match runs. And perhaps it will be illuminating to analyze them under three broad categories. The first category is the classical openers, copy book in defense, classical in stroke play, everything right like a demonstration of the coaching manual. The second category is the very effective, combative opener, who may not be classical or elegant but whose methods have proved successful for them. The third category among the openers will be the dashers and buccaneers who take risks; take the attack to the opposition from the first ball and in the process provide thrills which no one else can. But first we shall talk of Victor Trumper. Even today, he is among the most loved sportsmen in Australia and idolized by cricketers born many years after he has gone. But he gets pride of place not for being such a wonderful person but simply because he was the best batter before Bradman. Trumper's years were not batter friendly; the pitches were bad, they were left open to the elements, and as bowlers made balls bounce, grub or spit, it was a Test of pure batting skill to make runs. And Trumper made them in a style that even today evokes the greatest admiration. His teammates Carter (the wicketkeeper) and Charlie Macartney in many conversations with the famous cricketer-turned-journalist Jack Fingleton said, 'When you talk about batters, first put Trumper up there alone and then start comparing the rest.' When Macartney had played a breathtaking innings in England, a journalist in his report the next day said it was a Trumper-like knock. Macartney was livid saying 'What nonsense, I am not fit enough to tie his shoelaces.' Trumper was graceful, supremely athletic and played the ball so late to wherever he chose. There is the story of England's prime bowler Geoff Hirst telling his Captain (when he came over to decide the field placing), 'It doesn't matter where we put them, Sir, Victor will hit them where he pleases.' All Australians and most Englishmen thought he was the best ever to have graced the cricket field. C. B. Fry raised a toast to him at the House of Lords saying 'Charge your glasses, gentlemen to the greatest batter in the world, Victor Trumper, first man in and last man out on a Melbourne sticky against Hirst and Rhodes.' Trumper had made 74 the previous day on a particularly nasty drying Melbourne gluepot. So, as Carter and Macartney said, we shall place Trumper alone at the top and now discuss the rest.

The three greatest classical openers ever are Jack Hobbs, Len Hutton and Sunil Gavaskar. Each of them interestingly also represents three eras of cricket, with Hobbs representing the first 50 years of cricket, Hutton the next 40 years and Gavaskar the modern 50 years. Let us first pay tribute to these maestros and then lower the bar to allow some more illustrious classical openers into their company.

Hobbs: The greatness of Hobbs is that even though the game today is very different from his time, a 100 years ago, people still use Hobbs as the yardstick for perfection in opening batsmanship. He played every shot in the book, jumping out to drive, or cut and hook the short ball. It was Hobbs who found the answer to play leg breaks and googlies. He had such immaculate defense and such grace in attack. What adds charm and luster to the story of Hobbs is that he is idolized as a true sport and gentleman cricketer who won the affection of everyone. Stories of his modesty and humility despite great deeds might remind us of Tendulkar. Hobbs in two other aspects also has a striking similarity to Tendulkar. He played Test cricket for 22 years and that will strike a chord with millions of Indians who have enjoyed Tendulkar's batsmanship for 23 years. Hobbs was 48 years old when he played his last Test and in fact scored the last of his Test centuries when he was

46 years old. But for World War I he would have played more Tests. The other striking similarity with Tendulkar, the holder of many records, is that Hobbs holds the record for first-class centuries and in fact collected 197 first-class centuries, nearly a hundred of them after he crossed 40. When Hobbs passed away in December 1963, Wisden in its obituary wrote:

> His career was divided into two periods, each different from the other in style and tempo. Before the war of 1914–1918 he was Trumperesque, quick to the attack on springing feet, strokes all over the field, killing but never brutal, all executed at the wrists, after the preliminary getting together of the general muscular motive power. When cricket was resumed in 1919, Hobbs...ripened into a classic. His style became as serenely poised as any ever witnessed on a cricket field.

Again those who think there were two distinct periods of Tendulkar—the first 11 years and the next 11 years will see a parallel. Perhaps it would be fitting to conclude this section on Hobbs with what his opening partner Sutcliffe said:

> I was his partner on many occasions on extremely bad wickets, and I can say this without any doubt whatever that he was the most brilliant exponent of all time, and quite the best batter of my generation on all types of wickets. He was a man of the highest integrity who believed in sportsmanship in the highest sense, teamwork, fair-play and clean-living. His life was full of everything noble and true.

Hutton: The finest opener after Hobbs, and considered one of the best batters of all time, Hutton was technical perfection personified. This he achieved through immense discipline coupled with deep ambition to be the finest. Boycott, himself, one of the finest openers in cricket history, has this to say about Hutton a fellow Yorkshireman whom he idolized:

> He had great technique, on uncovered pitches he was the master, and that was allied to wonderful elegance when conditions were more favourable. He played all his life under

> the LBW law which changed in 1937 and made batting much harder, so his considerable achievements are all the more worthy.

Hutton was also the first professional cricketer to captain England, and he did not let his batting suffer under the burden of captaincy. He held the world record for the highest score in an innings, 364, till Garry Sobers broke his record in 1958. Twice he carried his bat through the innings. Hutton was the perfect combination of elegance, technical correctness and appetite for run making. No wonder he ended up with an average of over 56. Like many cricketers of his era, he too lost six years of cricket at the prime of his career due to World War II.

Sunil Gavaskar during his 23rd Test century
Photo Courtesy: Kasturi & Sons

Gavaskar: Here was someone so exceptional that just looking at his stance, the way he went back to defend or moved forward to push the ball to mid-off to get off the mark, one was sure that one was looking at the best opening batter. If defense can be beautiful to watch it had to be Gavaskar—he was so beautifully balanced. He announced himself to the world in a manner never done before by scoring 774 runs in four Tests in West Indies for an average of 154. Perhaps only in his maiden series did he play without burden, being just a debutante. After that series, right till he retired, Gavaskar carried India's batting on his shoulders. He played with the worry that if his defense was breached India would fold up. While Gavaskar played with such monumental self-denial to secure safety for India, many could not see beyond the mere fact that Gavaskar treasured his wicket. Occasionally Gavaskar indulged himself. When he did that he revealed a side to his batting that even today is like a whirlwind tour of Shangri-La. On a misty October day in 1983 against Holding, Marshall, Winston Davis and Wayne Daniel, Gavaskar hit a hundred that had a dozen full-blooded hooks for fours. In no time he had raced to a century in just 94 balls. It was also his 29th century that brought him level with Don Bradman. Actually Gavaskar had a great sense of occasion. Be it the way he hit that century to equal Bradman or his swan song innings of 96 against Pakistan, considered by many to be one of the finest innings ever played on a minefield pitch. How like Gavaskar to answer those skeptics who so often said he was not that good on bad wickets to sign off with such an innings! As captaincy wore him down, he showed his petulant side, he could be stubborn and whimsical and the media feasted on all that. Actually Gavaskar for us was at his most endearing when he captained India for the last time in the Benson and Hedges World Cup in 1985. Remember the jaunty and distinctive cap that he wore, the Zen-like calm with which he captained, the way he had the boyish Sivaramakrishnan bowl at his best. He was happy, contented and at peace, and it showed through those two weeks of the tournament.

Let us now open the gates to allow the other fine classical opening batters into the hallowed company of Hobbs, Hutton and Gavaskar (see Table 23.2).

TABLE 23.2: The Classical Openers

Player	*Country*	*Span*	*Matches*	*Innings*	*Runs*	*Score*	*Average*	*100s*
J. B. Hobbs	England	1908–1930	58	97	5,130	211	56.4	14
H. Sutcliffe	England	1924–1935	54	83	4,522	194	61.1	16
W. M. Woodfull	Australia	1926–1934	27	44	2,036	161	50.9	7
B. Mitchell	South Africa	1929–1949	27	48	2,390	189*	56.9	7
E. A. B. Rowan	South Africa	1935–1951	15	29	1,300	236	50.0	3
C. Washbrook	England	1937–1951	34	62	2,456	195	43.9	6
L. Hutton	England	1937–1955	76	131	6,721	364	56.5	19
A. Melville	South Africa	1939–1949	7	12	708	189	64.4	3
J. B. Stollmeyer	West Indies	1939–1955	32	55	2,139	160	41.9	4
A. R. Morris	Australia	1946–1955	45	76	3,381	206	45.7	11
B. Sutcliffe	New Zealand	1947–1958	23	41	1,763	230*	45.2	4
D. J. McGlew	South Africa	1952 1962	31	57	2,316	255*	44.5	7
Hanif Mohammad	Pakistan	1952–1969	39	65	2,638	337	41.9	7
C. C. Hunte	West Indies	1958–1967	44	78	3,245	260	45.1	8
R. B. Simpson	Australia	1960–1968	38	70	3,664	311	55.5	8
G. Boycott	England	1964–1982	107	191	8,091	246*	48.2	22
G. M. Turner	New Zealand	1969–1983	38	67	2,828	259	45.6	7
S. M. Gavaskar	India	1971–1987	119	203	9,607	221	50.3	33

C. G. Greenidge	West Indies	1974–1991	107	182	7,488	226	45.1	19
D. L. Haynes	West Indies	1978–1994	116	201	7,472	184	42.5	18
M. A. Taylor	Australia	1989–1999	104	186	7,525	334*	43.5	19
Saeed Anwar	Pakistan	1990–2001	54	86	3,957	188*	47.1	11
M. A. Atherton	England	1990–2001	108	197	7,476	185*	39.1	16
J. L. Langer	Australia	1993–2007	65	115	5,112	250	48.2	16
M. S. Atapattu	Sri Lanka	1997–2007	79	136	5,317	249	43.2	16
M. P. Vaughan	England	2002–2008	38	72	3,093	197	45.5	10
A. N. Cook	England	2006–2012	80	142	6,539	294	49.2	21

Source: Data from espncricinfo.com. Analysis and tabular compilation by authors.
Note: *Remained not out.

We do not think many will have objections to seeing Langer, Cook, Boycott and Hanif Mohammed in this list. Or for that matter Hobbs' old mate Sutcliffe, Jeff Stollmeyer and Conrad Hunte who were among the best openers in the classical tradition from West Indies. In our list is a less familiar name from South Africa: Bruce Mitchell. Mitchell was South Africa's finest batsman during his playing days. In fact he played in every Test that South Africa played between 1929 and 1949. He was technically competent and correct in his play but tended to be over cautious and defensive. It was something that he imposed upon himself because South Africa in his days was not a strong batting side. Mitchell's greatest triumph came on the tour of England when he scored 164 to set up a victory at Lords. He followed this up with a match-saving century in the final Test and ensured that South Africa won the series.

Boycott in his book *The Best XI*, picks Mitchell in his all-time South African XI saying 'studious, careful and very determined to occupy the crease for as long as possible, he was a man after my own heart.'

Ask anyone over 70 and he will insist that Arthur Morris who opened for Bradman's Invincibles was among the best. Like Mitchell, he too was before our time, so we will rely on what Wisden and cricket writers of those days have to say about him. Of Morris it was said that he was the epitome of classical batsmanship, full of elegance and poise. He was also a wonderful human being and a role model for sportsmanship. There were two interesting aspects that struck us as we read of Morris. One, that in his batsmanship and gentlemanly behavior, he reminds us of our own Rahul Dravid. The second that after his pairing with fellow opener Sid Barnes was broken, Morris was not really himself thereafter. This second tidbit reminds us of how our own musical pairs like Shankar Jaikishan or Alathur Brothers withered away after the demise of one of the partners.

There are two striking omissions in our list. One is Barry Richards, considered by almost everyone who played with him as the finest opener of his time along with Gavaskar. Our reason for omitting him is that he played just four Tests; the series against Australia at home in 1970. While he hit two centuries and two fifties and clearly seemed destined for greatness that was actually the end of his career. In our view this brief window to his prowess at Test level is not enough for us to include him in our list. For a similar reason that he too played just seven Tests, we excluded Vijay Merchant—India's finest opener apart from Gavaskar. Merchant hit three centuries, two fifties, had an average of over 47 and was technique personified with all the attributes of an opener.

Some in our list are special. For instance Greenidge's batting was based on sound technique and the unflappable opener's temperament but he erupted into belligerent stroke play unlike many of the others on our list of classical openers. Similarly, Saeed Anwar will bring to mind flashy strokes on the off side and a reputation as a huge success in one-day cricket but he was a fine and serious Test opener whose audacious stroke play was not easily curbed.

At the other end of this spectrum in our list is Jackie McGlew of South Africa, who was a self-denying Spartan at the wicket, grim, determined and adhesive at the crease. Hanif Mohammed was also a technically correct batter who could stay forever at the wicket—a monument of patience and temperament. Starting his career at 17, he carried the opening burden for Pakistan in their first decade in Test cricket. Hanif played the longest innings in Test cricket when he batted for 970 minutes for 337 runs at Barbados to save the match against West Indies. There is a story around this knock. So defensive was Hanif that a spectator perched on a tree above the ground fell asleep, toppled to ground and was taken unconscious to hospital. When he regained consciousness two days later, he asked about the match and was told that Hanif was still at the crease. How this affected that man's health has not been recorded. Uncharitable though it may seem, such excessively slow and cautious batting gave a bad name to technically correct batsmanship and to Test cricket.

If these were the finest classical openers with great technique then we must also find space to recognize those excellent openers who may not have looked elegant or technically perfect but who were so effective that they achieved great results. Some names in this category will spring to mind without bidding, such as Graeme Smith and Mathew Hayden, but there were others. So we trawled through the names of openers who had scored at least 2,000 Test runs and had an average of near 40 and more. Great names in this list too, with runs and averages to show how superbly they served their team. Table 23.3 is our short list of such openers.

These players were worth their weight in gold. Overcoming technical limitations with unmatched powers of determination, combativeness and ability to counter punch at every opportunity; these are traits that you can recognize in each one of them. Grit, ability to overcome physical pain, their focus is on accumulating runs. Batters like Hayden, Graham Gooch and Smith stood like mountains between bowler and stumps, there seemed no possible way to get past them. No wonder they have played over a 100 Tests each, scored 8,000 runs and have 74 centuries between them.

For Indians it will be interesting to observe that their team performed at its best when John Wright and Gary Kirsten—both in our list above—were their coaches. Is there something in this observation? That for Indian cricketers, perhaps such gritty but remarkable cricketers prove to be the most effective coaches. And on the lighter side, pause and think about Lawry and Navjot Sidhu. Both of them were obdurate and dour personalities on the ground during their playing days but have transformed into ebullient, highly excitable and voluble (that is putting it mildly in the case of Sidhu) commentators.

While opening the batting in Test cricket is serious business, it must also be fun and entertainment. Nothing can rival the

TABLE 23.3: Very Effective, Invaluable and Utterly Reliable—Some Great Openers Here

Player	*Country*	*Span*	*Matches*	*Innings*	*Runs*	*Highest score*	*Average*	*100s*
M. L. Hayden	Australia	1994–2009	103	184	8,625	380	50.7	30
G. C. Smith	South Africa	2002–2012	102	176	8,334	277	50.5	26
G. A. Gooch	England	1978–1995	100	184	7,811	333	43.9	18
A. J. Strauss	England	2004–2012	97	171	6,741	169	40.9	20
M. E. Trescothick	England	2000–2006	76	142	5,824	219	43.8	14
G. Kirsten	South Africa	1993–2002	84	149	5,726	275	41.8	14
J. G. Wright	New Zealand	1978–1993	80	144	5,260	185	38.1	12
W. M. Lawry	Australia	1961–1971	67	123	5,234	210	47.2	13
G. Gambhir	India	2004–2012	53	93	3,986	206	45.3	9
Mudassar Nazar	Pakistan	1976–1989	70	109	3,787	231	36.8	9
J. H. Edrich	England	1963–1976	47	82	3,430	310*	44.5	8
D. L. Amiss	England	1972–1977	39	69	3,276	262*	53.7	11
C. C. McDonald	Australia	1952–1961	47	81	3,073	170	39.4	5
S. M. Katich	Australia	2008–2010	33	61	2,928	157	50.5	8
N. S. Sidhu	India	1983–1999	45	69	2,911	201	42.8	8
D. C. Boon	Australia	1985–1993	36	63	2,614	200	45.1	8
E. J. Barlow	South Africa	1961–1970	28	52	2,290	201	45.8	5
W. Bardsley	Australia	1909–1926	33	47	1,755	193*	41.8	4

Source: Data from espncricinfo.com. Analysis and tabular compilation by authors.
Note: *Remained not out.

air of excitement and expectation at the start of a series or Test match if the openers happen to be attacking and thrilling stroke players. These openers send the pulse racing, they bring in the crowds and the buzz in the air is because of them. How much richer cricket is because of these Robin Hoods? So the third and last section of our story is a tribute to the dashers. This section on dashing openers is essentially what we wrote in our blog, 'Dashing openers—A priceless tribe' in espncricinfo.com in July 2010.

Indians of our generation grew up listening to tales of Mushtaq Ali the cavalier opening batter of the 1930s and 1940s. Forty years later, when Srikkanth made it to the Indian team, Mushtaq was remembered. When Sehwag began blazing away, Mushtaq was still being remembered. The allure of the dasher as a Test match opener is simply eternal.

Should not the Test opener play sensibly, see off the new ball, take the spite out of the wicket, tire the fast bowlers, and set up a platform for the batters to follow? Not for the dashing opener! 70 for no loss at lunch may be alright for normal openers but for the dasher, it is better to be 123 for 1 at lunch! He stirs the senses like nobody else can. And that alone is reason enough to celebrate this priceless gift to cricket.

The vision is intoxicating; of a knight on a steed, rapier in hand, cutting a swathe for the batters to follow. The pitch might be green, the ball swinging prodigiously or bouncing sharply. But these blithe spirits—they see the ball, their eyes light up and they go for it. Audacity, instinct, hand-eye coordination certainly but most important of all, technique is their servant and not the other way around. Because they bring off outrageous shots, people tend to think they have a loose technique. Far from it! Sehwag brings down his bat as straight as any 'technically sound batter'. The dasher often fails because he chooses to attack a ball that should not have been so belligerently addressed. Their very vulnerability adds to their irresistible charm. Table 23.4 is our list of the death or glory buccaneers among Test openers.

TABLE 23.4: Thrilling the Senses—the Dashing Openers

Player	*Country*	*Span*	*Match*	*Innings*	*Runs*	*Highest score*	*Average*	*100s*	*50s*	*Strike rate*
V. Sehwag	India	2002–2012	97	167	8,180	319	50.8	22	30	82.4
Shahid Afridi	Pakistan	1998–2005	15	24	892	141	37.16	2	6	75
D. A. Warner	Australia	2011–2012	13	23	921	180	43.85	3	3	71.4
T. M. Dilshan	Sri Lanka	2009–2012	25	45	1,883	193	43.79	7	8	64.8
S. T. Jayasuriya	Sri Lanka	1994–2007	90	152	5,932	340	41.48	13	25	64
Tamim Iqbal	Bangladesh	2008–2012	26	50	1,885	151	37.7	4	11	60.9
M. L. Hayden	Australia	1994–2009	103	184	8,625	380	50.73	30	29	60.1
C. H. Gayle	West Indies	2000–2012	91	158	6,505	333	43.07	14	33	59.7
G. C. Smith	South Africa	2002–2012	102	176	8,334	277	50.5	26	33	59.7
K. Srikkanth	India	1981–1992	43	72	2,062	123	29.88	2	12	58.6
V. T. Trumper	Australia	1901–1912	32	52	1,650	159	33	3	9	

Source: Data from espncricinfo.com. Analysis and tabular compilation by authors.

We have included a couple of the hardy combative batters who featured in our list of 'effective batters' because their scoring rate was as good as or better than some of the well-known dashers. Figures against the names pertain only to those Tests where they played as opening batters.

It is not that the dasher scores at a run a minute or run a ball. It is more to do with the image he has created for himself; of an audacious risk taking batter who takes the attack to the opposition. Let us whet our appetite by recalling some of the innings they played to set the grounds on fire. We will of course begin with Trumper, the first and most endearing of these breathtaking batters and end with Sehwag, unarguably the greatest torch bearer of this tribe.

1. V. T. Trumper: 1901–1912; 32 Tests; 1,650 runs, average: 33

This paragraph, as other paragraphs earlier about Trumper, is written in sheer yearning, for Trumper played his cricket 100 years ago! Our school boy impressions are from the stories of Trumper by Cardus, Fingleton and Robinson. The pictures that accompanied the prose always showed Trumper jumping out of his crease, and finishing a straight hit. Trumper was one in a million. Take your pick from these glorious run a minute centuries against England: Manchester in 1902, 104 runs in just 115 minutes; Sydney in 1908, 166 runs in 241 minutes; Against South Africa: Melbourne in 1910, 158 runs of 159 balls and then in Adelaide in the same series 214 runs of 247 balls. Trumper died tragically young at 38 years.

2. K. Srikkanth: 1981–1992; 43 Tests, 2,062 runs, average 29.88

In January 1986, on the first morning of the Sydney Test, we both left home around 7 a.m. for a net session in preparation for a city tournament. Srikkanth was 27 not out when we set off. By 7.30 a.m., when we reached the ground, Srikkanth was 10 runs away from his century. The man had simply gone berserk. His fans will feel cheated if we do not mention how he belted Imran and company out of Chepauk in January 1987, hitting 123 runs of just 147 balls. He had many bumbling dismissals but his bended knee square drive of Roberts was voted the shot of the 1983 World Cup tournament. With the kind of outrageous risks he took, it was inevitable that Srikkanth often failed. But he is acknowledged as the pioneer of the aggressive opener in one-day cricket and the lofted drive in the early overs against pace remains an undisputed contribution by him to the one-day game.

3. F. M. Engineer: 1965–1975; 26 Tests; 1,577 runs; average 32.85

For the thousands of cricket-crazy spectators at Madras, on the first morning of the Test match against West Indies in January 1967, it was excruciating to watch Sardesai sedately play out all six balls of the last over before lunch. It prevented Farokh Engineer from recording a century before lunch for Engineer had already belted 97 runs that morning against Wesley Hall, Charlie Griffith, Garry Sobers and Lance Gibbs. It is an innings that even now gives us goosebumps. He was the 'suicide pilot' opener for Lancashire in their Gillette Cup matches.

4. B. K. Kunderan: 1960–1967; 12 Tests; 782 runs; average: 41.15

In his second Test, some mastermind promoted him to open for India against Davidson and Meckiff of Australia at Madras in 1960. The first over he faced went for 14 runs—four hits and two misses. Kunderan continued in the same vein to score 71. Called in to replace the injured Engineer for the 1964 Test match at the same city against England, this dynamo blasted nearly 200 runs on the opening day. There was minimum movement of feet, amazing hand–eye coordination and a flashing blade. Kunderan was a huge crowd puller in his day.

5. C. Milburn: 1966–1969; 7 Tests; 500 runs; average: 41.66

There was a rare cheerfulness to English batting during Milburn's days, a combination of Milburn's bulk and his attacking batting. Given his build, Milburn sensibly preferred boundaries to running his singles. England may have lost the Old Trafford Test to West Indies in 1966, but Milburn with a belligerent 94 made sure the ship went down with guns blazing. His stop–start Test career was finished when he lost an eye in a car crash.

6. R. C. Fredericks: 1968–1977; 58 Tests, 4,329 runs, average: 42.86

An abiding memory of the winter break in December 1975 is listening to the peerless McGilvray over radio bring alive Roy Fredericks' red hot innings at Perth against Lillee, Thomson, Gilmour and Walker. A small made man, Fredericks packed enormous angst in his shots. His 169 runs of just 144 balls with 27 fours was sheer violence. In fact, in the Inaugural World Cup in 1975, Fredericks hooked the 13th ball of the match for a six but in the process he dislodged a bail, leaving everyone thinking what might have been!

7. Shahid Afridi: 1998–2005; 15 Tests; 892 runs; average: 37.16

In at least three Tests against India in India, Afridi opened the Pakistan innings at a blistering pace. Two of those set up the platform for Pakistan wins. Although he stopped opening for Pakistan and became even more erratic down the order, Afridi is clearly the most bludgeoning bat to ever open for Pakistan. The fact that his strike rate as a Test opener is over 86 runs per 100 balls says it all. And 75 per cent of his runs have come in boundaries and sixes!

8. K. R. Stackpole: 1969–1974; 33 Tests, 2,390 runs; average: 40.5

Stackpole became an opening bat for Australia only after a few years as a middle-order batter. But once he became the dour Lawry's opening partner, he opened up great options for Australia. An attacking captain like Ian Chappell relished a belligerent opener who took the attack to opposing bowlers. On his only tour to India in 1969, he carved a century at Brabourne Stadium but was rather quiet by his standards in the other matches.

9. C. J. Barnett: 1934–1938; 12 Tests; 793 runs; average: 39.65

A prolific county player, Barnett is best remembered for his knock of 126 in the Nottingham Test against Australia when he narrowly missed a 100 before lunch. Barnett was a punishing batter feared for his ferocious cuts and scorching drives played on the up. In many a county game, he hit the first ball he faced for six.

10. C. H. Gayle: 91 Tests; 6,505 runs; average: 43.07

Modern-day cricket evokes images of Gayle hitting sizes at will in the T20 version of the game. But it will be good to remember that he has hit 85 sixes in Test matches. That in fact is only marginally below Sehwag. Like Sehwag and Jayasuriya, Gayle too has hit a triple century, something which only a few of the great classical openers with their monumental patience have managed.

11. Sanath Jayasuriya: 90 Tests as opener; 5,932 runs; average: 41.48

It was captain Arjuna Ranatunga's master stroke on the tour to Australia in 1985–1986 that Jayasuriya became an opener. It was sheer carnage after that. Devastating with strokes square off the wicket and a game where his strong wrists and forearms gave him great power and timing, Jayasuriya was a powerhouse who brought exceptional hand-eye coordination to hit perfectly good balls for boundaries. Perhaps among openers, after Sehwag it was Jayasuriya who thrilled spectators out of their senses.

12. V. Sehwag: 104 Tests as opener; 8,586 runs; average: 49.34

By coming last to Sehwag, we are actually according him pride of place. He in fact belongs in a class of his own. And it is best seen when his runs, average and strike rate are compared with the others. Sehwag simply stands apart. Jewel in the crown, there has never been an opener like him and it is difficult to think there will be another in a lifetime. The stats are astounding: 23 centuries, of which two are triple centuries, four are double centuries and most are big centuries. His average of around 50 is only below the illustrious all-time great classical openers like Hobbs, Sutcliffe and Hutton and above many other all-time greats. Add too, the number of wins that he has set up through his explosive opening. To achieve such astonishingly high yields at a strike rate of 82.2 puts the 'Nawab of Najafgarh' at a peak that nobody has scaled. As his pile of centuries grew, they only got faster! Don't get colored by his failures in his last few Test matches as he lost his place in the Indian side. Please ask yourself, has anybody thrilled our senses like this man?

How appropriate it is that that this story about opening batsmen is bookended between the timeless and classical openers like Trumper, Hobbs, Gavaskar and the greatest entertainers of all time like Jayasuriya and Sehwag. Between them how much pleasure they have given cricket lovers!

24

THE CHINAMAN AND MYSTERY BOWLER*

We set off to do a story on Chinaman bowlers and to our dismay found that many of the names that rolled deliciously off our tongues just did not have enough wickets to qualify for any kind of assessment. So we said, to hell with all that—let us just enjoy ourselves writing about our favorite Chinaman and mystery bowlers—the nonconformists, conjurors and sleight of hand purveyors.

The left-arm Chinaman is a mirror image of the right-arm leg break—bowled by turning the wrist so that the ball turns the opposite way to left-arm finger spin. When bowled back of the hand, it becomes the googly, it turns the other way. We identified 10 Chinaman bowlers as we trawled through the history of the game. Even if you were to add up all the wickets taken by the Chinaman bowlers it would be less than a combined tally of Bedi and Underwood. There are 45 left-arm spinners who have more than 40 wickets each but just four Chinaman bowlers who meet this criterion. The strike rate of the Chinaman bowler is superior (a wicket every 70 balls as compared to 79 for the orthodox left arm); the bowling average

---

* Although prevalent earlier, the term 'Chinaman' is not used anymore because of its racial implications. Bowlers of this style are referred to as left-arm wrist spinners.

is similar, 31.6 as compared to 31.2. The difference is that while the 45 left-arm spinners have taken over 4,800 wickets in 1,605 matches, the 10 Chinaman bowlers have played only 184 matches to take 427 wickets.

Old timers had the great fortune to see the peerless Sobers bowl a lot of this stuff. In fact they were so fortunate that they saw the great man bowl left-arm fast, slow orthodox and Chinaman all on the same afternoon. His 235 Test wickets are a wonderful mix of all three. In the 1950s, Johnny Wardle played for England. A maverick—and that sat badly in England—he bowled orthodox finger spin in England, but served up Chinaman and googlies abroad. He bowled the way his heart dictated and he bowled really well—28 Tests, 102 wickets at a strike rate of 65 balls per wicket. His average of 20.4 is the best for any post-war spinner who has over 100 wickets. In our statistical analysis, he is seventh best among left-arm spinners since 1900, which is awesome. But he rubbed the administrators and his captain Peter May the wrong way. He would have played a lot more games for England but for May's preference for his Surrey team mate Tony Lock.

Time for a lovely story: Johnny Martin who played for Australia in the 1960s bowled his Chinaman very slowly through the air. In a Sheffield Shield match, Martin beat a batters all ends up and struck him on the back foot in front of the stumps. To his utter disgust, the umpire turned down his appeal. Martin asks the umpire: 'What's wrong, Ump, isn't he in front?' Umpire: 'Yes son, he is.' Martin: 'Then why isn't he out?' Umpire: 'Because the ball wouldn't have reached the stumps, Johnny!'

Why is it that most of the Chinaman bowlers are from Australia? Is there something in the Australian air that makes spinners bowl back of the hand wrist spin rather than finger spin? Just as they have given cricket many famous leg spinners from Mailey to Warne and MacGill, so too have they provided us a line of left-arm Chinaman bowlers, from Fleetwood Smith to Brad Hogg. Strangely, Australia hardly has a worthy presence among orthodox left-arm spinners.

Fleetwood Smith (10 Tests, 42 wickets) in spite of some sterling performances in the 1930s is unfortunately best remembered as the bowler who conceded the highest number of runs in an innings—one for 298 out of an England score of 903 for 7. This was the Oval Test where Hutton made 364.

Much later, Lindsay Kline (13 Tests, 34 wickets) and the same Johnny Martin (eight Tests, 17 wickets) had their unforgettable moments too: Kline took a hat-trick against South Africa in 1957 but his moment of glory was as a no. 11 bat for Australia in the famous 1960–1961 series against West Indies. Coming in as the last batter he stayed for more than 100 minutes with Slasher Mackay to earn Australia a draw at Adelaide. More than the fact that he lasted against Hall, Sobers, Worrell and Gibbs for that long, what was amazing was that he was practicing at the nets in the afternoon against similar bowling for more than an hour as if anticipating what he would be called upon to do later that day! Immediately after, he was dropped for the final Test—typical of Australian cricket, no sentiment at all.

Martin's moment came in the same series. After the famous Tie at Brisbane, Australia won the second Test comfortably at Melbourne, thanks to Davidson and Martin's bowling. In a golden spell, Martin removed Kanhai, Sobers and Worrell in four balls. Had he done it in three, it would surely have ranked as the grandest hat-trick ever!

Time once more to pull the leg of the Chinaman bowler: This story was told with great relish by Dilip Sardesai. India's tour of West Indies in 1971—the series belonged as much to Sardesai as it did to Gavaskar—began ominously for India at Jamaica. In no time India was 70 for 5 and Sardesai was left with Solkar to repair the damage. Sobers the West Indies captain had Inshan Ali their Chinaman bowler on at one end. Now, for the Indians this slow bowler was a far happier proposition and not wanting Sobers to change him, Sardesai and Solkar decided that in every Inshan Ali over they would deliberately appear to be beaten by the odd delivery, as though they had failed to pick him. Sardesai chortled that the extended spell to Inshan Ali actually helped the Indian cause. Knowing Sardesai, this could well be a true story!

Not much need be said about the Chinaman bowlers of the last 25 years. We have watched them in close detail on television.

None more so than Paul Adams of South Africa, perhaps the only bowler to have ever had his face toward the umpire while delivering! His action—called frog in the blender—caused great consternation to the English batters when he was first unleashed. But batters sorted him out in time, because although Adams bowled good length and line he became too predictable. Nevertheless, by the time he finished, he had 134 wickets in 45 matches. More recently, we have seen Hogg—tongue hanging out—bowl for Australia. Katich bowled well too and ought to have been used a lot more by his captain Ponting.

It is surprising that the subcontinent that produced many left-arm orthodox spinners (Vinoo Mankad, Bishan Bedi, Dilip Doshi and Iqbal Qasim to name just a few) does not have a single Chinaman bowler in its Test history. The one Chinaman bowler who could have played for India was a wonderfully gifted bowler from Hyderabad—Mumtaz Hussain. A contemporary of Gavaskar, Mumtaz promised a lot when he made his name in university and Ranji Trophy cricket with a mesmerizing mix of orthodox left arm, Chinaman and the googly. He was so difficult to read that the keeper had to devise a set of hand signals to read him. Sadly within a couple of seasons Mumtaz had greatly reduced his Chinaman and bowled mainly orthodox finger spin. Soon—for it was the time when Bedi ruled—Mumtaz faded away into the anonymity of first-class cricket. It is probably the closest that India came to having an international Chinaman bowler.

The Mystery Bowlers

Sometime during World War II: An Australian is spinning a Ping-Pong ball to pass time. Iverson is trying out different grips to flick and turn the Ping-Pong ball against the wall. He finds he can turn the ball both ways by flicking the bent middle finger on either side of the ball and keeps practicing. When the war is over, Iverson unleashes this in Sheffield Shield. Called to play against Freddie Brown's English team in 50–51, he takes 6 for 27 in the second innings of the third Test at Sydney.

Jack Iverson is the pioneer, the 'first man ever' in this story about right-arm finger spin mystery bowlers. If Bosanquet introduced the googly to the repertoire of the wrist spinner and if Saqlain discovered the Doosra to spice up off spin, then Iverson was the one who first showed the world the magic of imparting spin either way with fingers in a manner difficult for the batter to fathom.

How rare is the mystery finger spinner can be gauged from the fact that the title of our article could itself contain the names of all the well-known exponents of this art form. There are over 150 spinners in Test history but only Jack Iverson, Sonny Ramadhin, Johnny Gleeson and Ajantha Mendis occupy the rare table of mystique—the Harry Potters of cricket.

There is a truly wonderful close-up photograph of Iverson's grip in the *Wisden Cricketers' Almanack*. And an identical close-up of Gleeson showing how he gripped the ball. And we who have watched Mendis' grip in great detail over television would be completely forgiven if we thought the hand holding the ball in that photograph was that of Iverson or Gleeson. The grip is all about how with thumb and middle finger the ball will be flicked or propelled. It will be the middle finger that will decide whether the ball will go one way or the other. Not much turn but that lethal amount enough for an edge, LBW or bowled. Bowlers, who know what is involved in delivering the ball, will be the first to acknowledge that to propel a cricket ball over 20 yards with the middle finger imparting spin calls for extraordinarily strong fingers. It is probably many times harder than the flipper which is squeezed out between thumb and finger.

Iverson played just one Test series in 1950–1951 in which he took 21 wickets. An injury and he was gone forever. Yet 20 years later when an unknown bowler called Gleeson was spotted in New South Wales, they said, 'Look at Gleeson, he is bowling Iversons!' The lure of mystery is something irresistible. Perhaps that was the reason Gideon Haigh, the cricket historian, wrote his painstakingly researched biography of Iverson—a biography of a cricketer who played just five Tests but one who took his own life many years later.

The Magician's Demeanor: Food served by Cordon Bleu chefs looks and tastes great but the diners have already been floored by the chef who performs like a conjuror. It was a similar mystique that Sonny Ramadhin brought to his bowling. Sleeves buttoned up always, wearing a cap when bowling, fast whirring action, Ramadhin created a Houdini-like atmosphere when he bowled.

Ramadhin appeared on the world stage in the early 1950s around this time but played for a full decade. In 43 Tests, Ramadhin took 158 wickets. Bowling in tandem with the left-arm spinner Alf Valentine, Ramadhin caused havoc in England. His match figures of 11 for 182 in the famous series win against England in 1952 and his partnership with Valentine immortalized him in calypso. Ramadhin bowled his off break with his middle finger down the seam (a conventional off spinner would have this across the seam) and surprised batters with the odd ball from the leg with no apparent change of action. The hype over his disguised leggie mesmerized the English batters who were even more tied to the crease than usual—doubt and demon freezing their minds. However, down under, the Australians decided to play him with better footwork and go down the wicket to play him off the pitch, a ploy that made him much less of a problem. In his second tour of England in 1957, Ramadhin started sensationally by spinning England out in the first innings of the first Test at Edgbaston. But in the second innings, May and Cowdrey made a record third-wicket partnership of 411. They played a lot with their pads stretched forward, playing outside the line and treating him as an off spinner, ending his ascendancy forever. An amazing facet of Ramadhin's bowling is that he got a whopping 61.5 per cent of his dismissals entirely by himself—that is he got them bowled or LBW or caught and bowled (C&B). In this aspect, he is no. 1 among all bowlers—fast and slow—with 150 or more wickets.

Johnny Gleeson started late—and was in his late twenties when he made his debut in Sheffield Shield cricket. Catching the eye of Benaud and Bradman, Gleeson was pitch forked into the Australian team. Off a long run, Gleeson spun the ball both ways but used as a stock bowler by Lawry, he lost his nip soon. Gleeson played 28 Tests for 93 wickets and on only three occasions did he take a five for in an innings. Uncharitable though it may seem, Gleeson among the four mystery spinners appears the most prosaic. Perhaps we are biased by the fact that we saw him bowl against India in 1969 along with Mallet and found Mallet to be the more dangerous. He seemed accurate enough but not dangerous and the Indians seemed to pick him. Chandu Borde, the stalwart Indian batter, said that was because Indians read the bowler from his hand rather than off the pitch.

And after Gleeson, for a long time—36 years to be precise—there was not a whiff of the mystery spinner till Mendis burst on the scene. In nine matches, he had 42 wickets; he had notched up a 10-wicket haul too. The picture of Dravid completely bamboozled by the carrom ball that knocked his off stump was played and replayed on television endlessly. But the television is an inexorable enemy. Every bit of his action was minutely examined. His googly anyway was easier to pick as it came of a clearly loopier trajectory. Pakistan played him so well that soon he was dropped. He made a comeback but Herath was clearly Sri Lanka's main spinner and Mendis got only the occasional game. All of India know that Ravichandran Ashwin, the off spinner, does not bowl the Doosra but employs the carrom ball. Over used, he becomes predictable but sparingly used, he gets reward. However, Ashwin is essentially an off spinner. The problem with mystery spinners is that the minute they are sorted by batters, they seem to wither away. We can do no better than conclude with these words of Gideon Haigh:

> [W]hen mystery wears off there must be a residue of skill and resilience. Indeed, many international cricket careers now unfold like whodunits solved in the first 30 pages; after that, the player is a quarry on the run, trying to stay a step ahead of his opponents.... The acid Test of Ajantha Mendis, then, is not what he is doing now, but how his game is standing up in two years' time.

25

EVERY FORM OF SPIN: THAT'S INDIA

Quiz time:

Can you name an Australian left-arm spinner with more than 74 Test wickets?

Or a leg spinner from England who played with any success in the last 60 years?

Apart from Muralitharan, Rangana Herath and Dilruwan Perera, can you name a Lankan spinner with over 100 wickets?

Is there a Pakistani left-arm spinner apart from Iqbal Qasim who has more than 70 Test wickets?

Has any West Indian leg spinner captured at least 60 wickets?

Imran Tahir is the leg spinner playing for South Africa now, but did any leg spinner play for them in the last 80 years?

Name a New Zealand spinner other Daniel Vettori with more than 110 wickets.

Actually all these questions can be answered with a simple 'None,' or 'No.' If a similar set of questions were to be asked about India, each of the questions would be answered with a resounding 'Yes' and the accompanying details!

Sometime in November 2011, we culled and massaged facts and figures about all three kinds of spin—left-arm spin, right-arm off spin and leg spin—and we realized that India alone among all Test-playing nations has an even and strong presence in all three forms of spin bowling. All the other countries have lacked in at least one kind of spin and when you consider a composite picture, India clearly emerges as the only country that is equally strong in all three. Our analysis is based on data as of early November 2011; we have also only considered data of spinners who have a minimum of 30 Test wickets. And this is what our analysis shows.

- Indian spinners have taken 3,380 wickets and distributed this among themselves so evenly that off spin accounts for 32 per cent, leg spin for 34 per cent and left-arm spin for the other 33 per cent.
- The Tests that spinners have played for India are also nicely distributed: off spin 444; leg spin 311 and left-arm spin 384.
- Their workload too has been even: around 87,000 balls bowled by off spinners, 81,000 by leg spinners and nearly 100,000 balls by left-arm spinners.
- At most times through India's Test history, one will always find a pair of spinners or a spin trio in its lineup.
- If one were to name the great spinners over the ages, India would be the only country that is represented in all three forms of spin bowling. Take a look: Mankad and Bedi in left-arm spin; Gupte, Chandra and Kumble in leg spin, and Prasanna, Venkataraghavan and Harbhajan in off spin.
- Indian spinners have taken 10 wickets in a match on 29 occasions. As a percentage of the number of Tests their spinners have played, this may be inferior to England, West Indies and of course Sri Lanka (read Muralitharan). But the point is that these 29 occasions are quite nicely shared by all three tribes—on 9, 12 and 8 occasions by off spin, leg spin and left-arm spin, respectively.

- Similarly India's list of spinners who have 100 wickets and more, has four off spinners, three leg spinners and four left-arm spinners.
- None of the other countries even remotely have this kind of evenness of strength. While Australia is absolutely dominant in leg spin, it is completely absent in left-arm spin. In the case of England, it is top of the charts on left-arm spin but cuts a forlorn figure in leg spin.
- It is only in off spin that the major cricket-playing countries seem to be fairly evenly matched over the ages. Each country has a fair representation of wickets taken by off spinners as a percentage of their country's spin tally. Thus, 29 per cent of Aussie spin wickets have gone to the off spinner, England 38 per cent, India 32 per cent, New Zealand 38 per cent and Pakistan 26 per cent. West Indies, because of the exploits of Lance Gibbs and Sonny Ramadhin and the longevity of Carl Hooper, has most of its spin victims in its off-spin column. Every country has an off spinner in the '100 wickets plus' club; England leading the way with six of them, India close behind with four, while Australia and West Indies each have three such bowlers. Clearly there is an even distribution of success in off spin, unlike leg spin or left-arm spin across Test-playing nations.

To appreciate why this evenness of strength in spin is such a special feature, one must scan the other cricketing nations. Pakistan like Australia has a strong and successful tradition in leg spin, with great spinners like Abdul Qadir and Mushtaq Ahmed but conspicuous in its low share of left-arm spin. Take out Iqbal Qasim and they have a negligible presence in this department. West Indies spin revolves around three spinners. Lance Gibbs their off spinner, Sonny Ramadhin the mystery spinner and Alf Valentine the left-arm spin twin of Ramadhin. South Africa about 100 years ago had three googly bowlers and in fact trounced England in a series using this spin trio. Much later they had the formidable off spinner 'Toey Tayfield,' of whom it was said that if you waited for him to bowl a bad ball, you would have to wait forever. Their left-arm spin is only remembered for the Chinaman bowler Adams. Sri Lanka is Muralitharan and Muralitharan is Sri Lanka. In that one sentence, which can be seen as absolutely infuriating or extremely inspiring is the story of Lankan spin. New Zealand's spin can similarly be told in just two words: Daniel Vettori.

The compelling fact that sets India apart is its rich and consistent line of spinners of all three varieties through the ages. The spin quartet of Bedi, Chandra, Prasanna and Venkat playing together for more than a decade perhaps has no parallel in cricket history. The 1950s too were rich for India. Subhash Gupte was easily the best leg spinner of his time and complementing him from the other end was Vinoo Mankad, the left-arm spinner, perhaps the greatest spinning all-rounder the game has ever produced. Playing alongside Mankad and Gupte was Ghulam Ahmed, an off spinner of distinction. The years between Vinoo Mankad and Bedi belonged to Nadkarni and Durani and by then Chandrasekhar had also arrived and the famous quartet was round the corner.

It was only during the entire 1980s that India did not have a great spin combination. In fact none of the spinners who played in that period rose to greatness. Left armer Dilip Doshi was the best of them. Shivlal Yadav, the off spinner, never rose above the ordinary and frustrated his captain's carefully planned field setting. Sivaramakrishnan, the prodigiously talented leg spinner came and disappeared like a shooting star. Maninder Singh, a genuine talent like Siva, never lived up to his early promise. And then Kumble arrived in 1990! With Harbhajan joining him some years later, India again had a potent pair of spinners and between them they took over 1,000 wickets as India tasted success against every country. With the retirement of Kumble and the waning of Harbhajan the cupboard was again bare for a short while. And then came Ravichandran Ashwin and Ravindra Jadeja. Debuting in November 2011 and December 2012 respectively, they have formed one of the most lethal spin combinations in cricket history. The Ashwin-Jadeja duo has taken 500 Tests in the 49 Tests they have played together and are just one wicket adrift of the Kumble-Harbhajan combination. Times have changed and no longer does India play more than one spinner when they go abroad. Spinners hunting in a pack may be a thing of the past, at least outside the subcontinent.

26

NOBILITY AND COURAGE: THE VERY SPIRIT OF THE GAME

We are both incurable cricket romantics and will carry with us to the end of our lives the belief that much that is noble about the game will remain unsullied by passage of time. However, much the external attributes of cricket may change, we believe that the intrinsic quintessential qualities of courage and nobility remain forever entwined with the game.

There is something innate, something unique about how every person is wired that determines the sporting spirit quotient of an individual. What is special about cricket is that from the time we begin to play the game, expectations are set—of upholding the spirit of the game, that spirit signifying integrity, uprightness, honesty, keeping team interest above self-interest and so on. In this essay, we describe some of the most moving incidents of warmth, generosity and nobility seen on the ground to show that sportsman spirit transcends times, cultures and geographies. Many of these sporting gestures extracted their price—the games turned in favor of the opponent; some of these players lost their places in the Test team but none of these considerations ever entered their mind.

Often, in fact almost always, it is the captain who sets the tone. In the Jubilee Test (1982) at Mumbai, with England tottering on 85 for 5, Bob Taylor was given out caught behind.

But India's captain for the Test match G. R. Viswanath pleaded with the umpires to recall Taylor because he thought the batter was not out. Taylor returned to forge a match-winning partnership with Ian Botham. Nothing of all this ever mattered to Viswanath, because he simply did not know any other way to play the game. Indian captains—Rahul Dravid, Anil Kumble and Mahendra Singh Dhoni in recent times have done no harm at all to this spirit of the game. Kumble's statesmanlike conduct during and after the tumultuous Test against Australia in Sydney in 2008 is fresh in our minds. He emerged stature enhanced while his opposing number Ponting did enough to tarnish his own reputation. Dhoni in the Test match at Trent Bridge, Nottingham in August 2011, allowed Ian Bell to resume batting after he had, due to his own carelessness, been adjudged run out of the last ball before tea. Asked why Dhoni decided to allow Ian Bell to continue batting, Rahul Dravid said: 'When the guys came in at tea there was a sense of awkwardness. While he was out in the laws of the game, it didn't feel right in spirit and Dhoni and the boys felt it was the right thing to do.'

In a one-day international match in the summer of 2009, Andrew Strauss, the captain of England, recalled Sri Lanka's Angelo Mathews after he had been declared run out. When asked, Strauss simply said that was the only thing he could have done once he saw that the batter had collided with the bowler Graham Onions. Strauss has since retired, but he will be remembered for this gem even if all his batting has faded from memory.

Nearly 100 years ago Arthur Gilligan, the England captain, while leading his county Sussex against Warwickshire did something that needs to be narrated here. In a rain-affected match, Warwickshire need just 14 runs to win, with less than an hour's play left. The rain came pouring down; there seemed no earthly chance of play. But Gilligan led his men into the ground and in pelting rain gave Warwickshire the chance to try for victory. It is just one's inner conscience or one's soul that will dictate what to us is the right thing to do. But by setting such standards these cricketers do the game great service, for the players who follow will have to emulate them.

Peter May was another England captain who demonstrated such generosity, when they toured West Indies in 1959–1960. With Barbados requiring around 20 runs to win, there was a downpour that would have driven any team indoors. May asked his men to stay on because he believed Barbados should not be robbed of victory by the rain.

Sports and cricket in particular, cannot survive merely through rules and regulations. The spirit of the game and the principles of behavior of the players are what will keep the game alive. The excuse that the game is now professional and cannot adhere to archaic standards of amateur days is not really valid. Could there be a more hard-boiled professional cricketer than Len Hutton? Yet here is an instance of the respect he had for a worthy opponent: George Headley, the immortal West Indian batter, was making a comeback to Test cricket in 1953–1954 against Hutton's Englishmen. Recognizing the enormous pressure on the great man, Hutton asked his bowler Tony Lock to bowl Headley a gentle half volley so that he could push it for a single to deep cover and get off the mark. And having done that, the game went back to being fiercely fought again.

At Trent Bridge, Nottingham in 1964 in an Ashes Test, Geoff Boycott the English opener placed a ball and set off for a quick single. His partner Fred Titmus, in responding to the call, collided with the Aussie bowler Neil Hawke and fell down, hopelessly stranded mid-pitch. The Australian wicketkeeper Wally Grout, who had meanwhile received the throw, merely paused and calmly rolled the ball back to the bowler, thus allowing Titmus to regain his ground. In Grout's book taking advantage of a mishap like that was simply not cricket. Grout is famous for another magnificent act of sportsmanship. At Melbourne in the last Test of the famous 1960–1961 series against West Indies, as Grout played the ball and ran two runs, Gerry Alexander, the West Indian keeper, was pointing out that a bail had been dislodged. With no one sure of what had happened the umpire gave Grout the benefit of doubt. But Grout felt he should not have been reprieved and simply gave his wicket away the next ball. Our generation has grown used to the combative Australian cricketer and his 'take no prisoners' attitude. It feels good that two of their keepers (Adam Gilchrist is the other) were wonderful examples of sportsmanship.

Whatever we may say, one plays to compete and win and nothing exemplifies this as much as the battle for the Ashes. As England beat Australia by two runs in the Ashes Test of 2005, Brett Lee, the batter, sank to his knees in utter despair. The English players embraced and celebrated but Andrew Flintoff, the hero of England's triumph, had already slipped away to Brett Lee to console him. The picture of Flintoff putting his hands around the disconsolate Lee is probably the most memorable one of the year. Such spirit is not restricted to players. Certain cricket grounds are blessed with a special bond with the spirit of the game. In December 1999, all of India was disappointed when India lost to Pakistan by just 12 runs and one of Tendulkar's greatest tons went in vain. The crowd at Chennai ought to have been the ones who were most devastated. Somehow, 60,000 people at the stadium found the nobility to rise up and give the Pakistan team a standing ovation and the picture of the Pakistani team's victory lap is etched in memory forever.

The first towering personality of cricket from around 1880, Dr W. G. Grace was known to take advantage of his position and stature at every opportunity and would intimidate umpires even in village matches (remember the famous 'they have come to see me bat, not to see this fellow bowl'). On one occasion, an exasperated bowler, having been denied Grace's wicket earlier, finally clean bowled him and then told Grace with all the scorn he could summon, 'Doc, why are you going, there is still one stump standing.' Luckily some of the great batters who followed Grace were wonderful sportsmen. Jack Hobbs was an epitome of sportsmanship. In a Test match, he asked Aussie keeper Bert Oldfield if he was out and when Oldfield confirmed this, Hobbs walked. And the Australian hero Victor Trumper—revered by all as the perfect human being, naïve and kind hearted to a fault—played the game as it should be played, with joy and respect for the game. One of the finest instances of sportsmanship amongst teammates was in 1949 when Australia played South Africa. Neil Harvey was in superb form. Batting with him was Arthur Morris on 99 when they were stranded at the same end as a result of Harvey's poor call for a run. Without a thought, Morris simply sacrificed his wicket, run out 99. As he passed a crestfallen Harvey, he is supposed to have told him—Son, you better make up for my missed century and score a double hundred. Harvey indeed did go on to make his first Test double century. Quite in contrast, is an incident from a match where Australia was batting against Pakistan. Shane Watson and Simon Katich, the two batters in the middle got into an awful muddle over a run and both of them literally competed against each other to regain the sanctuary of the nearest crease. They had to be separated in a photo finish!

Should batters walk or not has always been a hot debate. To Viswanath, it was no debate. How many times have we seen Vishy simply tuck his bat and walk the minute he snicked the ball, even before the fielders could appeal. Brian Lara too was priceless in this aspect. To the consternation of umpires, he would turn and walk on LBW appeals, even as umpires were making up their minds. Dravid, Indian readers will remember, walked when he was on 95 in his maiden Test innings in England in 1996. How many would do such a thing? Among the Aussies, Gilchrist was the sole exception, walking even before the umpire gave him out. In the World Cup semi-final in 2003 against Sri Lanka, Gilchrist walked although the umpire had turned down the catch against him. He set such high standards for himself that it became an embarrassment for the rest of the Australian team. Although we need not look down upon batters who wait for the umpire's verdict, we certainly have a warm feeling for these walkers simply because they embellish the game with the spirit with which they play the game.

Among the bowlers who have been great ambassadors for the spirit of cricket, we cannot think of a better example than Courtney Walsh. In the 1987 World Cup match against Pakistan, Walsh earned eternal respect as a gentleman cricketer because in a needle situation he refused to run out the Pakistan batter who kept running out of the non-striker's crease despite being warned not to do so. Walsh's sporting gesture cost West Indies the match (and they were knocked out of the tournament) but Walsh quite simply did not want to win any other way.

Bowlers' large heartedness toward their fellow tribesmen is legendary. Bishan Bedi, probably of the largest heart among Indian bowlers, did not hesitate to bowl to English batters at their nets; nor did he hesitate to share his immense knowledge of left-arm spin with Iqbal Qasim when Pakistan visited India. In fact Pakistan beat India in the decider at Bangalore in 1987, and Qasim later said that it was Bedi's precious advice—the right way to bowl on that minefield of a wicket at Chinnaswamy Stadium was to impart minimal spin—that helped him spin Pakistan to victory. Chuck Fleetwood-Smith of Australia was another kindred spirit, sharing the secret of a special grip of the ball with Hedley Verity the English spinner. Asked if this would not be to Australia's disadvantage in the Test matches, Fleetwood-Smith is said to have retorted, 'Art is universal'.

Sportsman spirit in cricket has usually been discussed in rather simplistic frameworks. There is a section of opinion which believes that when the game moved from amateur to professional status and then to the intense commercialization of modern days, it lost the gentility associated with the game. The other section is of the view that because we see and hear everything on television, we feel the spirit has deteriorated whereas it may not be really so. Both may be correct to an extent but there is much more to it. We hope that through this essay we have been able to bring out some evidence to show that magnanimous gestures have embellished modern times as much as the earlier times. In an ironic sense, perhaps modern-day television coverage might well become the reason that the spirit of cricket is preserved, for no cricketer would want to be shown up as a boor or have his integrity questioned. From there to more voluntary acts of sportsmanship may not be such a big leap after all.

Courage while batting evokes much vivid imagery. Batters hit on the face, spitting out blood to take guard again and so on. No story of Indian batters grievously injured is more poignant than that of Charlie Griffith felling Nari Contractor in West Indies over 50 years ago. Grainy photographs, black and white in our newspapers, showed Frank Worrell, the West Indies captain, distraught and first in the queue at the hospital to donate blood for the emergency operation. Contractor never played for India again but both of us saw him bat with undiminished commitment in Ranji and Duleep Trophy matches after recovering from the near fatal injury.

At Madras in 1964, chasing a modest fourth innings target set by Australia, India lost four wickets cheaply by the end of the fourth day. On the fifth day morning, Manjrekar who had injured his thumb while fielding, now came out to bat with Hanumant Singh. Manjrekar had to cut off the part of the glove since his swollen thumb could not go into any protective covering. Injured thumb exposed, wincing with pain every time he played the rampaging McKenzie, he gave company to Hanumant (playing beautifully) for almost the entire morning session. Finally, at the stroke of lunch, Manjrekar was dismissed. The batters who followed failed to take India home and Manjrekar's heroics went in vain.

The one-off Centenary Test between England and Australia

at Melbourne in 1977 to commemorate 100 years of Test cricket was a historic occasion. The build-up to the Test match was such that even cricket followers in far off India looked forward to the event. We set up alarms on our clocks to wake up in pre-dawn darkness. By 5 a.m., and even before the cock had crowed, we had tuned our radio sets to receive the running commentary. That Test is remembered as an outstanding advertisement for Test cricket, with Australia winning by 45 runs, with centuries by Derek Randall (for England) and Rodney Marsh (for Australia) and hostile bowling by Bob Willis and Dennis Lillee. David Hookes hit 5 fours in an over from Tony Greig to announce his arrival. Buried among all this is a vignette of great courage. McCosker unwisely, and early on the first day, tried to hook Willis and had his jaw smashed. He made just four and was off to the hospital. The doctors wired his jaw up, bandaged him to hold it in place. He was in no condition to leave his bed but as Australia began batting in the second innings, he hauled himself up and arrived at the ground on the third day of the match and offered to bat. Every run was precious. Greg Chappell held him back as much as he could but when Australia's eighth wicket fell, he came out to help the team add precious runs and also to help Marsh complete his century. He looked a fearful apparition, swollen face, jaw swathed in bandages. This was Test cricket and he received no mercy. He got a bouncer to greet him and he instinctively hooked. He connected well and collected a boundary. He stayed to get 25 and he put on 50 with Marsh. McCosker was as much the hero of the Centenary Test as Randall, Marsh, Hookes and Lillee.

Australian spectators were simply won over in 2009 by Graeme Smith of South Africa with a display of great courage. South Africa had already won the Test series and the final Test was, therefore, not of great consequence. Smith had badly damaged his right elbow and also broken his right arm in the first innings. On the last day of the Test, with still some overs left in the game, South Africa lost their ninth wicket. Smith who had not batted because of injury in that innings was not expected to show up. But to the consternation of his team and the admiration of Australian players and spectators, Smith walked out to join Makhaya Ntini in the middle. Heroically, and in great pain, Smith staved off the Australians for some time. But when they were within 10 minutes of securing a draw, Smith was unable to keep out a ball from Australian left-arm fast bowler Mitchell Johnson. The Test match could not be saved but as Smith and Ntini walked back, the crowd's ovation was almost entirely for Smith and his heroic act.

Pakistan beat West Indies in October 1986 at Faisalabad. The 'man of the match' was Abdul Qadir as he routed the West Indies in their second innings with a spell of six for 16. But for all his teammates and his countrymen, Salim Malik was the hero of the Test. Malik broke his arm above the wrist in the first innings on the first day of the match, but came out as the last batter in the second innings on day four, so that Pakistan could add some precious runs. That they did, 32 of them with Malik batting literally one handed for 41 minutes, keeping out 13 balls in the process. Malik to his great shame is now only remembered as the man who brought great harm to the game with his match fixing shenanigans. Courage evokes great respect. People who watch the game, know that when a hard ball capable of causing great damage is coming to you at great speed, it requires not merely great skill but great concentration and tremendous courage to negotiate. India's tour of West Indies is remembered as much for India's fairytale chase of 403 in the fourth innings to win at Port of Spain as for the mayhem and bloodbath in the fourth and final Test of that series at Sabina Park, Jamaica. On a pitch which had developed a ridge, Holding, Roberts and Daniel relentlessly bounced Indi's batters. One man who stood through it all was bespectacled Anshuman Gaekwad, reaching 81 till he was felled by a bouncer and carried away bleeding from the ear. He had to be later operated. Those days India was not cricket's financial superpower. If it were to happen today, the ruckus it would create would be a 100 times that created by Jardine's Bodyline.

Mention of the infamous Bodyline series in 1932–1933 is usually associated with the bravery of the Aussie batters. But the series is also remembered for an Englishman who demonstrated remarkable strength of will. Eddie Paynter, the left hander, was hospitalized with tonsillitis and fever but with England's batting wobbling, Jardine asked Paynter to report at the ground and bat. Sick and groggy with medication, Paynter batted for over 4 hours, spending another intervening night at hospital to make a gallant 87. England won this Test.

About Jardine's own courage, Bill Bowes narrates this episode in his book, *Express Deliveries*:

> After the Adelaide match, 'Body-line' was on everyone's tongue by now. When the crowd saw Jardine coming out in his jaunty Harlequin cap, they howled for the aborigine fast bowler, Gilbert to attend to him, for they had had a demonstration of leg-theory earlier in the day. The Queensland fast bowler, for a period of about six overs, was nearly as fast as Larwood, but he couldn't stay the pace. However, by skill or accident, he managed to get one through Jardine's defense, and DRJ was hit full on the hip bone. Momentarily, he looked as if he was going to fall, but straightening himself, waved back the fielders who were running to assist him, took another guard, and batted for nearly an hour till the end of play. Then with head erect, and escorted by police, he walked through the surging crowds into the players' cage. 'Close the door,' he said in the dressing room, and when it was shut, he collapsed on the masseur's table. This man had guts and would not let anyone know how badly he had been hurt and had batted for an hour in unrelieved agony.

Of the montages of courage from the 1980s, there is one story much told, the other rarely told. Mohinder Amarnath, hit by Marshall, spat out teeth and blood and had to walk away to hospital. Returning to bat next day in the same blood splattered shirt he hit the first ball—a bouncer predictably greeted him—out of the ground. Never a backward step was his motto. Mohinder's courage is folklore. Two years earlier, in Australia, India's Sandeep Patil was felled by a bouncer. Carried off and groggy for the rest of the match, his captain wanted Patil to bat again. Sick and wobbly, Patil came out, battled for only a few balls and was duly dismissed. Gavaskar, his captain, applauded him all the way back. For what mattered was that by coming out to bat, Patil had exorcised fear and also communicated that he had done so.

Examples of raw guts and courage are many across the world of cricket over the years. The most moving and compelling story is that of an injured Bert Sutcliffe batting to save the Test for New Zealand against South Africa in December 1953. Badly injured by a bouncer from Neil Adcock, Sutcliffe returned from hospital with a heavily bandaged head and hit seven sixes in an unbelievable counter attack. If Sutcliffe battled physical injury it was even more poignant that Bob Blair, the man who partnered him in this effort, had suffered even more grievously. News had just come that Blair's fiancée had been killed in a train accident. How Blair found the courage to keep his mind in a heroic 10th wicket stand with Sutcliffe will forever be one of the most moving stories of fortitude. Finally, Blair was dismissed and then he let the tears come. As the pair walked back, arms draped over each other, weeping and emotionally drained, there was not a dry eye that day in the crowd.

Another great story that comes to mind is Cowdrey coming to bat with his left arm in a plaster against West Indies at Lords in 1963 to ensure a draw for England. This, after Brian Close had played a great innings of courage taking Hall and Griffith repeatedly on his body and not flinching one bit. There is a photograph in Ian Wooldridge's book *Cricket, Lovely Cricket* on this series showing Close with a towel round his waist displaying the bruises all over his upper body. Many years later, in 1976, when he was already 45 years old, England's selectors turned to him to open the innings when confronted with the fearsome West Indies fast bowlers. His reflexes had waned but his ability to take blows on his body and grit it out in the middle was undiminished. Close simply knew no fear and it is no surprise that he was also a fearless short leg fielder. He stood at pick-pocketing distance from batters and in the 1963 series caught Sobers off a hook at that position!

Fielding close to the bat requires not only raw courage but incredible reflexes. Like batters of those days, fielders too wore no protective gear while fielding at hand-shaking distance from the batters. All of India remembers Eknath Solkar as their bravest and finest close-in fielder while there are others of his ilk of whom too we have written in our essay on close catching. But here, we will talk about the courage of Gavaskar the fielder, who is rarely remembered because he is overshadowed by Gavaskar the fearless batter. Standing in a Test match in New Zealand in 1976 at that same forward short leg, vacated by Solkar, Gavaskar's cheek bone was broken when Lance Cairns (the burly fierce hitting father of Chris Cairns) smashed a sweep into his face. A few years later—the summer of 1982—when Gavaskar was captain of a beleaguered Indian team, he stood at silly point and Botham broke Gavaskar's shin bone with a crack that sounded like a pistol shot. Remember, Gavaskar was the captain and could have stationed himself anywhere but opted to be in the line of fire. The fractured shin bone became famous as Gavaskar was photographed in crutches with India's Prime Minister Indira Gandhi and the US President Ronald Reagan, at a function in Washington a month later. Love him or hate him, one of the world's finest openers displayed guts while fielding too.

There are many stirring stories of bowlers transcending injury and great pain to bowl unbelievable spells. Indians of course will never forget a lame Kapil Dev delivering them a victory at Melbourne in 1981.The most striking story in recent times is that of Anil Kumble on India's tour of the Caribbean

Kumble bowls with a fractured jaw in the India vs West Indies Test Match, Antigua

Photo Courtsey: Kasturi & Sons

Islands in 2002. Jaw fractured by Dillon, strapped up tight and scheduled to fly back to India for a surgery, Kumble came out to bowl as he always did—with fierce resolve and concentration; he got Lara with a gem and arms raised walked way. However often this vignette is played and replayed, the sheer power of the episode will never fade. To represent bowling heroes from other countries we pick Malcolm Marshall's spell of 7 for 53 at Headingley in 1984 as an example of indomitable will and courage. Bowling with his left hand encased in pink plaster, Marshall created a unique piece of cricket history. How did he overcome such pain? How could he despite such discomfiture still produce a spell of such match-winning hostility? We saw him in India for the first time in 1979 as a young boy of 20; little did we know that soon the world would recognize him as one of the greatest fast bowlers of all time. Marshall's life was however cruelly short. He died of cancer when he was just 41, cut off in the prime of his life.

No essay on courage will be complete unless we salute Mansur Ali Khan Pataudi. Having lost one eye in a motoring accident in England in 1962, Pataudi played almost all his Test cricket with one eye. That in itself has no parallel in cricket history. But at Melbourne, in 1967–1968, Pataudi also had to bat on one leg because he had an injured hamstring. Pataudi was resplendent in a losing cause as he produced two of the most combative innings (75 and 85) in cricket history. Listening to Alan McGilvray over radio and reading Jack Fingleton in *The Hindu* next morning, it was clear that here was something truly heroic. That is not all. In 1975, his powers and reflexes all but gone, Pataudi was smashed on the jaw by Roberts at his fastest in Calcutta. Coming back to cheers from the crowd, after stitches on his chin, Pataudi turned the clock back and exploded with a cascade of boundaries. The blazing counterattack was brief, he made just 36 but as Pataudi walked off, the crowd knowing that they will never see him bat again, stood up to give him an unforgettable farewell.

Obviously in an essay like this, one can only showcase a few heroes. For every heroic act that we have described, cricket's history will show us a dozen more. Before the advent of helmets, players of bygone eras faced Trueman and Tyson, McKenzie, Lillee and Thomson, Gilchrist, Griffith, Roberts and Holding. They had no arm guards and in many cases no chest guards either. They had a bat, and they had their eyes and reflexes. Like nobility, courage too has an umbilical relationship with cricket. Nothing can ever change that.

27

THE SUBLIME LEFT HANDERS

The elder amongst us has watched left handers from the days of the incomparable Neil Harvey and was a first-division left-handed batter in Chennai and Mumbai. The younger can recall the magic of Sobers whom he saw more than 46 years ago and bowled leg breaks without much success against left handers. We argued, debated and traded anecdotes to compile a list of what we believe are the most sublime of left handers. The dictionary defines sublime as something that is characterized by feelings of grandeur, nobility, awe, magnificence and something that is ennobling. Going by this definition, we let our memories guide us in our quest of pulling out 12 gems. Here they are in order of their appearance in Test cricket.

Clem Hill of Australia, Frank Woolley of England, Bert Sutcliffe of New Zealand, Neil Harvey of Australia, Garfield Sobers of West Indies, Graeme Pollock of South Africa, Alvin Kallicharan of West Indies, David Gower of England, Brian Lara of West Indies, Sourav Ganguly of India, Stephen Fleming of New Zealand and Kumara Sangakkara of Sri Lanka. The argument as usual may be over a couple of names. Should Mike Hussey and Arthur Morris not come in? Surely Saeed Anwar of Pakistan has given viewers more than enough pleasure to be counted. And just because Hayden smote the ball powerfully does it make him less sublime? Obviously we have not considered batters like Bill Lawry, Bob Cowper, John Edrich and Justin Langer and in more recent times Graeme Smith, Andrew Strauss and Alastair Cook because very good batters they might be but not with the silken touch and grace of the sublime left hander. Ranking these batsmen is meaningless and insulting for Mount Everest has enough space for all of them.

What makes the left hander so special? For one the rarity because we still get to see only two or at best three in a team. Among batters who have scored over 2,000 runs in Test cricket there is only one left hander for every three right-handed batter. And then there are these advantages:

- Bowlers find it difficult to switch their line and the left hander is given opportunities on the leg stump and outside to score from.
- The normal incoming ball from outside a right hander's off stump cannot get the leftie LBW since it pitches outside leg stump of the left hander.
- Wicketkeepers find the left side difficult and are prone to be clumsy keeping to left handers.
- Since the field has to change and the bowler has to switch line every time a single is taken—when batting with a right hander—the leftie irritates and disturbs their rhythm by his very presence. If there are enough left handers in the team, it makes sense to keep the batting order flexible to ensure a left–right combination at the crease as far as possible.
- Bowlers find it difficult to bowl from round the wicket even though it is an important option against the leftie. Spinners tend to bowl from wide of the crease while faster bowlers are always conscious of not running on to the pitch on their follow through.

Just as the right hander's on drive is the touch stone of his prowess, so is the cover drive for the left hander. Does it have anything to do with the batter's stance? Neil Harvey was a hero to many when he burst on the scene and such was his footwork, grace and artistry that even 50 years later there are many who swear that he cannot be surpassed.

Garfield 'Garry' Sobers
Photo Courtesy: Kasturi & Sons

Of Sobers and his unlimited magic so much has been told that we just share one incident—when Richie Benaud in the 1960–1961 Test in Australia thought he had beaten Sobers with the googly, that magician changed stroke even as the ball was sneaking past him and whipped it back to the sight screen. Till date no one has remotely matched the insouciant grace and lissomness that Sobers brought to the ground.

Following Harvey and Sobers was Graeme Pollock who perhaps could have ended up as the best of them all. Could he have sustained his initial tempo? Would he have been equally good when confronted by the best spinners from India and Pakistan? The jury will forever be out on that. Meanwhile West Indies unleashed a line of great left handers. From the 1960s till 2000, they produced a string of pearls—Clive Lloyd, Kallicharan, Roy Fredericks, Lara and Chris Gayle. Lara did enough in a magnificent career to keep the debate going about whether Sachin Tendulkar was the best batter after Don Bradman. Has there been anyone with as much magic in the high back lift as Lara? Has there been a batter who played as late as Lara—so much so that to mere mortals he looked supernatural as he seemed to have a choice of three shots for every ball. No one has ever faced Muttiah Muralitharan better than Lara and remember that for much of his career he carried a limp West Indian batting line up on his colossus like shoulders.

Stephen Fleming of New Zealand burst on the scene in 1994 when the purity of his cover-drive and all-round elegance made the media compare him to David Gower, with whom he interestingly shares a birthday. Fleming turned out to be a fine captain too (seven of the dozen in our list captained their country) and is the first Kiwi to play 100 Tests and score more than 7,000 runs for his country. His batting was always ethereal but was also unfulfilled promise. Fleming however will be wholeheartedly remembered for his captaincy.

Grace—the most often used expression to describe left handers sits most aptly on Gower. Gower gave you the impression that he never needed practice or a net. He could saunter in and caress the first ball away with a conjuror's wand. There could have been no better sight than Gower in lighting up the ground with the lightest of brush strokes. He would waive the ball away from him between point and cover and if you put a fielder to plug that gap then between them as well.

Aha, we are getting into hot water here—we are talking of batters splitting the offside and we have not said a word about Ganguly? Everything about his unparalleled offside play has been said by Dravid in that famous quote about Ganguly being the God of the offside. However, no less awesome was the shimmy to the left-arm spinner to hoist him over long on and long off. Ganguly, like many modern cricketers, used a heavy bat. It remains an eternal puzzle to us why he needed such a heavy willow for he could have played those gorgeous square drives even with grand pa's walking stick.

Kumar Sangakkara has been Sri Lanka's premier batter for over a decade along with Mahela Jayawardene and has been elegance and grace personified. To us he represents the dual words of style and substance better than most batters. He has graced the game in a manner that will always be an inspiration to his countrymen.

The first great left handers to grace cricket were Clem Hill of Australia and Frank Woolley of Kent and England. Clem Hill was Australia's best batter at the turn of the century and was equally effective against pace and spin with the most assured footwork and had centuries and successive nineties in Test cricket. He was overshadowed only by Victor Trumper whom he revered. Woolley's grace and timing were unique and his effortless big hits seemed so easy and casual; there are still Englishmen who consider him the finest left hander their country has produced.

There were few left-handed batters those days. All the great batters—Trumper, Hobbs, Sutcliffe, Macartney, Jackson, Foster, MacLaren, Fry and Ranji were right handers. Till 1950 and the advent of Arthur Morris and Neil Harvey, while one could reel of names of prolific right handers the left handers' club could hardly conjure the odd name or two. England had only Percy Chapman, Eddie Paynter and Maurice Leyland as left handers against right-handed legends like Hobbs, Sutcliffe, Hammond, Hutton and others. And Australia was even more impoverished as all they could offer was a dour accumulator called Warren Bardsley, against right handers like Bradman, Ponsford, Macartney and McCabe. India was even more bereft of left handers. Imagine, till the 1950s—C. K. Nayudu, Lala Amarnath, Vijay Merchant, Mushtaq Ali, Vijay Hazare, Polly Umrigar, Vijay Manjrekar, Pankaj Roy and not a single left hander amongst them. The first left hander who broke through was Deepak Shodhan who scored a hundred on debut against Pakistan in 1952 and sank without trace thereafter. Nari Contractor, a determined and not inelegant left hander, could have played longer for India but his Test career was finished by a near fatal bouncer from Griffith in West Indies. The most graceful of the Indians was undoubtedly Salim Durani—who could be dazzling when in the mood, had so much time to play the ball and such silken grace in everything he did. Many years after the languid but enigmatic Wadekar and the wasted talent of Surinder Amarnath, there was Vinod Kambli who made two double hundreds and a chockfull of runs in a couple of home series before fading away. The jinx on left-handed batters in India was broken by Ganguly, the most enduring and graceful of them all.

India contributes just three names to the list of 68 left-handed batters who have scored over 2,000 Test runs—Ganguly, Gambhir and Wadekar. Was batting the other way round discouraged for some reason in those days? No, for there have been a stream of left-handed batters in our first-class cricket, even though they may not have made a mark in Test cricket. And left-arm bowlers too. So surely those who might be looking for socio-cultural linkages and reasons for why we have produced fewer Test left handers may actually be chasing a red herring.

One-day cricket has its own strong contribution. No example could be more powerful than that of Sanath Jayasuriya. For five years after making his Test debut Jayasuriya was just an innocuous journeyman—till he was asked to open in ODI in 1995–1996 by his captain Ranatunga. And the talent that had been bottled up then announced itself to the world and strode it like a colossus. Adam Gilchrist made the no. 7 batting position the most feared one in Test cricket because he turned matches on their heads from this position. India's Yuvraj Singh gets his chances in Tests because he is such a splendid one-day cricketer. Test cricket is seeing changes—run rates are increasing, fewer Tests are ending up as draws and there is place for the aggressive genius and therefore for the maverick leftie too.

By saluting a dozen artists we are not blind to the impressive contribution of the others. As we have written in another essay if we wanted a left hander to bat us safely through two days of tsunami, we would always want Allan Border or Andy Flower or Shiv Chanderpaul in our middle order. If we wanted to take a tilt at the most daunting of targets, we would want the pugnacious Smith to open the batting for us; to put fear into the opposition, we would want the oak-like Hayden up front and the towering presence of Lloyd in the middle of our lineup. All these stalwarts have averages that are superior to some of the players in our sublime list. But because they give the ball a mighty thump with the bat as opposed to the satin-like touch of the artists, they have not been included in an essay devoted to sublime left handers.

28

WORLD CUP CAPTAINS—COURAGE AND STRATEGY

The muggy April night was dark, but Wankhede Stadium shone bright with lights beaming down from its giant towers. Forty-two thousand spectators had just been silenced as Virat Kohli drilled a return catch to Tillakaratne Dilshan, leaving India at 121 for 3. A target of 275 seemed far away. And down the pavilion steps came M. S. Dhoni. A collective buzz went around; the captain was not in form, but was still promoting himself above Yuvraj Singh who was. But Dhoni was not being impulsive or merely bold and innovative. He knew he had to tackle and neutralize Muralitharan before Yuvraj came to bat. Paddy Upton, the mental-conditioning expert with the Indian team, whispered to Kirsten, 'Dhoni will win the game for us.' In his book, *The Barefoot Coach*, Upton explains Dhoni to us, 'It is not emotional control but the lack of access to emotions...a performance enhancing gift from birth.' MSD began slowly, 2 off 10 balls, 13 off 24. And then he thumped Murali to cover off his back foot for a boundary. The rest is history. As Dhoni hit Kulasekara into the stands at long on, the crowd went berserk. The captain merely twirled his bat and picked his souvenir stump. Later as his teammates, danced, jumped and wept, Dhoni was by comparison, sphinx-like. Courage, brilliance, nerves of steel, but most important, a tranquil mind that realized long ago that triumph and disaster are mere imposters.

Perhaps the template for heroics by World Cup captains was set at the first-ever World Cup final in 1975. With West Indies tottering at 50 for 3, out came bespectacled Lloyd, in his characteristic stooping gait, with a bat that looked like a match stick in his hand. What followed was carnage as Lloyd tore into the Aussies. While white-haired, 40-year-old Kanhai, unrecognizable from the pomp of his youth, gave him sedate company, Lloyd pummeled 12 fours, 2 sixes and hit a century of 85 balls. The bowlers he belted were Lillee, Thomson, Gilmour and Walker. Remember, there were no field restrictions in those days. Chasing 292, Australia panicked their way to four run outs and a defeat that was bigger than the 17-run margin. West Indies in 1975 had not become the unstoppable juggernaut; they were just starting to rebuild after the Sobers era. Richards and Greenidge were new, as was Roberts. Holding, Marshall and Garner had not arrived. Lloyd made all this irrelevant that June evening. Face almost inscrutable, Clive Lloyd lifted the first ever cricket World Cup trophy.

The most vivid Indian cricket photograph is of course that of Kapil Dev lifting the Prudential Cup in June 1983. The team went as no-hopers, the odds deservedly 66 to 1 on India. Srikkanth, the irrepressible story-teller, says he asked his wife to join him on the World Cup tour so that they could 'watch the final' and proceed to USA on holiday. Kapil torpedoed all that. Every cricketer in that 1983 team will swear that Kapil's 175 not out to pull India from 17 for 5 against Zimbabwe, is the greatest one-day innings by an Indian. Defending just 183 in the final, it was Kapil's catch—running miles backwards to finish Richards—that opened the floodgates. Kapil's tactical nous was also fully tuned on through the tournament. The much higher use of Mohinder Amarnath in conditions that favored his gentle swing; preferring Kirti Azad to Shastri at the latter end of the tournament; and harnessing Balwinder, Binny and Madan Lal with himself for a canny bowling combination. But perhaps the first seeds were sown a few months earlier in Berbice,

Guyana when India beat West Indies in the second ODI of their bilateral series. It was further reinforced in the first game of the 1983 World Cup, when they beat the Windies on the back of Yashpal Sharma's heroics. People forget that India beat the mighty Windies thrice in four months. Kapil, the inspirational captain, his 1,000-Watt toothy grin has never been matched by any winning captain.

Australia went through their lowest period in the mid-eighties. Chappell, Marsh, Lillee, Thomson, they had all gone. Hughes had thrown in the towel, finding the burden of leading unbearable and Allan Border inherited a down-in-the-dumps team. But it was the perfect job for the most obdurate left-hander in cricket history. No one else could have snarled and berated, coaxed and shown teammates by personal example, what the baggy green cap meant. With Bob Simpson as coach, Border formed a partnership that reshaped Australian cricket history. The first step in the turnaround was that tied Test match in Chennai, exactly a year before WC 1987. A tie that felt like a loss to Indian cricketers and like a win for the Aussies. It was the game that lit their flame again. So connect this to their triumph in the lengthening shadows at Eden Gardens in November 1987. With England cruising at 135 for 2, just 119 to get, Border brought himself on. Branded forever in public memory is the visual of Gatting caught reverse-sweeping the part-time left-arm spinner. Border gambled and won. Finals usually claim all the attention but people also remember that Border won tough matches on the way, never afraid to throw his young teammates into the most challenging situations. Be it the one run win over India in their first game or the semifinal against Imran Khan's Pakistan at their citadel in Lahore.

The World Cup seems to bring out the best from the captains. Not only do they raise their game but their strategic and tactical acumen acquires an inspirational edge, often giving them match-winning breakthroughs. Many things that look common place in the game today, were path-breaking innovations when captains first tried them out. In 1992, Martin Crowe opened the bowling with off-spinner Dipak Patel and promoted a hard-hitting middle-order batter Mark Greatbatch to open. The long straight boundaries suited Patel's spin while the short square boundaries were tailor made for Greatbatch. Both moves were spectacular successes and became a template for other teams to emulate. And thus we had Jayasuriya, Tendulkar, Gilchrist and Ganguly pushed up to open in ODI. When leg-spinner Imran Tahir bowled the first ball in the World Cup 2019, it was a bold but accepted tactic. Team composition too has seen inspired moves and one recalls how the use of Rahul Dravid as wicket keeper in WC 2003 gave India the balance they needed. Sometimes though, even the best got it wrong. Brearley's gamble of filling the fifth bowler's quota with the part-time bowling of Gooch, Boycott and Larkins, boomeranged against West Indies in 1979.

England's captain, Morgan, had fashioned a completely new approach for England's 2019 campaign, honed over two years of practice. All out aggressive batting is their strategy, a mind-set that was alien to them. Kohli generously says, England might well be the first team to score 500. Talking of Kohli, perhaps the World Cup also inspires captains to be statesmen on the world stage. Kohli had already won hearts in 2019 with his gesture of asking the crowd to not jeer but clap for Steve Smith and by also 'walking' when he thought he had edged the ball.

Steve Waugh did not tell Herschelle Gibbs, 'Son, you have just dropped the Cup', when the South African messed a simple catch from Waugh in a must-win match for Australia in the Super Six of World Cup 1999. It is one of the many delicious, apocryphal quotes in cricket lore. Waugh, in his autobiography, *Out Of My Comfort Zone* (an impossibly fat brick of 800 pages), says what he told Gibbs was, 'Do you realise you have just cost your team the match?' Waugh, the master of mental disintegration who wore down opponents on the ground, had the measure of even as fine a captain as Hansie Cronje in that match. You can sense Waugh's exult, as he writes, that Cronje 'was on edge. The game's equilibrium had shifted.' Waugh's 120 not out, chasing 272, was the defining innings of the 1999 World Cup. If he had failed, Australia would have flown home. Instead Australia qualified for the semifinal where they met the Proteas again. The South Africans self-destructed at the doorstep of victory and that tragic Allan Donald–Lance Klusener run out will haunt South Africa forever. The final was so one-sided that Waugh's team beat Akram's Pakistan in a game that lasted less than 60 overs. India's Venkataraghavan, who umpired both the Australia–South Africa games told us that Waugh was the steeliest among captains, a strategist who brought preparation, thought, planning and determination to quell opponents. Waugh's successor, Ponting helped Australia make it a hat trick of triumphs. Indians will ruefully remember his punishing century that decided the 2003 final at the Wanderers in Johannesburg. Four years later, Ponting again held the trophy after an unbeaten run through the 2007 tournament. He had a very strong team—Hayden, Gilchrist, McGrath et al—but his use of left-arm wrist spinner Brad Hogg who finished with 21 wickets, was special.

Audacious and innovative

It was only in 1992, in Australia and New Zealand that colored clothes, black sight screen, white balls, floodlights and field restrictions were introduced.

Even as other captains struggled with these new rules, Martin Crowe swiftly crafted an audacious bowling and batting strategy that almost won New Zealand the Cup. Without doubt, one of the enduring memories of the 1992 World Cup is the stirring captaincy of Crowe. With just two fielders allowed outside the circle in the first 15 overs, Crowe caught the opposition off-guard by promoting aggressive, middle-order batter Mark Greatbatch to open the innings, giving him the license to attack the short square boundaries with his trademark slashes and cuts. Crowe also surprised the opposition by opening the bowling with off-spinner Dipak Patel, using long off and long on as outfielders. Patel had an outstanding tournament, snaring eight wickets at an economy rate of 3.1. Crowe's form was sublime during this tournament. Had he not pulled a hamstring in the semifinal against Pakistan while batting (he was forced to sit out when the Kiwis fielded) he might not have let Imran Khan's team win. New Zealand's semifinal loss was poignant but the innovations that Crowe introduced have stood the Test of time. He was a misunderstood man during his playing days, but later, as a cricket columnist and mentor of young cricketers, Crowe was liked immensely. The tributes that poured in when he passed, as a result of cancer, at 54, showed what an adornment he was for the game.

Towering leader

Imran's triumph in 1992 was not to be denied. Pushing 40, his tearaway speed a thing of the past, Imran was however at his field-marshal best. No one gave Pakistan a hope in hell at the half way stage, for they had won just one out of their first five round robin group matches. Saved by the skin of their teeth when rain washed out a game in which they were bowled out for 74 by England, Pakistan grabbed the lifeline that fortune had thrown them. Wasim Akram once recalled on air, how at every meeting outside the ground, Imran would keep saying that they will win. An unrecognizably brilliant team played the rest of the tournament, beating Australia, Sri Lanka and New Zealand to get into the semifinals. When they slacked even a little, Imran gave them a shellacking in choicest Punjabi. Every player quaked; even Miandad, never short of ideas or advice, approached his captain warily. Imran promoted himself to one-drop and his batting gained a Zen-like quality. Young Inzamam batted with the freedom his captain had granted him. Wasim's left-arm swing always lethal, acquired a spitting cobra quality. Aaqib's deliveries seemed invested with all sorts of guile. A tall, arresting figure always, Imran, during those last few games, seemed to have four hands as he commanded and marshalled his fielders. It was as though Imran was ordained to lift the 1992 World Cup.

Always a step ahead

1996 was Sri Lanka upstaging every team. Jayasuriya terrorized every bowler he faced. On a mean pitch at Eden Gardens, Aravinda de Silva's attacking fifty thwarted India in the semifinals. He went one better with a classic century in the finals against Australia. But the man who planned and plotted the Lankan campaign all the way was Arjuna Ranatunga. For foxiness, there were few to match the Lankan skipper. His body language itself was combative, as if to say, 'we are much better than you think, and you will find out soon.' Murali became a different bowler, after Ranatunga stood up for him in a series-threatening confrontation with the umpires in Australia after they called Murali for 'throwing'. Ranatunga and team manager Duleep Mendis, on that same Australian tour—just before the World Cup—converted Jayasuriya, who used to potter around in the middle order, into a superhero opening batter. They chose pocket dynamite Romesh Kaluwitharana as Jayasuriya's partner. Sri Lanka's batting was transformed. With the explosive Jayasuriya at the top, Gurusinha, Aravinda de Silva and Ranatunga in the middle order, and Muralitharan and Dharmasena as spinners, the Lankans had created a champion team for sub-continental conditions. How canny was Ranatunga? One can get an oblique answer to that question from his running between the wickets. The roly-poly man would waddle between the wickets but one will not remember him missing a run or getting run out. Never out of breath, the wily Lankan skipper, throughout World Cup 1996, was a step ahead of the others.

Winning hearts

Brendon McCullum won everyone's hearts in 2015. Like his compatriot, Martin Crowe, McCullum too was unfortunate, losing the final. But such was the goodwill for New Zealand and McCullum, that the Kiwis were everyone's favorite team. McCullum showed the world that aggressive cricket can co-exist with fine sporting spirit. It was a fairy-tale path all the way to the final for the Kiwis as McCullum led them from the front, opening the batting with a belligerence that made the senses sing. He failed a few times—and heartbreakingly in the final—but he hit four fifties at a mind boggling strike rate of 188.5. As fielding captain, he set a new benchmark for aggression by providing three slips to his fast bowlers. All this while playing with great cheer, an ever-present smile, never a sledge and accepting every umpiring decision with equanimity. Four years later, taking them forward with the same good cheer and building even more goodwill for his country is Kane Williamson. A calm, organized and thoughtful leader, Williamson is among the world's top three all-format batter. All class and grace, he has already overtaken Crowe as New Zealand's best-ever batter.

More than money

Test cricket was nearly a century old in 1975 but the game had nothing in the nature of a 'world championship'. Cricket seemed strangely satisfied with bilateral jousting. It was with the arrival of one-day cricket that the sport had a 'world championship'. And since the inaugural event in 1975, every four years, the best of cricketing nations compete for what has become the most cherished trophy in the sport. The winners in 2023 will take home £4.0 million, which is 1,000 times the £4,000 that Lloyd's team got in 1975. The commerce is overwhelming but even the cynics will concede that for the young athletes passionately competing for the World Cup, all thought of the prize money is incidental. What has driven every player and captain from Clive Lloyd to Eoin Morgan is the indescribable elation of holding the trophy in their hands.

29

NEIL HARVEY: EVERY LEFT HANDER'S IDOL

When I (Raghunath) met Rajan Bala, the noted cricket columnist, a few months before he passed away, we managed about two hours of cricket talk. One of the first things he said when we realized both of us were born in 1946 was, 'If you were born in 46, Harvey must have been your hero.'

It was impossible in the 1950s not to be a great admirer of Neil Harvey—boyishly good-looking, he was a left hander with such grace that captivated and there was joyousness when he batted. He was naturally attacking, so it was natural that he danced out to spinners. His footwork had to be seen to be believed. And the Australians themselves believed he was their greatest batter after Bradman.

As a boy of 10, when I saw him score 37 at Chennai, I was mesmerized by the flair, dancing feet and the flashing blade. But it was not just the 10-year-old boy who was enthralled. *Sport & Pastime*, that venerable magazine also was, for they carried three pictures of him batting, in their next issue. And these three pictures were stuck on the School Sports Notice Board for weeks. The same magazine carried the sequence of photographs that showed Harvey playing all the shots—the drives, pulls and cuts—in the subsequent issues that followed.

Looking back now, I am not sure whether I batted left

handed because of Harvey, or liked him so much because I was a left hander. But I was so obsessed with him that I hated Jim Laker for getting him out for ducks at Manchester in 1956. It took me 15 more years or so to start liking Laker and see the whole thing in a more balanced fashion. But what the hell, you are not rational at 10, especially about your heroes!

Harvey was just 18 years old when he made his debut in 1947 against the Indian team led by Lala Amarnath. He scored a 150 plus in his second Test against India. But Australia was such a strong batting side then under Bradman that in the subsequent tour to England he had to wait till the fourth Test to get into the playing 11. In that Test, England first posted a healthy 400 plus total and then had Australia in trouble, capturing four wickets for around 100 runs. Harvey made a wonderful 112 to give the Australians a respectable total. That match was historic because Australia became the first ever country to win a Test match by scoring over 400 runs in the fourth innings.

Harvey simply captured the hearts of the Australian public after World War II. With Bradman nearing 40 years of age, likely to call it a day anytime, the Australian cricket fan needed a new batting star to complement the dashing Keith Miller. Harvey was not only brilliant and spectacular; he was also a schoolboy idol with his good looks, definitely one aspect where the great Bradman was lacking! In the next four years he had two fantastic series against South Africa. The first was an away tour in 1949 and this was followed by the home series against the Springboks in 1952. In 10 Tests against them, he scored eight centuries including a double century. Those eight centuries were like a priceless string of pearls. Among these, one of his greatest knocks was his 150 at Durban. Batting second, Australia collapsed for 75 in their first innings but then struck back by bowling out South Africa for just 99 in their second innings. Now it was all down to Australia's fourth innings chase of 300 to win the match. In conditions that were certainly no better than when 20 wickets had tumbled for 175, Harvey played an unforgettable innings to take Australia to victory by five wickets, remaining unconquered with 151. Harvey's innings was an outstanding exhibition of splendid footwork on a turning pitch against two fine spinners, Toey Tayfield and Tufty Mann. Miller and Whittington wrote, 'Harvey, we thought, became that day as great a batter as he had always been a spectacular and attractive one.' At the end of the series, Miller and Whittington added, 'When Harvey went to South Africa three summers ago to have his 21st birthday, they complained to him that they had never seen Don Bradman bat. Harvey has since done his utmost to remedy this deficiency in their cricket education.'

In his first 10 Tests, Harvey hit six centuries and 1,045 runs at a Bradmanesque average of 95. By the time he had played 24 Tests, Harvey had scored 2,415 runs at an average of 65 with 10 hundreds, and most importantly he had performed against England, South Africa, West Indies and India.

When people talk about Graeme Pollock and rate him the greatest left hander along with Lara and Sobers, I cannot

Neil Harvey at a practice session
Photo Courtesy: Kasturi & Sons

agree with such a facile conclusion. Pollock played only against England and Australia and did not face Indian spinners like Subhash Gupte, Ghulam Ahmed and Vinoo Mankad. Nor did he play the West Indians Ramadhin and Valentine or Fazal Mohammed in Pakistan. And yet Harvey matched Pollock's record in his first 25 Tests playing against all the nations at home and away.

Harvey was no batting machine and his cavalier batting style with spectacular footwork and attacking batsmanship made him fallible. His appetite for runs too waned in his later period and in his next 55 Tests, Harvey made just 3,700 runs at an average of 43. After a successful tour to West Indies in 1955 under Johnson where he scored 650 runs with three centuries (including a double hundred), his consistency dropped and his major efforts thereafter came only at crucial junctures. Now a mellow and seasoned campaigner, Harvey started scoring against tough opposition when his teammates were struggling. Against Tyson and Statham, Fazal Mohammed on matting, against the spin of Gupte and Mankad, Valentine and Ramadhin—all on their home wickets—he played great match saving hands with his exemplary technique and footwork. His attacking instincts were never subdued for he was always willing to take the initiative in these attractive efforts which came in every series he played. He played superlative knocks that were remembered by all who saw them—his unbeaten 92 against Tyson, the 167 at Melbourne against Laker and Statham (when nobody else made any runs), 96 against Fazal when only one of his teammates reached double figures, fighting sixties against Laker and Lock, 85 against Gibbs at Sydney, 70 and 50 against a rampaging Trueman in 1960 at Headingley. All these knocks except the 96 and 167 at Melbourne were in lost matches. Harvey was immensely likeable because he was also one of the most unselfish of cricketers. He was passed over twice for the captaincy by Australia. First it was Ian Craig who led them on tour to South Africa, and after that the captaincy went to

Richie Benaud. Harvey was a wonderful support to them, and was Benaud's vice captain and advisor, as Australia became top dogs in Test cricket again. In the only Test that he captained—Benaud could not play because of a shoulder injury—Harvey marshaled his forces intelligently to win the Lords Test against England to give them a series lead in the Ashes. Till the end he was an outstanding fielder. In his early years, he was brilliant in the outfield, a star in a team which was considered the best fielding side in the world. In his later years, he moved to slips where he was a safe catcher.

When finally he, Benaud and Davidson retired after that Test series against England, Australian cricket had a vacuum as it suddenly lost three champions at the same time. Harvey finished with 21 hundreds and an average of over 48 while scoring 6,149 runs in 79 Tests. Significantly, 13 of his 21 tons were made away from home; four against South Africa and three each against England, West Indies and India.

Having also seen Brian Lara, David Gower and Garry Sobers play in India, how would I rate Harvey alongside them? In a pantheon of stylish attractive left handers, Harvey, Lara and Gower would be the top three. Gower was the most effortless with exquisite timing as his forte; Lara was a prodigious big innings batter with a big back-lift and flourish in his follow-through, the entire arc from back-lift to finish was elaborate and exaggerated; Harvey was twinkle footed and combined style, timing and elegance. All three of them were risk-taking and adventurous—dangerous once they got in. Harvey at his peak was perhaps tighter and more solid than the other two, although this statement will have many counter points and arguments, especially from those who haven't seen Harvey in action.

Those who saw cricket in India in the 1950s confirm that no batter other than Harvey ever had the full measure of Subhash Gupte, the wondrous leg spinner. Spectators in Mumbai were lucky enough to see the master hit two centuries in 1956 and

1960. So what made Neil Harvey so special that 50 years after he retired, people still talk about him with such awe and affection? The quality of his batting was simply divine—driving, cutting and pulling with wonderful precision and timing; the spirit of adventure that was integral to his batsmanship; the buzz that went around every ground in the world when he entered to bat; he could never ever be boring or ugly at the crease. He was a selfless team man and it was probably this laidback persona that robbed him of the chance to captain Australia. Who knows, if he had taken over from Lindsay Hassett in 1954, what Australia might have done against Tyson, Statham, Laker and Lock, in the two consecutive Ashes series that Australia lost during that time.

Australian cricket writer, Ray Robinson, had no doubts why Harvey was special. In praise of Harvey, Robinson wrote:

> His bat and hands have flashed magically before more eyes than have watched any other of his countrymen. It takes a star of the first magnitude to gleam in regions bedazzled by Bradman, the only Aussie to have made more runs and centuries than Harvey. To the challenge of this situation, Neil has responded by making himself the only man in Cricket history to score Test centuries in fifteen different cities. The only cricketer (at that time) to put together 20 centuries in a post-war period marked at times by wickets of strange uncertainty—that sent Test teams' totals in the last decade (52–62) dipping one-third below the average of the era when the only other two who scored more than 20 centuries batted (Bradman and Hammond 29 and 22). It is no accident that Bradman, Harvey and the legendary Trumper are the only three, British crowds have seen twice reel off hundreds before lunch. Or that the fastest Test hundred Australian crowds have witnessed for thirty years have gushed from Harvey's bat at a rate not equalled by the spectacular Kanhai or Sobers. Against the left-handed batsman's occupational hazard of boot-roughened turf in a vulnerable area (outside the off stump for left handers), this nimblest of left handers has

> intruded into the right-hand champion's preserve, the big six who have amassed most runs since Tests began: Hammond, Bradman, Hutton, Harvey, Compton and Hobbs.

For the magical moments he gave so many of us, he remains the finest of that rare breed—the supremely gifted, graceful, stylish, twinkle-toed left-handed batter we have ever seen.

30

FOR AN EVEN GAME BETWEEN BAT AND BALL

Cricket has seen many significant changes over the last 110 years. Some have been marvelous innovations that have heightened the thrill of bat versus ball, while other changes have seriously disturbed the golden balance. The most significant of the pre-World War I change was that pitches instead of being 'natural' began to be 'prepared.' Thus a game that was wickedly and capriciously slanted in favor of bowlers (the bowling averages and figures of George Lohmann, Demon Spofforth and Colin Blythe at the turn of the 20th century bear testimony to this) began to bestow better chances for batters. Yet, even on these prepared wickets, great bowlers reaped almost the same rewards; none exemplifying this better than Wilfred Rhodes, the torch bearer for the tribe of spinners. Many years later, the covering of pitches was another great change—less play was lost because of this simple measure and it also ensured that the weather did not provide undue advantage to a bowling side to demolish the batting side on a drying pitch. Covered pitches did swing the game well in favor of batters. The changes in the laws governing LBW and the front foot no ball rules and a few others have been made in responding and sometimes reacting to the way the game is being played at that point in time.

Science and technology have obviously been the biggest

influence. Everything has undergone such change that Trumper and Ranji will not recognize today's batter. The bat is becoming stronger by the day. Gone are the days of thin handles, linseed oil seasoning; instead we have thick multi-rubbered handles and compressed wood, with such lethal weight distribution that almost the entire bat is a 'sweet spot'. It means that a mistimed hit that Trumper or Ranji would have holed out to, now regularly clear the ropes. Pads, inner guards and gloves have all become lighter, and batters and keepers as a result are much more mobile. As though this was not enough, grounds have been becoming smaller. At numerous small venues and in the IPL T20 a 65 yard hit is a six these days where earlier a six would have to clear 80 yards or more. Till the 1980s, the benefit of doubt to batters while deciding on a LBW appeal was another factor in favor of the batters. Cricket, not so subtly, post-World War II became even more of a batter's game.

As the game tilted toward batters, the oppressed bowlers found ways and means to restore balance and wrest some rights for themselves. There have been three significant changes that bowlers have succeeded in creating for themselves. The first is of course reverse swing. On benign pitches, because of 'ball management' a bowler of speed today confounds well-set batsmen. A sense of unpredictability, suspense and balance has been introduced. What Sarfraz Nawaz started, Steyn and Zaheer have converted into fine art. Conventional principles of aerodynamics tell us that the shiny side of the ball moves faster through the air because it will encounter less friction or resistance. However now, fielding sides manage the ball in a manner that the shiny side gets a lot of saliva and sweat while the rough side is left scuffed and dry. The result is that the shiny side becomes heavier. The result is that the shiny side moves slower through the air while the rough and drier half of the ball moves faster through the air. But reverse swing will also remind people of bottle caps, strong teeth, finger nails and pockets full of sand. Today with television keeping a close watch and umpires inspecting the ball closely and frequently, tampering of the ball has been reduced greatly.

The other great change is of course the Doosra. What Bosanquet's googly was to leg spin, Saqlain Mushtaq's Doosra is to off spin. Saqlain delivered the ball perfectly legitimately, perhaps because he had a long-last stride like a wrist spinner. But after him there have been a slew of off spinners who have been under scrutiny, whether it is a Harbhajan or a Johann Botha or a Saeed Ajmal. The Doosra is never without a faint whiff of suspicion. Ashwin, Nathan Lyon and Graeme Swann are purveyors of off spin who have not resorted to the Doosra.

Both these changes in bowling have actually been thrust on the game because of the manner in which the game is loaded in favor of the batter. And because the laws of the game do not firmly address these imbalances, the bowlers will find newer ways; the lines between right and wrong will get blurred in an uncontrollable spiral.

And that brings us to the third major change that has been forced upon the game after the ICC had to find a solution to the controversy over Muralitharan's action. The laws of the game now allow bowlers a 15 degree flex of elbow. So from an era when the bowler had to really adhere to a 'bowling action', today's bowler is allowed a certain straightening of the arm that still shocks the purists. One of the finest essays on this issue has been written by Mike Atherton ('Hail Muttiah Muralitharan, the Humble Hero who Changed the Game', in the *Times*, July 22, 2010) where he brings balance, perspective and candor in equal measure.

Even as the game was grappling with batters already having it mostly their way, a couple of things further loaded the game in favor of batters. One was the annoying luxury of a runner for a batter suffering from cramps in the one-day game. The one-day game is as much about fitness and agility as about talent, technique and temperament. If after a stay of about

35 overs, a batter suffers from cramps, it is a sign of lack of fitness to last the course. To afford him a runner, when he is fully set was a travesty of justice and fair play. For this reason we would rate Kapil's 175 and Viv Richards' World Cup final knock of '79 higher than Saeed Anwar's knock against India. Sachin, nearly 37 years old, scored 200 on his own legs putting our argument in the best possible perspective. We believe that if fatigue, cramps or a muscle pull hampers a batter's mobility, that's part of the game and his fitness level; he cannot ask for assistance and must decide to either bat on with discomfort or retire. Contrast this facility given to batters with the rule which forbids bowlers from bowling immediately if they leave the field for an extended period of time to attend to injuries. If batters with cramps are allowed runners then bowlers must be allowed to bowl as soon as they return to the field after repairs or rest. One of the best things therefore to have happened in recent times is the change in rules that now forbid the use of runners in one-day cricket for cramps and pulled muscles suffered during the course of an innings.

The second unfair advantage that batters are employing is the switch hit. The reverse sweep can be viewed as dexterity because it is played the other way without changing the grip and in that sense clearly legitimate. But when you change grip, become a left hander and sweep or slog the bowler through point or covers, you are actually cheating the bowler and the field set for you. Allowing a switch hit is akin to bowlers being permitted to change without notice from over the wicket to around the wicket. Perhaps one way of restoring balance with regard to the switch hit, is to declare the batters LBW if he is struck on the pads while playing the switch hit to a ball pitched outside the leg stump and turning in. If the switch hit has come to stay make sure it is balanced by something for the bowler. Do not goad and frustrate the bowlers further. Hopefully, there will a change in rules in the matter of 'switch hit' too.

Cricket in its relentless march will see wonderful innovations as well as unwelcome irreversible changes. The sport is commercialized but it is wrong to assume that audiences respond in larger numbers only to a batting blitzkrieg. The same audiences respond magnificently to tight well fought matches even if they are not raining fours and sixes. We have enough evidence of this even in T20 let alone Test matches. The challenge for people in charge of the game is to credit the audiences with discernment and ensure that the contest between bat and ball at all times remains even. For balance is what provides harmony to cricket as it does to all things in the life.

31

PRASANNA, LAKER AND THE TRIBE OF OFF SPINNERS

In the winter of 1969, both of us saw two of the best-ever spells of off-spin bowling within a week of each other. The younger of us, not yet 13, saw Erapalli Prasanna bring Australia down to its knees with a spell of six for 14 in 11 overs, as South Zone almost pulled off a nail biting victory at Bangalore. A few days later, the elder among us watched the same Prasanna reduce the same Australians to 24 for 6 at Chepauk in Madras. Whenever we discuss off-spin bowling, our mind's eye takes us back to those magical moments. Prasanna beating the batter who survives; Prasanna then cockily walking 'backwards' to his bowing mark, with mincing steps, a teasing smirk on his face and his taunting eyes never leaving the batter! If Prasanna represents the ultimate artist

Indian off-spinner, E. A. S. Prasanna
Photo Courtesy: Kasturi & Sons

among off spinners, then surely the finest of craftsmen among them has to be Venkataraghavan. People talk of the floater as the supreme weapon of beguilement in an off spinner's armory. In his first Test series, and not yet out of his teens, Venkat had the skill to bowl that ball to claim Jarvis of New Zealand in the Kotla Test of 1965. It was a delivery that was so good that newspapers next morning waxed eloquent about the prodigious talent of the young man.

Off spin has always been an integral part of a good bowling attack. Good leg spin provides the X factor; fast bowlers provide the essential cutting edge but plugging and plotting away on friendly and unfriendly tracks with patience, resilience and guile is the off spinner. Some will be the quickish type, almost medium pace and quite deadly on helpful tracks. The others will be slow, accurate and relentless. Both are every captain's dream. On a hot day, on a benign track, it will be the off spinner who will bowl for figures of 1 for 75 in 33 overs!

Over the years, tons of wickets have been taken by the off spinners. There are, at this moment in August 2012, 35 off spinners who taken at least 50 Test wickets. All of them have been valiant servants of the game, and the spectrum ranges from the wide-eyed Muralitharan on a summit of 800 wickets that no bowler will ever surpass (the cliché that records are meant to be broken will not apply here) to W. Bates who took 50 wickets more than 125 years ago, surely forgotten even in his own homeland but whom Wisden in its *Almanack* describes with a lot of respect for exceptional ability.

If we were to poll cricketers and knowledgeable cricket followers to rank these 35 off spinners, there will never be any kind of agreement. And yet, cricket statistics has its own fatal charm, seducing the keen follower of the game to try and stack cricketers on some key statistical parameters. We were no exceptions. We decided to massage the bowlers' statistics using five parameters—number of wickets, strike rate, bowling average, five- and 10-wicket hauls, and proportion of wickets taken away from home—and created a composite effectiveness index for each of the 35 off spinners with over 50 Test wickets. We have described the model earlier in our essay on the leg spinners and will therefore merely place before you Table 31.1 that ranks the off spinners based on their overall effectiveness index.

Based on our model of computing the bowling effectiveness index, the top 20 off spinners are: Muttiah Muralitharan, Jim Laker, Harbhajan Singh, Hugh Trumble, William Bates, Graeme Swann, Saqlain Mushtaq, Lance Gibbs, Hugh 'Toey' Tayfield, E. A. S. Prasanna, G. E. Palmer, Saeed Ajmal, Ashley Mallett, I. W. G. Johnson, Fred Titmus, D. A. Allen, Roy Tattersall, Shivlal Yadav, S. Venkataraghavan and Tauseef Ahmed.

Quite predictably, we both agreed with some of the rankings our statistical massaging threw up, and equally predictably we vehemently disagreed with some of the rankings. All our perceptions about what constitutes quality off-spin bowling were in fearful conflict with what mere numbers throw up. Which is why, we need to remind ourselves every time that while numbers are important they do not tell the whole story.

We realized that we must stick our neck out and make our own subjective but informed estimates of quality. While facts and figures were at the back of our mind we brought in our own assessment of factors such as guile, the beauty of their bowling action and so on. To begin with, we agreed that the three spinners of the long ago generation—Trumble, Bates and Palmer—would be included in the top 20 but will not be ranked, for we were in no position to argue one way or the other about their place. But for the remaining 17 we would rank them.

And so we arrived at our own list of the 17 greatest off spinners of all time. See Table 31.2.

Off spin unfortunately has regularly thrown up—with good reason—controversial actions. A leg spinner's action has never been questioned and our theory is that it is simply because one uses the wrist to bowl leg spin and it would be impossible to

TABLE 31.1: Off Spinners Ranked on the Effectiveness Index Created by the Authors

Sl. no.	*Bowler*	*Country*	*Span*	*Tests*	*Wickets*	*Strike rate*	*Average*	*5 wickets/ inning*	*10 wickets/ match*	*Overall effectiveness index*
1	M. Muralitharan	Sri Lanka	1992–2010	133	800	55	22.72	67	22	2.0
2	J. C. Laker	England	1948–1959	46	193	62.3	21.24	9	3	2.9
3	Harbhajan Singh	India	1998–2011	98	406	68.1	32.22	25	5	2.9
4	H. Trumble	Australia	1890–1904	32	141	57.4	21.78	9	3	2.9
5	W. Bates	England	1881–1887	15	50	47.2	16.42	4	1	3.0
6	G. P. Swann	England	2008–2012	45	188	58	28.64	13	2	3.0
7	Saqlain Mushtaq	Pakistan	1995–2004	49	208	67.6	29.83	13	3	3.2
8	L. R. Gibbs	West Indies	1958–1976	79	309	87.7	29.09	18	2	3.2
9	H. J. Tayfield	South Africa	1949–1960	37	170	79.8	25.91	14	2	3.4
10	E. A. S. Prasanna	India	1962–1978	49	189	75.9	30.38	10	2	3.4
11	G. E. Palmer	Australia	1880–1886	17	78	57.9	21.51	6	2	3.5
12	Saeed Ajmal	Pakistan	2009–2012	23	122	61.3	27.09	6	2	3.6
13	A. A. Mallett	Australia	1968–1980	38	132	75.6	29.84	6	1	3.6
14	I. W. G. Johnson	Australia	1946–1956	45	109	80.5	29.19	3	0	3.9
15	F. J. Titmus	England	1955–1975	53	153	98.8	32.22	7	0	3.9
16	D. A. Allen	England	1960–1966	39	122	92.5	30.97	4	0	3.9
17	R. Tattersall	England	1951–1954	16	58	72.8	26.08	4	1	4.1
18	N. S. Yadav	India	1979–1987	41	102	81.9	35.09	3	0	4.1

(Table 24.1 Contd)

(Table 24.1 Contd)

Sl. no.	*Bowler*	*Country*	*Span*	*Tests*	*Wickets*	*Strike rate*	*Average*	*5 wickets/ inning*	*10 wickets/ match*	*Overall effectiveness index*
19	S. Venkataraghavan	India	1965–1983	57	156	95.3	36.11	3	1	4.1
20	Tauseef Ahmed	Pakistan	1980 1993	34	93	83.6	31.72	3	0	4.2
21	R. Illingworth	England	1958–1973	61	122	97.8	31.2	3	0	4.3
22	J. G. Bracewell	New Zealand	1980–1990	35	102	82.3	35.81	4	1	4.3
23	J. E. Emburey	England	1978–1995	64	147	104.7	38.4	6	0	4.3
24	N. M. Hauritz	Australia	2004–2010	17	63	66.6	34.98	2	0	4.4
25	Ghulam Ahmed	India	1948–1959	22	68	83	30.17	4	1	4.4
26	G. Miller	England	1976–1984	34	60	85.8	30.98	1	0	4.5
27	T. B. A. May	Australia	1987–1995	24	75	87.6	34.74	3	0	4.5
28	D. N. Patel	New Zealand	1987–1997	37	75	87.9	42.05	3	0	5.0
29	C. H. Gayle	West Indies	2000–2010	91	72	95.2	41.59	2	0	5.1
30	P. I. Pocock	England	1968–1985	25	67	99.2	44.41	3	0	5.2
31	A. M. B. Rowan	South Africa	1947–1951	15	54	96.1	38.59	4	0	5.3
32	H. D. P. K. Dharmasena	Sri Lanka	1993–2004	31	69	100.5	42.31	3	0	5.3
33	C. L. Hooper	West Indies	1987–2002	102	114	121	49.42	4	0	5.4
34	P. J. Wiseman	Australia	1998–2005	33	61	92.7	47.59	2	0	5.5
35	G. R. J. Matthews	Australia	1983–1993	25	61	102.8	48.22	2	1	5.6

Source: Data from espncricinfo.com. Analysis and tabular compilation by authors.

TABLE 31.2: The Authors' Ranking of the Off Spinners—Subjective, Contentious, but Fun

Sl. no.	*Player*	*Matches*	*Wickets*	*Bowling average*	*Economy rate*	*Strike rate*	*5 wickets/ innings*	*10 wickets/ match*
1	J. C. Laker	46	193	21.24	2.04	62.3	9	3
2	E. A. S. Prasanna	49	189	30.38	2.4	75.9	10	2
3	L. R. Gibbs	79	309	29.09	1.98	87.7	18	2
4	M. Muralitharan	133	800	22.72	2.47	55	67	22
5	H. J. Tayfield	37	170	25.91	1.94	79.8	14	2
6	Saqlain Mushtaq	49	208	29.83	2.64	67.6	13	3
7	Harbhajan Singh	98	406	32.22	2.83	68.1	25	5
8	G. P. Swann	45	188	28.64	2.96	58	13	2
9	S. Venkataraghavan	57	156	36.11	2.27	95.3	3	1
10	Saeed Ajmal	23	122	27.09	2.65	61.3	6	2
11	A. A. Mallett	38	132	29.84	2.36	75.6	6	1
12	F. J. Titmus	53	153	32.22	1.95	98.8	7	0
13	Ghulam Ahmed	22	68	30.17	2.17	83	4	1
14	D. A. Allen	39	122	30.97	2	92.5	4	0
15	R. Tattersall	16	58	26.08	2.14	72.8	4	1
16	R. Illingworth	61	122	31.2	1.91	97.8	3	0
17	I. W. G. Johnson	45	109	29.19	2.17	80.5	3	0

Source: Data from espncricinfo.com. Analysis and tabular compilation by authors.

do so with a bent arm. Off spin however is finger spin and there is always the likelihood of a bent arm, even more so if the bowler is not quite side on and gets more open chested. To add to its woes, recently the Doosra has become the single biggest reason for off spinners to be under scrutiny. In the days before Saqlain demonstrated the Doosra with the cleanest of actions and with wonderful subterfuge, our classical off spinners had the beautiful over spinner, the floater and the leg cutter. Today, every off spinner bowls the Doosra and sorry, we find many of these deliveries obnoxiously suspicious. Which is why, the two of us place such a premium on the bowling action.

Who had the loveliest actions? Venkat had the most languid effortless action. Five easy steps, the fifth a short one to allow him to pivot and as his bowling arm reached high, the left arm would be right down, all weight on his front foot, the left foot. He was a tall man and yet his release was so beautifully calibrated that not only was his bounce menacing, he also caught batters short on the drive. Prasanna's action was divine, for the sheer merriment and drama of it all. The busy small steps of a short man and then the toss of the ball with such a wonderful pivot that the ball would hum, buzz and then change flight as if pulled on a string. Many years after he has retired, very perceptively, like a litany, Prasanna says that for an off spinner, length is mandatory, line is optional. Gibbs had a long career and many wickets; in fact, for a long time after he overtook Trueman, his record stood unchallenged. Gibbs, one

Srinivas Venkataraghavan's beautiful bowling action
Photo Courtesy: Kasturi & Sons

remembers had a unique bowling action, a springy loopy style and at the end of his follow through, the weight was not fully transferred to the front foot. He had a more square on action unlike the side on actions of Venkat or Prasanna. Gibbs had very long fingers, and spun and bounced the ball prodigiously. He was relentlessly accurate and had wickets in every country he played in. And of course we cannot resist adding that a certain Mr. Sobers often stood at short leg to pluck catches of Gibbs' bowling.

Saqlain Mushtaq is remembered most as the bowler who unfurled the Doosra but he deserves much more than that. For a few years, between 1998 and 2002, he was the world's outstanding off spinner. He was deceptive and often got batters committed to the wrong shot. He was the fastest bowler to 100 wickets in one-day internationals. He was the reason Pakistan beat India in the Chennai Test of January 1999 and thus Tendulkar's fabulous century in that match is unfortunately remembered as among the greatest in a losing cause. Saqlain bowled with a long last stride with his bowling coming over in a manner that no eyebrows could be raised.

Why is Laker on top of the pile for us? Not for his immortal 19 for 90 against Australia at Manchester in 1956, which feat anyway would rank as the most remarkable in the entire history of Test cricket. He was for us indisputably the first ever off spinner of great impact and the most complete off spinner. *The Wisden Illustrated History of Cricket* (1989) by Vic Marks (English off spinner incidentally), says, 'Laker possessed all the necessary qualities—a classical action, superb control of flight and spin, and the ability to assess swiftly his opponent's strengths and weaknesses.' Apparently batters could hear the ball fizzing on its way to them and many found the ball was not really there when they went to drive it. We have this memorable story about Laker: After finishing off Australia at Manchester (the 19 wickets), Laker quietly drove off home. On his way, he stopped at a pub for a pint of ale. A group of people at the pub were watching the Test match highlights, saw Laker on the bar stool and remarked that the chap looks like Laker. Laker, enigmatic as ever, quietly continued quaffing on his ale!

Laker, incredibly had taken all 10 wickets earlier that season for Surrey against the Australians on a not particularly spiteful wicket—a fact that many do not remember. So his subsequent performance in the Manchester Test was not a flash in the pan. Five years earlier in a Test trial at Bradford, he had the unbelievable figures of eight wickets for two runs against the rest of England. In spite of all these figures and the fact that from 1948 he was the best off spinner in the country over the next decade, Laker was overlooked for both the 1951 tour and the 54–55 trips to Australia. Simply because he was always viewed distrustfully by the establishment! So whimsical selection policies everywhere seems to be a part of cricket history.

Laker's shoes were impossible to fill for the Englishmen who followed him. Titmus and Allen no doubt had their own golden moments. Titmus was such a chirpy loquacious character, that one of his team mates memorably said, that he probably took catches in mid-sentence! But these bowlers had clean classical actions as does Graeme Swann today. Swann has never bowled the Doosra, but he has a wicked well-disguised straighter one and complete control of his spin, flight and pace. He is right up there among the greatest for us, although the recent Tests against Sri Lanka and South Africa in 2012 are forgettable for him.

Saqlain Mushtaq played his last Test for Pakistan in 2004. Five years later, at the ripe age of 32 Saeed Ajmal made his debut. He became Pakistan's main strike bowler, harvesting a bucketful of wickets. The Doosra was his chosen weapon. His action was dubious to put it mildly but that was the time many off spinners got away with questionable actions. Our views on the Doosra and suspect actions (Bishan Bedi insists we are too mild) are hopefully clear from the fact that our essay has Prasanna and Laker on a pedestal separate from some others whose wickets and strike rates might have been better but whose bowling actions made us grimace.

Young readers might be puzzled to see Ghulam Ahmed's name in our list. But know thee well; he was a lovely off spinner, one of the wiliest. While Gupte and Mankad provided India with leg spin and left-arm spin in the 1950s, Ghulam was the counter foil to both of them. His action was known for its complete economy and seemingly minimal effect that enabled him to bowl long spells without fatigue. But he was a terrible fielder and one could safely predict he would drop the ball if a catch came toward him.

Toey Tayfield is South Africa's finest spinner ever and so accurate that, as we have written earlier, a batter could wait all day for a bad ball to hit. He was not a prodigious turner of the ball but he bowled from close to the stumps, over the wicket, to get maximum drift. The drift ensured that the spin he generated was enough to make batters commit errors. Tayfield would set strange but remarkably well-planned fields with two short mid-ons, one straighter and one squarer to the right hander and two silly mid-offs similarly for the left hander. There is a remarkable sequence of photographs that captures Tayfield make a sensational return catch of his bowling. Arthur Morris, the Australian, drove Tayfield and it hit the silly mid-off fielder and rebounded. The next picture shows Tayfield diving full length to catch this. Tayfield got his nickname Toey because he would stub his toes into the ground after every delivery. It became a mannerism that never left him. And unlike Ghulam, this man was an excellent fielder, one of the best! Actually some of these off spinners in our list are absolutely top drawer fielders. Tayfield of course and then Mallett and Venkat right there among the best.

Murali on sheer numbers is so far and above the rest that he can sit on the summit impervious to anything that people might say about his bowling. The interesting thing is that Murali was probably as much a wrist spinner as a finger spinner, which is why he could spin the ball on a marble top. Harbhajan, second in the wicket list, enjoyed his greatest moments when he singlehandedly bowled India to a series win against Australia in 2001. Harbhajan relies greatly on bounce, not so much on drift. If he gets a wicket early, he is terror but if denied a wicket early, he gets fretful. As purists, both of us give a lot of emphasis to the purity of action and on that count alone we are unable to rate both these giants above Laker and Prasanna.

Finally, let us look at Hugh Trumble, one of the three great off spinners who played in the late-nineteenth and early-twentieth century. Trumble played 32 Test matches between 1890 and 1904. His 141 Test wickets came at less than 22 runs apiece. He was tall and his quickish off spin was unplayable on wet wickets. His exploits are best encapsulated in the Australia–England Ashes series of 1902. Two of the three Tests were nail bitingly close. Australia beat England by three runs at Manchester and then England beat Australia by one wicket a few days later at Oval. In both matches, Trumble was simply marvelous, 10 wickets in the win at Manchester and then 12 wickets in the heartbreak at Oval.

Off spin is no bridesmaid. There is as much guile, cunning, skill and art in this as in any other form of bowling. And to add to it is the fact that the off spinner is the ultimate soldier—ready for the long battle. On flat unresponsive pitches, in hot and unhelpful conditions, the fast bowler may flag, the leg spinner may feel deflated but the off spinner will go on. Right arm over the wicket most times, sometimes round the wicket... probing away.

Note: R. Ashwin and Nathan Lyon made their Test debut in 2011. During the past 12 years where their careers have overlapped, they have, between them, taken nearly 1,000 wickets. On almost every indicator of bowling effectiveness these two will feature among the best. What is more, between them, they have ensured that the Doosra is castaway and pure actions once again rule the world of offspin. Surely Prasanna and Laker would gladly make way for these two in the title to this essay.

OH, FOR A CLEAN OFF SPINNER'S ACTION!

A few years ago, with every off spinner trying to bowl the Doosra even before he had mastered the stock off break, we saw a rash of dubious actions across the country. And it seemed that the body governing the game was not taking quick and corrective action.

Concerned by this disturbing trend, Giridhar wrote this blog in espncricinfo.com on December 6, 2008.

It was a Sunday morning in the last week of October and the sun was rather pleasant, of the kind that you seem to get only in Bengaluru. I was walking to the market rolling between thumb and forefinger the piece of paper on which my wife had written the list of things required at home. Just 100 yards away from my home is a rather large play ground where invariably a couple of teams square up against each other for intense tennis ball cricket during weekends. This Sunday morning was no different and even as I was striding purposefully to the market, I could see beyond the compound wall of the ground, two teams had already commenced battle. The noise emanating from the spectators aligned to the two camps was equal and I guessed that it was an even scrap. The sights and sounds of cricket are like a magnet and so I paused and told myself, okay just a few minutes of this action before I resume the expedition to the market. I put my elbows on the compound wall and peered down on a match that had just begun.

The batting seemed to be of good quality and I rather suspect that one of the batters was of a league cricket caliber because he played a cover drive and then unfurled a square cut of some elegance. The opening bowlers were also good—they ran in smoothly and delivered decent deliveries and not a wide bowled. But a wicket had not fallen and the captain of the fielding side with some visible impatience summoned his first change.

The new bowler sets his field elaborately, in fact rather too elaborately with much gesticulation. But we are finally ready. Aha, seems to be a spinner, only four steps to the bowling crease! And what does he deliver? An entire over of extremely accurate off spin, every ball was like a dart, with the third ball he took out the ' league cricket' caliber batter' s middle stump and with his sixth ball he plucked out the off stump of the completely clueless no. 3 batter. Raucous cheers, much leaping around, high fives, lots of hugs—I straightened up, dusted my elbows and resumed my walk to the market. But this time my head was bowed and even from the other side of the road you could see that I was not a happy man. The reason was simple. This match-winning off spinner bowled with an abominable action.

Of course tennis ball cricket bowling heroes have always been bowlers like our friend here. But these day s, the story of the maverick off spinner does not end in the neighborhood maidan. Our friend already 19 or 20 y ears old must be bowling like this for a few y ears and by now display ing this brand of bowling in inter-college matches too. He would be wrecking teams and may soon play a higher grade of cricket. So I muttered to myself as I continued on my way.

It was not even 24 hours later that I saw some live cricket again. This time it was on television, a match between two teams called India Blue and Green or Yellow or whatever. Both teams had an off spinner each. One of them was being spoken of very highly by the commentators, as the man to watch out for, he can put the brakes, he is a tricky customer, he is the one who will...

This young man, Mohnish Parmar, has already played first-class cricket, play ed for India A or equivalent teams and therefore must have passed muster with umpires in India, the national committee that reviews actions. But boy, what I saw made me rub my eyes in disbelief! Here he came on a diagonal run up as though measured and marked by Muralitharan. And then he contorts himself and delivers unbelievably copy ing Muralitharan. And of course he beats batters; he gets a wicket here, a wicket there and of the 24 deliveries that he bowled at least 16 of them were the Doosra! The pernicious Doosra is difficult enough to bowl and obviously places the maximum strain on the legality of the action. And through this entire per od when this young man is bowling, the commentators make only the occasional apologetic reference to his action. If it is legal who am I argue with that? But if I say it was bloody out right ugly to watch, can you deny me the right to say that? Later that evening in the same match, a rather studious-looking chap named Ashwin bowled a spell of off spin for the other team—neat clean action, no Doosra, the straighter one of course and he got a wicket bowling a well set batter through the gate.

Something is badly wrong somewhere. A bowler with a dubious action in neighborhood cricket is perfectly acceptable and in fact provides the much-needed sharpness to the fielding side. It is okay so long as he knows that he will play and enjoy cricket as a pastime. But it is an altogether different matter if he is allowed to graduate to higher grades of cricket. In the long run, we are doing the greatest disservice to him. Take the case of this bowler with the strange action from the Challenger series match. If he were to continue play ing, he would put everything else in his life on the back burner—his studies, his office career, his family. How will he cope if just a short while later, umpires finally do what should have been done when he first began to play serious cricket? Won't it be too late to change his action? Will he be as effective? What if all his dreams and aspirations come shattering down? Most importantly who is to blame? Why is our cricket administration turning such a blind eye to what is obviously a problem of endemic proportion. I am willing to bet that nearly every Ranji team has an off spinner with a dicey action either in the team or in the fringes of the team. And simply because our system does not have the discipline or courage to stop such bowlers and tell them to correct their actions before they bowl in a match again. I typed in these words and in a not too pleasant mood filed this piece away and out of sight.

Four weeks later and as November is drawing to a close, two news items in quick succession tell us that the off spinners in our country are in trouble. Mohnish Parmar' s action has been questioned by the umpire in a Ranji Trophy match, and Sunil Rao the off spinner from Karnataka has also been told that his action is not what it should be. Why did it take so long? What the umpire spotted in the actions of Mohnish Parmar and Sunil Raju must have been cry ing out loud for a couple of seasons. How much more traumatic it would be for the young men now and how much easier it could have been if our cricket system had done its duty earlier. Leg spin by the very nature of the action and delivery is impossible to be bowled with an illegitimate action but an off spinner if not careful can easily end up with an action that will bring grief to the bowler and the game.

32

RUBBING SHOULDERS WITH THE BEST: STORIES FROM MADRAS AND BOMBAY LEAGUE

When one has been bitten by the cricket bug early in one's life, it is but natural that as a youngster you dream and fantasize.

My (Raghunath) dream was the image of returning to the pavilion at Lords bat aloft after scoring a century with the members standing up in the long-room applauding. If this didn't quite happen at least I had the satisfaction of playing cricket with some of my heroes—Polly Umrigar, Salim Durani, Kripal Singh, V. V. Kumar to name a few. While I played the Madras heroes in league and Collegiate cricket during the 1960s, I also had the wonderful opportunity of playing with many of India's best cricketers in Bombay's fiercely competitive league tournaments for five years.

I captained a representative under-25 side to Bombay during my final year in the college and we played sides captained by Ashok Mankad, Vijay Manjrekar and Vasu Paranjpe. This helped me to step into a first-division side during my stint in Bombay, playing the prestigious Kanga league besides Purshottam and Talim Shield matches. All matches in Bombay were played on turf wickets and no quarter was given or claimed; everyone was very professional in his approach and discipline was taken for granted. Stalwarts like Madhav Mantri, V. S. Patil and Vijay Manjrekar practiced what they preached and set an example for youngsters to follow. I remember Manjrekar admonishing me for rolling the ball back down the pitch. (I was keeping wickets with our regular keeper injured.) Polly Umrigar in a friendly match at CCI, as soon as he came in, would not play balls on his leg toward short leg preferring to take them on his thigh-pad till he was set; such was the seriousness and professional attitude the Bombay player displayed. And the more senior you were, the greater was the discipline for they saw themselves as role models. This was not evident in Madras or Bangalore where players who had made the grade often thought they were above the law and the code of conduct that was preached. Venkataraghavan was the exception—apart from talent, his discipline, fitness and work ethic has ensured that he is till today, the most successful cricketer from Tamil Nadu.

Here are some memories of brilliant performances I was lucky enough to catch during my playing days.

The first recognized Test star I played with was Kripal Singh. I remember Kripal standing at silly-mid-off to intimidate me the first time I played against him. I also remember him telling me that a clever bowler needs to turn only one ball in an over. I will always remember him farming the strike in the *Sports & Pastime* matches to keep his less-talented partners from facing good bowling and the ease with which he would skip down the wicket to place the ball between mid-on and mid-wicket for the single every fifth or sixth ball was amazing. Son of Ram Singh who still did business then (in the early 1960s) from his sports shop in Bells Road next to Chepauk ground, Kripal was the local hero of the neighborhood. When he came down the steps of the Presidency College pavilion, the cheers could be heard all over Triplicane. An unforgettable memory in the closely fought duels between Parry and State Bank is that of Kripal hitting V. V. Kumar for a winning straight six; the ball cleared the ground and bounced off the top of a Route no. 13 bus on Pycrofts road!

I have seen two great knocks of his. Fifty-three against Hall and Gilchrist at Chepauk hooking and square-driving them with panache and then a great knock of 133 against Bombay at Chepauk which clinched him a place for the England tour of 1959. He was always a player with grace, elegance and technique. On that tour of England, he is supposed to have played a knock of 178 against Lancashire which made Statham wonder how he could be kept out of a side which was getting white-washed 5–0. Kripal played just one Test in that series and scored a 40 plus in one of the innings. The next two Test players I faced off with were Kumar and Venkat—though I played with and against Venkat before he broke into national ranks. Kumar was another early hero, but was not popular with the Madras cricket follower—he would explode in his squeaky voice at batters and umpires losing his temper. He was an excellent accurate leg spinner with all the variations and a good googly and top spinner. He was an attacking bowler with a lot of self-confidence and bowled with great control in long spells—he was extremely economical and would often bowl long spells giving away less than three runs an over. After a great debut against Pakistan, he played just one more Test against England carrying an injury when all our bowlers were hammered by Geoff Pullar, Ted Dexter and Ken Barrington. He should certainly have played more Tests for India. In spite of this shabby treatment, he continued to coach spinners in the state and for the country with great commitment.

Venkat was the epitome of physical fitness and was perhaps the finest close-in fielder the South has produced. Outstanding at gully, he was very good at slips or short leg too. He never bowled a bad ball in all the matches I played against him and was quick off the wicket even on matting where the ball doesn't skid through. Consequently, I played forward to him all the time but rarely got a half-volley to drive. Occasionally being, a left hander, I would get something to guide through the off-side square of the wicket. He was stern and unforgiving with his close-in fielders.

Most of his teammates were scared to stand at short leg when he bowled. Another feature of Venkat was his self-confidence and he always believed his team would win, irrespective of the opposition's strength. Venkat was clear about his goals and I can never forget how after he passed his umpire's examination he met me at Chepauk and declared he would be a Test umpire in three years and become one of the world's best in five years. Talk about SMART goals!

T. E. Srinivasan—a very talented, stylish batter, who was a few years my junior, was a thrilling batter to watch.

Srinivasan was a great personality with tremendous ability—he played the rising ball very well having honed his technique on concrete pitches in his school. He talked a lot and was mistakenly thought to be arrogant, but was an endearing friend who spoke his mind. My mother-in-law gave him some addresses when he went to play league cricket in Yorkshire and he went and charmed them with his personality. His innings against West Zone that clinched him a place in the Indian team touring Australia and New Zealand was special with blazing drives and spectacular shots played on the rise to good length balls. T. E. Srinivasan died after suffering a paralytic stroke and surgery to remove a tumor, but was brave and cheerful till the end.

Around 1968, I left Madras and went to work in Bombay. I joined Indian Gymkhana and playing cricket in Bombay was a unique experience. The cricketers in that city made me understand how serious cricket should be played. To have played against legends like Polly Umrigar, Nari Contractor, Bapu Nadkarni, Dilip Sardesai, Vijay Manjrekar and others, even today gives me an indescribable happiness.

Umrigar was my boyhood Indian hero. He was tall, long-nosed with a booming voice and was a majestic figure in an Indian side of portly players. I played two matches against CCI during my Bombay days; a Kanga league match when we caught them on a wet wicket and surprisingly beat them and then in a practice match a year later; he was well into his forties but still played with concentration and seriousness soon after he came to bat. He was taking balls on the leg stump on his thigh pad just because there was a short leg and played patiently to score around 40. He was India's best fielder—both at slips and out-field, and in the first Test match I saw in '56, made great catches of Sutcliffe and Reid, their two best batters.

Manjrekar was not a particular favorite when I was a callow youth. Rotund and often slow in Test matches, I had seen him in quite a few Tests and his favorite stroke was dispatching the ball between cover and backward-point placing the ball with great precision; his bad knees preventing him from sweeping or pulling on the leg-side. When I was captaining a representative Madras colts side against Indian Airlines during my final year in college-playing at Shivaji Park, his home ground, he came in at no. 4 and patiently made a century against us; remembering what I had seen of him we tried to keep him quiet by bowling on the leg stump and placing a few extra men in the cover to point region. It made no difference to him and he played the bowling with respect but no difficulty and without one ugly stroke made a hundred plus. He was encouraging to our bowlers and passed on friendly tips to them all the time—a thorough professional if ever there was one.

P. K. Shivalkar—a clever and accurate bowler with a good armer, it was a challenge to bat against him and I usually played him with a lot of care not trying to do anything unduly risky or foolish. He would give the ball more air and constantly goad me to show him my cover drive. He was devastating on turning wickets and was a match winner for Bombay—unfortunately not breaking into the Test scene due to a career spanning with first Nadkarni and then Bedi.

Dadar Union and Shivaji Park were the two best teams in Bombay cricket in the 1960s and 1970s—adjoining neighborhood teams separated by the Central Railway line. If Shivaji Park was the team that boasted of Manjrekar, Ramakant Desai and Ajit

Wadekar, Dadar Union was fed on the deeds of Madhav Mantri, Naren Tamhane and V. S. Patil and was just then unleashing Sunil Gavaskar, Ramnath Parkar and Dilip Vengsarkar. There was great rivalry between the teams; in the early 1970s, Dadar Union was led by Vasu Paranjpe, as clever a captain as you can hope to see; a white kerchief tied around his neck, Vasu didn't miss a trick and was respected and admired by his teammates. I will never forget a Kanga league match we played against them. After making a good score they were trying to get us out cheaply to make us bat again for an innings victory. Their left-arm fast bowler Urmikant Modi was in great form and had taken six wickets. Our captain Satyamurthy was playing a lone hand; with a few runs to avoid the follow-on Modi bowled him a bouncer which Satya failed to hook and thereafter got him in the next over so they did enforce the follow-on. As their team applauded Modi into the pavilion when the innings ended and they reached the Pavilion, Vasu Paranjpe blasted Modi for bowling the bouncer to Satyamurthy—if he had hooked him for a boundary we would have saved the follow-on—Vasu's shelling the hero for not using his brain and getting carried away (after he had taken seven wickets) was an unforgettable episode in my cricket education. Another Dadar Union memory was Vasu putting himself on to bowl his Chinaman slows after I had made a good score and getting me caught at square leg—I felt such a fool to have fallen for that trap.

Ashok Mankad led Mafatlal in the Times Shield matches and Jolly cricketers in the league. He was a wonderful captain and I remember him moving over to short extra-cover to catch a new batter as soon as he came in. Earlier in a two-day match against the Madras colts, I remember him give a piece of his mind to a bowler who turned up late on the second day even though they were batting and the bowler in question was a tail-ender; Mankad really made that player feel bad and apologize profusely for not observing a basic etiquette that was the part of Bombay professionalism. In similar fashion,

Hanumant Singh leading State Bank dropped a Test cricketer from his playing 11 because he was five minutes late. Bombay cricket's discipline and professionalism made a deep impression on me and throughout my playing career a lackadaisical, casual attitude to the game that I saw in Madras cricket made me very angry and disappointed.

Dilip Sardesai was another great batter I played against and I was staggered at his constant chatter, especially when he was batting; he was talking nonstop when he was the non-striker, with the bowler, umpire, nearby fieldsmen and all within earshot. I remember him shouting 'sixer' and hitting me for six at the P. J. Hindu Gymkhana into the tennis courts to win the match for them. Soon after, he played his best series for India against West Indies in 1971. He was a wonderful batter who used his feet and played all-around the wicket and was great to watch even if you were at the receiving end.

Salim Durani was a magnificent all-rounder; we had seen him bowling brilliantly against Dexter's MCC at Madras and by the time I went to Bombay, although his bowling had fallen away a bit, he was still a great batter. We were playing Khar Gymkhana in a Talim Shield match at Khar. We batted first and Durani bowled a few great overs and then seemed to have lost the mood. After we had posted a good total it was their turn to bat. They lost a few wickets when Durani came in to bat. There was nothing sensational in his beginning and he pottered around till he reached his thirties. Then all hell broke loose—he hit the last two balls of our leg spinner for two straight sixes. In the next over, he hit our fastest bowler for two sixes—the second a pull of an attempted bouncer in front of mid-wicket. He had so much time and seemed to have played that stroke without any hurry at all. At the other end, the leg spinner was promptly removed from the attack and a left-arm medium pacer brought on. I remember fielding at cover boundary and twice in the next over barely moved as a couple of cover hits hit the railings just a few yards from me; the grace and the timing which generated such speed from the time the ball left the bat was unbelievable. The empty ground had suddenly filled with people rushing to see Durani at his best. He plundered 60 runs in about 20 balls to race to the 90s. Then suddenly, he became pedestrian and the mood seemed to have left him—he proceeded fitfully to his century and then got out to a lame stroke. Those 20 minutes were unforgettable and I still get goosebumps remembering those moments of sheer joy. It is indeed a pity that India never realized the full potential of Durani, one of the few left handers who at least once in a while brought comparisons with the genius of Garfield Sobers.

By the time I played against Nari Contractor, he was but a shadow of the great batter he was before his injury and he looked ordinary and vulnerable in the match that we played against Parsi Cyclists at Azad Maidan on a rain-affected wicket where the ball was stopping and shooting through. We won the match and I took four catches at short leg, Contractor being one of my victims. Madhav Apte who played during the early 1970s for Jolly cricketers was gentleman personified, so soft-spoken, civilized and cultured. Though well past his best, one could still see the technique and soundness in his batting.

Around 1974, I returned to Madras from Bombay. I was almost 28-year-old and started a manufacturing unit for brake linings. But I had the weekends free to play first-division cricket and this time I joined the Bharath Reddy-led Gandhi Nagar team. Over the next few years before I gave up league cricket, I had occasion to play with Krish Srikkanth, L. Sivaramakrishnan, Bharath Reddy and also a few other very talented players who could not make it to the Test scene—players like V. Sivaramakrishnan and Sunil Subramaniam to name a few. Krish Srikkanth touted as an attacking opener got out quickly—I caught him at slip and didn't make much of an impression in that match. L. Sivaramakrishnan—LS—as he was called in Chennai cricket circles was a good bat and extraordinarily agile, alert fielder besides being a leg spinner of top class. I remember hitting a full-toss powerfully to square leg only to find Siva jumping up to catch the ball one-handed quite nonchalantly in a Hindu Trophy match. V. Sivaramakrishnan was a fluent left hander with a nice swing of the bat and timed the ball sweetly. Once he was set he played big knocks and seemed to have a lot of time to play the ball.

Playing against all these top cricketers, one realized that besides talent, technique, sound defense and fundamentals of orthodoxy, one also required a great amount of patience, commitment and hard work to succeed in this game. This allied to big match temperament—the grit to fight and succeed when it counts—is what makes a talented, skillful player break into the big league. But if I can be permitted to add without a whiff of sour grapes, one also needs a dose of Luck!

33

SACHIN RAMESH TENDULKAR: FROM ABHIMANYU TO BHISHMA FOR A BILLION INDIANS

The date, November 16, 2013. The place, Wankhede Stadium, Mumbai. The event, a Test match against West Indies. The historic moment, Sachin Ramesh Tendulkar steps out for India for the last time. And we are not there, watching. Having seen almost all his innings either on the ground or on TV, it is wicked irony that we did not watch a single ball of his final Test. Facilitating a teachers' workshop at a remote block of Almora district, we hardly followed that game.

When Tendulkar bid adieu, it seemed as though the stoutest chapter in Indian cricket had ended. Cricket may be a team sport, but its uniqueness is that at every moment, it is a duel between two individuals—the bowler and the batter. For the Indian—perhaps that is the way we are—an individual's runs or wickets can assume great importance, even take precedence over a team's collective achievement, in contrast to the Australian fan, for whom a Bradman or a Ponting century holds little meaning if Australia does not win. For the Indian fan, a century by Gavaskar or Tendulkar, even in a losing cause, gives greater satisfaction than a 30 even if India wins. This can be traced to the initial years when Indian cricket victories were occasional highs. Thus, the fan found joy, satisfaction or solace in the exploits of a C. K. Nayudu, an Amarnath, a Mankad, a Hazare, an Umrigar or a Pataudi. Even after we experienced the thrill of beating England and West Indies in the 1970s and winning the World Cup in 1983, our enjoyment of cricket had become hard-wired into celebrating individuals. Gavaskar and Kapil Dev were heroes in every household.

And then came Tendulkar.

Surrounded as he may have been by the finest batters, Dravid, Laxman, Ganguly and Sehwag, the Little Master was the uncrowned king. From the early 1990s till his retirement, whenever India played a Test match at home and when the second wicket fell, there would rise an incredible crescendo, a reverberation of clapping, cheering fans. Tendulkar was coming out to bat! To a non-Indian, it might seem bizarre that the fall of the home side's wicket should be greeted in such an uproarious fashion. Fans of other batters might valiantly point to the undeniable exploits of their heroes, but in the nation's collective consciousness, Sachin spun in an exalted orbit. His century of international tons may one day be surpassed, but it is unlikely that his 50 centuries in Tests will ever be outdone. With the 50-over games likely to taper away, it may well be that the total runs amassed by Tendulkar also remain at the summit.

The last time we saw Tendulkar live on the ground was in February 2013 at Chennai in a Test against Australia. India was tottering at 12 for 2. The crowd should have been distraught that a supreme entertainer like Sehwag had been sent back and India were in dire straits. But the man replacing Sehwag at the wicket was not a mere cricketer. It was Sachin Tendulkar. As he adjusted his box and other protective gear and took guard, invisible to the human eye, sat the mountain of a billion hopes on his shoulders. And when he bent low to loft Nathan Lyon to mid-wicket, he was carrying that burden of responsibility. When he was finally bowled, it was not merely personal disappointment that he carried back to the pavilion but the crushing weight of the collective disappointment of a billion people.

This had been his story for 24 years, since he had made his debut. Not the story about his records: those are at the fingertips of every India. Nor the quiz trivia to describe his longevity in the game. When did the Berlin Wall fall? Before Tendulkar or after Tendulkar? When did Glasnost and Perestroika happen? Before Tendulkar or after Tendulkar? How many Prime Ministers in India since Tendulkar? To us, the story of Tendulkar is unlike any other in cricketing story. How did he remain so calm? How did he handle this unimaginable pressure? How supreme was his love for the game that an entire nation's expectations did not weigh him down? How did he always find time to greet the young boy who came to him for an autograph and be ever polite to the hordes of journalists wanting a sound bite? Later cricketers like Dhoni have been lauded for their legendary calmness, but we can stop for a moment to marvel at Sachin Ramesh Tendulkar, who even under the unrelenting microscopic dissection of his batting by a billion people always retained his poise and composure.

The best of great monuments have simple lines and sound foundations. The foundation of Tendulkar's batting was his purity of technique. The straight bat, the perfect left elbow, the decisive movement of feet, the ability to judge length, line, and movement earlier than other batters and the comfort in playing of either foot were all key components of Tendulkar's technique. He had every shot in the book and, more importantly, the ability to play them off the right balls. But all this still does not explain Tendulkar, the legend. We could analyze, dissect, and watch his best innings to construct our version of Tendulkar. What would help in our search for Tendulkar's significance to a cricket-crazy India is to go beyond and consider the remarkable facets of his approach to the game. Bear in mind that, despite his iconic status, he remained the team man, eager to do his best for his country; that he had the wisdom never to throw his weight around to influence selection or strategy. Can one recall even one occasion of Tendulkar expressing dissent with an umpiring howler?

Abhimanyu. At an age when many boys had not begun shaving, Tendulkar was squaring up to Waqar Younis, Wasim Akram and Imran Khan. Still just 20, such was his self-confidence that he practically snatched the ball to bowl the last over against South Africa in a championship semi-final and bowled six balls of such cricketing nous that it entranced an entire nation. A year later, knowing that he could provide the start India sorely needed in one-day matches, he pleaded with his coach and his captain to agree to the experiment. It was an epochal moment in India's one-day cricket history.

Bhishma. In the 2003 World Cup, India had been soundly beaten by Australia in an early-group match. Our cricket-crazy nation, boiled over with indignation and acts of hooliganism, with vandals targeting the residences of the team members. It was Tendulkar who, on behalf of the team, went on air, asking Indian supporters to keep the faith, assuring them that the team would rebound dramatically. India calmed down and the team won every match thereafter before falling at the last hurdle, the Championship Final. It is not common for undisputed champions and heroes—in military, politics, or sport—to decline wearing the leader's mantle and step back to support others without creating problems for their successors. But Tendulkar was different. After a brief and unhappy stint as captain, he steadfastly abstained from giving in to the temptation of assuming that responsibility; happy, instead, always to support Ganguly, Dravid, Kumble, and Dhoni with timely advice and wise counsel. And finally, at an age, when good cricketers put their feet up to watch the game from the comfort of their drawing rooms, Tendulkar was cover-driving James Pattinson's bowling at 145 kmph.

We sought out Rahul Dravid, to talk to us about Tendulkar. Dravid had played over 143 Tests and numerous One-Day Internationals with the Master Blaster and watched him from the non-striker's end for over 15 years. In Test cricket alone, their partnership resulted in 6,920 runs with 20 century stands and 29 stands of over 50 runs. They have traveled as young men across the cricketing globe, spending months together on overseas tours. We said, 'Rahul, the chapter on Tendulkar is the most difficult for us to write. Tell us about Sachin, and we will be able to understand the phenomenon better.' Over coffee, sitting in the clubhouse overlooking the Chinnaswamy Stadium, the man who scored 13,288 Test runs talked to us about the man who scored 15,921 runs.

Dravid spoke easily, quickly, fluently. 'Tendulkar is quite simply a unique package, a perfect combination of everything: balance, technique, hunger for runs, ability to read a game, understand his own game and make subtle changes depending on his own mind and body. He loves the game more than anybody else. Remember that he is as human as any other guy. He brings together hunger for the game, hard work, and perseverance. I can show you 10 cricketers who might have been equally hardworking and humble, but here one needs to recognize that Sachin also has immeasurable God-given talent. International cricket is all about being able to answer new and difficult questions repeatedly and Tendulkar is unique because he has always found answers. If you ask me which would be the greatest Tendulkar innings, I will pick his 248 not out at Sydney in 2004. Why do I say that? Because it was an innings that came after a sequence of failures, at a time when he was struggling, and Sachin was determined to succeed despite this. I saw Sachin's character in that innings—humble, realistic about his form, cutting out all his off-side strokes, accepting his weakness and playing around it. In a word, that innings was truly inspirational.'

More from Rahul: 'He was very lucky that his coach did not mess with his technique. You are right in that he holds the bat very low near the neck, completely against what coaching manuals prescribe, but Sachin's coach was wise and could see that this grip worked well for Sachin. He let him be. His bat is heavy and perhaps one reason for that was that he began to play using his brother's bat. His brother was nine years older, so obviously the bat was going to be quite heavy for Sachin. My bat is much lighter, among the lightest in the team. Azhar too had a light bat. Laxman's bat would be somewhere between Sachin's and my bat's weight. It was great that we played together at the same time. We had huge admiration and respect for each other, and we were also conscious that, on the ground, we should uphold the highest standards of conduct. When people say we are very balanced, it is a combination of school, home and society that has shaped us this way. Somehow, we have been able to treat fame, money, and people's adulation with a sense of humility and perspective. We are deeply grateful for the adulation of our fans.'

Master Blaster
Sachin Tendulkar
Credit: V. Balaji

Later that evening, we compared notes of Tendulkar's knocks that for us were enduring memories. We are spoilt for choice, but we decide to write just about his finest knocks at Chennai, for he saved some of his best for this city. His first Test century in India was in 1993, at

Chepauk, against England. We remember Sachin easing his way to 70 not out by end of day's play after Sidhu had made a dogged ton. Next morning, he unfurled a series of straight drives against the pace of Devon Malcolm and Paul Jarvis and motored to his hundred with nine scoring strokes—seven boundaries and two singles. The enchanted crowd had found their new hero.

And then we remember two other contrasting, yet equally fabulous, centuries at Chennai. The first, in 1998, was that breathtaking assault on Shane Warne in the third innings. It was a master class in attacking batting, as he repeatedly hit against the spin. It seemed so easy, but behind it was intense preparation at the nets in Mumbai, practicing his attacking shots to leg spin pitched on the rough outside leg stump. The second century was the heartbreakingly magnificent fourth innings effort in a losing cause against Pakistan in 1999. If there is a story of ecstasy and agony for the Indian cricket lover, it would be this Tendulkar innings. On a difficult fifth-day pitch against Saqlain Mushtaq bowling at his best, as well as Waqar Younis and Wasim Akram, Tendulkar played one of the greatest lone hands. Half the side was out for little, the target was far away, and he only had that feisty keeper, Nayan Mongia, for company. Tendulkar first repaired the innings and then craftily started taking the attack to the opposition. In those days, Tendulkar was by nature a batter whose instincts were to dominate the bowling attack. Midway through his innings, an excruciating backache; still the maestro battled on. Step by step, he brought India to within sight of victory. And then at the doorstep, he faltered. How well one remembers that final denouement! Another Doosra from Saqlain, Sachin out of his crease, playing the lofted drive. But this time, it catches the outside half of the bat. As Wasim ran around to catch the mishit, 50,000 hearts at Chepauk groaned and sank in despair. The rest of the wickets fell in a heap. The ache from that loss has probably never left Sachin, though if it is some balm, we would like to tell him that all of India believe this knock was his greatest ever.

In the famous 2001–2002 series that Ganguly's men won against Steve Waugh's Aussies, Tendulkar scored another century, again at Chennai in the deciding Test, bringing out a perfect blend of attacking batting and stout defense against some very good bowling from McGrath and Gillespie. In any case, it seemed that whenever we went to Chepauk for a Test match, Sachin would make a hundred. For yet again in December 2008, Chennai got lucky, watching Tendulkar score a century to take India to a target of almost 400 against England. Carping critics had till that day often remarked that Tendulkar had never been able to pull off a fourth innings winning effort. With Yuvraj Singh for company, Sachin finally ticked that box with a match-winning ton. There was such serenity to that innings that it had a palpably calming effect on the crowd. As he stitched his partnership with Yuvraj, the crowd flowed with the game.

A 24-year long playing career will obviously have clear and distinct phases. In the first phase, Sachin the 'child-man' won us over with his precocious ability and talent, to play the way he did when most others of his age were worrying about high school exams. His innings at Old Trafford, Sydney and Perth convinced even hardened experts that we were looking at the next star of cricket.

However, Sachin had not yet achieved his celebrity status. All of that changed in early 1994 in New Zealand when he opened the Indian innings for the first time in an ODI. We remember getting up at around 3 a.m. to watch the match on television and what followed took our breath away. The perfection of his approach to opening in the ODIs and batting was both breathtakingly simple yet incredibly difficult for anyone else to execute. It lay in his unparalleled ability to play straight, hit the ball on the rise and through the line with the field up in the first 15 overs, Sachin was a natural. When he was done that day, everyone wondered why he had not opened earlier.

Sachin's batting in ODIs made him a phenomenon in a nation that had now become more invested in ODIs than in Test cricket, as the penetration of television and media worked their magic across a billion Indians. His classical technique, honed over the longer version of the game, was a great advantage in the opening overs of an ODI. By the late 1990s, he was certainly the best batter in the world.

Thrilled as we were by the beauty of his stroke play, we marveled that he could play such cricket while retaining the calmness of a Zen Buddhist. One wonders if he developed this to cocoon himself from the vagaries of the adulation and worship of cricket-crazy fans and remain sufficiently immune to them. His fans had unreasonably high expectations and anticipated a miracle every time the Little Man went out to bat. And that begs the question: why are we so unfeeling toward our heroes that we do not allow them human flaws and imperfections?

In the early 2000s, he seemed to go through a patch that to most of his critics indicated a decline in his powers. He seemed tentative and fallible against bowlers he would have summarily dismissed earlier in his career. The period between 2004 and 2008, coinciding with the ill-fated tenure of Greg Chappell as the coach of the Indian team, were troubled years. Tendulkar battled injuries and form. His critics, especially the armchair ones, said he must go. Somehow, somewhere, Tendulkar found the composure and sagacity to ignore all this and concentrated on getting healthier, fitter and back to his best. He rediscovered himself and everyone knows how incandescent this second coming of Tendulkar was, for he blazed away, like a latter-day Bradman, culminating in the 2011 World Cup victory. Back to his attacking best, he pummeled the bowling, and it was clear that he was enjoying his cricket more than ever before. When Dravid spoke of his powers of execution, he was possibly referring to his straight drive for which it was impossible to place a fielder; to his trademark leg-side shot where he turned his wrists to guide the ball exactly where he wanted; to his uppercut over slips invented for the ODI, but audaciously improvised and used in Test cricket too. In each case, here was the modern master of the game having spent two decades at the top, reinventing himself.

In all this we must not forget to mention what a canny change bowler he was. He could bowl medium pace, seam up and both off and leg spin. Everyone remembers Laxman's 281 in that unforgettable victory in Kolkata against Australia in 2001, along with Dravid's supporting ton and Harbhajan's 13 wickets. Amidst all that was a dream spell of 3 for 31 from the Little Master as he got Hayden, Gilchristand Warne. Oh, he bowled a well-concealed googly for sure! What a cricketer!

All this brings us to the Bharat Ratna, the highest civilian award in India. While earlier the Bharat Ratna was only awarded to statesmen, great leaders and scientists, it has been also bestowed on legends from the field of art and music. Even in the best of times, awards have political calculations and messages. National stalwarts like Dr Ambedkar, Sardar Patel, Jayaprakash Narayan and Madan Mohan Malaviya, to name just a few, were honored only many years (decades even) after they had passed. In 2014, sensing the mood of the nation, for the first—and till now the only—time, a sports icon was conferred the Bharat Ratna. Just weeks after he retired and only 40, Tendulkar, the heartbeat of a cricket-crazy nation, a man who had carried the hopes of a billion people on his shoulders for over 20 years was conferred the honor. Could the Bharat Ratna for Tendulkar have waited? Most importantly, would our adoration or respect for the cricketing genius have in any way been reduced if he were not a Bharat Ratna? Difficult to tell. Many years ago, as we shared an evening with Salim Durani, he looked deeply into his glass of rum and said, 'God made Tendulkar and said, son, go and play cricket.' That is what Tendulkar did from 16 to 40; and every fan lived and breathed his every run, every catch, and every wicket. If he fielded on the boundary and just waved a hand, 50,000 spectators swooned in ecstasy. If you ask him, that was his biggest award, all that he cared for.

Bhishma. There are some questions that remain unanswered. Should Tendulkar not have spoken out loud and clear during the terrible match-fixing saga? Or about Greg Chappell's methods, if he felt they were not helping India? Then the quest for the 100th hundred, which was tortuous and painful. The Great Man might have misjudged the timing of his curtain call. But surely, we can summon enough kindliness to accept that human as he is, the temptation of that milestone must have been irresistible. Consign to forgetfulness all these glitches, the mere guttering of a candle before going out. Instead recall and remember with joy and empathy the incandescence that illuminated Indian cricket for nearly a quarter of a century.

34

THE 360 DEGREE CRICKETER: IN CONVERSATION WITH S. VENKATARAGHAVAN—PLAYER, CAPTAIN, UMPIRE AND ADMINISTRATOR

This essay was written in January 2013

Late January is probably the best time of the year in Chennai. Venkat's house is in a quiet tree-lined street and as the two of us walk in, Venkat greets us with a broad smile. Raghu knows Venkat for over 40 years since the two have played with and against each other in league cricket. Now as senior

Venkat umpired the 100th Test match at Lords—here he shows his off spinner's grip with the historic ball used in the Test match
Credit: S. Giridhar

citizens, they play the occasional round of golf. Giri is meeting Venkat for the third time in his life. The first was a memorable meeting, as a school cricketer, spending an hour in the company of Venkat who was then the vice-captain of the Indian cricket team. The second occasion was much later in the 1980s during a Hindu Trophy match when Venkat was playing for India Pistons.

Venkat has read our earlier essays and perhaps as much because of this as his friendship, is ready to share his views on every aspect of the game with us. For us it is a coup for what could be better than the views of one who had spent a lifetime in the middle, playing and umpiring at the highest level. Those who know Venkat are aware that he is not only an outstanding cricketer but one of those rare cricketers who have read extensively about the game. It is not easy to get close to Venkat but on the subjects that he wants to speak about he is forthright, extremely illuminating and surprises you with scintillating anecdotes. As we settled into the comfortable sofas of his living room, we began a conversation that lasted over three hours broken only by lunch. We took furious notes but there were some things said that will remain only between the three of us. Here is what Venkat said.

How will Test cricket survive?

If cricket is to survive then Test cricket must thrive. Five-day cricket is the lifeblood of the game. Connoisseurs of course will find this form of the game most watchable but the support of the larger public is a must. If it lives only on limited overs cricket, the game will wither away. Youngsters must learn to play proper cricket first and then adapt to the shorter form. It just cannot happen the other way around. One-day cricket and T20 cricket is all about improvisation and so is it not logical that learning orthodox cricket can be the best foundation to be good in all three forms of the game? Basil D'Oliveira and Cowdrey played the vertical sweep and Ranji the leg glance in the traditional form of the game. That was improvisation that they built on the foundation of solid technique. Why even great West Indian batters like Vivian Richards, Clive Lloyd, and Gordon Greenidge played orthodox cricket although their aggressive hitting might make you think otherwise. Go back in time, and you will see that Bradman was also such a fast scorer. So were Sobers and Kanhai. Having said all this, one must realize that things must be done to make sure that the Test cricket is in tune with the times that we live in. We have a lesson from the 1960s. Back then, because England allowed Test and county cricket to get boring, the crowds voted with their feet; and the English Board had to introduce limited overs cricket—Gillette and John Player—to bring back the crowds that had stopped coming to watch Test and county cricket. Simple things could be tried to rejuvenate Test cricket. Like ensuring that both teams complete their first innings by the third day and make the fifth decisive. Already in the past few years we are seeing a lot more decisive Test matches with over 300 runs being scored in a day. That is a great sign. Test cricket is attracting good crowds in England and Australia. We must get the crowds back in India too. There must be a sensible balance and distribution of Tests and limited overs cricket in the Indian calendar. If Australia can designate Boxing Day, 26th of December, as the first day of the Melbourne Test then why can't India too earmark Pongal and New Year's Day as the first day of the Test matches in Chennai and Kolkata?

Are cricketers playing too much cricket these days?

Not really. Television and one-day cricket makes it seem so. In our days, we played a lot of cricket, maybe not Test matches but a whole lot of year round first-class cricket and league cricket. We played every league match apart from the Ranji, Duleep and Irani trophy matches. Don't forget that cricketers like me also played four months of nonstop county cricket. The value of playing such first-class cricket can never be overemphasized. Our top players must find the time to play in India's first-class tournaments not only for the sake of the game in India but also to ensure that their skills are being continuously honed. Learning is a continuous process. I attribute a lot of my success in Test cricket to the games I played in first-class cricket. Against Hyderabad I would bowl to Jaisimha, Abbas Ali Baig, Pataudi and other solid batters. Getting their wickets was so important for my confidence. When I played for Derbyshire against Kent I was not merely bowling to county journeymen but in fact to a world-class batting lineup consisting of Brian Luckhurst, Mike Denness, Bob Woolmer, Colin Cowdrey, Asif Iqbal and Alan Knott.

But what about the fitness levels which do seem to be getting affected?

There's a lot of talk about fitness these days and that it has to do with too much cricket. I do not agree. I've already said that we played cricket round the year in our days too. My view on fitness is that players must be cricket fit and not Olympics fit. I think I have a right to say this because I never ever left the cricket field because of injury! Cricket, everyone knows, is a wonderful combination of brain and brawn. Mental fitness, therefore, is required a lot more in this game as compared to the others. The physical fitness for cricket has its own requirement and regimen. Therefore, I find this aspect of playing football to keep fit shocking and silly. I played a lot of sport in my younger days but avoided football because it was contact sport more likely to cause me an injury rather than help me keep fit. Cricket fitness is best achieved through cricket practice. Not mechanical, mindless practice. Only perfect practice makes perfect. Into such perfect practice go thought, planning and strategy. When I practiced, I would visualize my field placing and communicate that to the batter. In a nutshell I kept fit playing cricket. So did Kapil Dev, and the two of us never missed a match due to injury. You never found us doing calisthenics. We practiced our cricket for hours and kept fit. Another example is Fred Trueman, the great fast bowler, who bowled in 33 county championship matches every year apart from his duties for the country. He never complained of overwork or injury. I remember meeting Bradman in 1985 when I went to Australia as the manager of the Indian cricket team. We saw some players doing their calisthenics routines and I turned to him and asked him, 'Sir, how did you keep fit during your playing days?' To which that great man simply said, 'I kept fit playing cricket.'

We pause and a moment later Venkat offers a wonderful insight into the great man. He asks us, how many of us know that the Don was an exceptional cover point and spent hours of practice in the evening, after the game, hitting a single stump over and over again. And that takes us neatly to the subject of close-in fielding.

What made you such a superb close-in fielder?

I was a good fielder simply because I practiced like hell. You know the parabolic drum and the roller in the ground. I would ask the groundsman's assistant to bounce the ball at speed on the drum and take the ricochets as they flew off the surface. Endlessly, I would take hundreds of catches every day, till the poor man said his arm was aching. I would place two gloves on either side of me a couple of yards away and if any of the balls passed me within those markers, I would take it as a personal insult. I learned to dive correctly without hurting myself.

At this stage of the narration, Venkat gets up and asks us to come with him to a room inside his home where there are framed photographs from his playing days. Not surprisingly quite a few of those photographs are of Venkat taking some fabulous diving catches close in. Venkat relives those days for a few minutes and we walk back to the living room to continue our conversation.

We change the track and ask him about umpiring.

I was always interested in the laws of the game and I believe that every cricketer must know these laws well. In 1971, when

India played West Indies in the first Test at Jamaica, the match was reduced to four days because the first day was washed off due to rain. When India took a lead of 170 runs, it was I who informed Wadekar our skipper about the rules that stated that when a Test match was reduced to four days, the follow on was enforceable with a lead of over 150 and did not have to be 200. Wadekar mumbled something about 'do sau,' which is 200 in Hindi but I said, 'Ajit believe me I'm right.' Sure enough Umpire Sang Hue agreed and told a stunned Sobers that West Indies would have to bat again. In a nutshell the attributes of a good, consistent umpire are: concentration, self-confidence, observation, gathering facts, applying the laws of the game and ability to decide in a fraction of a second.

So why was Venkat such a good umpire? Venkat thankfully does not suffer from false modesty and is able to identify his strengths. First is self-confidence. I have always been a confident person. At this stage Raghu interjects with a laugh to say he knows that well, for even in their college days Venkat would be the one player who would exude confidence that his team would win. His second clear strength according to Venkat is concentration. Venkat says that because he had to field close-in all day long, he developed that kind of concentration and proceeds to narrate a gem to prove this point. 'I have taken a catch of the last ball of the day three times in Test cricket and that is clinching proof of my ability to concentrate. While my colleague Chandra could afford to relax at fine leg, I had to be alert at slip or gully. And that helped me in my umpiring.'

We ask Venkat to tell us some stories from his umpiring days.

And Venkat obliges. The first story is West Indies versus Australia at Adelaide. Glen McGrath appeals for caught behind joined by nine teammates and 9,000 Aussies in the crowd. Not out, says Venkat in his instant and emphatic fashion. They cannot believe it till the big screen shows Venkat got it right.

Next over, there is again a huge appeal for a catch at the wicket. This time all 11 players and 11,000 in the stands join the chorus. Not out, says Venkat and as the screen shows Venkat got it spot on once again, McGrath walks up to Venkat and says, how glad he is that at least one person is watching the game! The other story Venkat tells us with some relish is his friendly challenge to the Channel 9 commentary team who keep dissecting umpiring decisions with the benefit of slow motion replays and hindsight. Venkat tells them that in order to get a real assessment of umpiring, the commentators too, just for one day, should commit to a decision real time and then compare results with the umpire at the end of the day's play. That day, in the middle, Venkat got four out of four correct and then walked up to the Channel 9 team to ask how they had fared. Tony Greig said, 'Venks, I got all four wrong'; Ian Chappell said that he got one out of four correct while the others simply kept quiet. Venkat said it taught them enough to realize how skilled an occupation it is to get a decision right in 0.4 seconds with the ball travelling at 90 miles an hour. On technology Venkat has clear views. Use it for line decisions such as run outs. Use it for boundary-line decisions. But on the use of Hawk eye for LBW, Venkat is categorical that Hawk eye cannot predict the trajectory after hitting the pad. The age of the ball, new, 20 or 40 or 80 overs will make a difference—the softer the ball the less it will bounce; depending on whether it pitches on the seam or side, the turn and bounce will be different. The age of the pitch too, depending on whether it is day one or day five will make a difference to bounce and trajectory. Sorry Hawk eye! As an umpire, however, he would still like umpires to make stumping decisions if only because it is a Test of concentration! He was half serious though. Venkat says, there is a charm to the game which is over 120 years old, and we must infuse technology in a manner that does not reduce the charm.

We switch back to his playing days. And Giri tells Venkat, that in our essays on opening batters, we have not included

Barry Richards among the greatest because he played just a few Tests and never played in the subcontinent. Venkat disagrees, and is absolutely certain—like most of his contemporaries—that Barry was among the best. 'He read line and length earlier than anybody else and had three different strokes for every ball. To get him out meant a monumental victory.'

Three great knocks on three consecutive days

Here is a gem of a story. Venkat watched a World Series match and on the first day, Barry Richards hit 160 that he thought must surely be the greatest knock he had seen. Next day, however Viv Richards blazed to a 180 that made Venkat pause to think if this was perhaps better. And on the third day, Greg Chappell hit such a classically sublime 185 that Venkat knew that he had seen the three best innings ever, incredibly, on three consecutive days! Venkat also remembers his old colleagues very fondly. He says that the best players of spin during his days were Vijay Manjrekar, Ramesh Saxena and Hanumant Singh. Sardesai and Jaisimha were almost as good. The talk slows down because Venkat is thinking of these old mates, who sadly have passed on.

On wicketkeepers

'Bob Taylor and Alan Knott have been the best we have seen. In fact, Taylor was as good as Knott but Knott was the better batter and got to play a lot more Tests for England.' Venkat should know for Taylor kept to Venkat during his county stint with Derbyshire. Standing up to keepers is of course the deciding hallmark of keepers but Venkat says, do not ignore the way the keeper receives the ball in his gloves for that often tell you how good he is. Among Indian stumpers he rates Naren Tamhane highest of all. He was superb and his keeping to the spinners and Subhash Gupte with his two googlies, was particularly brilliant. He was better than Engineer but if Venkat had to pick the team, he would go for Engineer who gave the team flexible batting options as opener and as no. 7. After Tamhane, Venkat has high regard for P. Krishnamurthy the late Hyderabad keeper who played just the five Tests against West Indies in 1971. Very reliable, very good is Venkat's categorical assessment. Kirmani was brilliant but inconsistent, and Giri unwisely reminds Venkat of the dozen catches—almost entirely of the luckless Venkat—that Kirmani dropped on the 1976 tour to West Indies. Venkat can now look at the lighter side and shrug this away with a laugh. For some strange reason, he says Kirmani found it difficult to read Venkat's straighter one and the one that went the other way. And it was natural that we spent a few minutes to discuss Venkat's own bowling.

Captaincy and captains

Venkat's initial comments seem to be on predictable lines. It is a team game, so the captain is as good as his team; and, therefore, how to motivate and get the best out of his team is critical. And then Venkat warms up. He takes us to the story of Hanuman who is not aware of his own potential and strength till wise old Jambhavan reminds him and exhorts him. Much the same way, Brearley could bring the best out of Botham. It is a skill that only a few have for Botham himself could never do the same when he was captain. The captain has the difficult role of being within and outside. He has to himself perform his role as a player and at the same time have the sagacity of a neutral dispassionate observer to help the others. Captaining India is a very different challenge with our socio-cultural diversity. The communication, the language, the motivation, all these have to be pitched differently and individually. So, captains need to be sensitive and aware that the way they handle Gavaskar will have to be different from the way they manage Solkar. Venkat what did you do? I was perhaps hard on those who had potential but were not performing adequately. So I would cajole, exhort and pull up those cricketers. I wanted to see effort. Tiger Pataudi did it very differently. He came from a different background and despite his young age—remember he was the youngest when pitchforked into captaincy in the West Indies and had Umrigar, Manjrekar and others in the team—people looked up to him. He was tactically and strategically not very good but he had the charisma. Raghu, a huge fan of Kripal Singh, asks Venkat about his impressions of Kripal who was his first Ranji captain. Venkat, ever the pragmatic, does not take the bait and simply says, 'It was very easy for Kripal to captain us. He was the senior Test player in the team. We listened to him.' Among international captains, apart from Brearley, Venkat rates Ian Chappell, Richie Benaud and Steve Waugh highly.

'Chappell, for instance, even in the commentary box is able to bring out points that the others do not see. He was also a very good motivator. Richie Benaud was special for two reasons. He was an excellent communicator and absolutely top class for his critical analysis and sizing up strategic possibilities. He was very astute. While everybody talks highly of Mark Taylor with good reason, Steve Waugh actually should get a lot of credit too for he was very good at strategy,' says Venkat.

And he adds in similar vein that another fine captain in recent years whom we all tend to forget is Michael Vaughan of England. Of Clive Lloyd who led the invincible West Indies from 1974 to 1985, Venkat feels he was in the royal position of not having to do anything! When he led the Windies on the 1974–1975 tour, he was tactically very poor. But soon he had four great fast bowlers and a formidable batting line up and they ensured that the West Indies ruled the world. Venkat wraps up our discussion on captaincy with a wry laugh and comment that we feel is almost directed at himself, 'Above all a captain requires luck.'

It is almost 3 p.m. in the afternoon now and we need to just discuss some of the remaining aspects of the game almost like a freewheeling closing session. The best fast bowlers you have seen—Andy Roberts, Malcolm Marshall, Michael Holding, Curtly Ambrose and Dennis Lillee. What about the huge emphasis on coaching in modern cricket? 'Now, that is a bone of contention,' says Venkat. 'A coach at Test level can only point out flaws that have inadvertently crept in. Perhaps, a coach can anticipate, spot, tell and demonstrate. You cannot tell Sachin much! You can only be a motivator and a psychologist.' Both of us, unabashed but frustrated supporters of the Tamil Nadu team, ask Venkat why is there such a difference in the approach of a Chennai cricketer and Mumbai cricketer. Pat comes the reply: 'It is the sheer competition for places. You have to play every match with a seriousness knowing if you fail, you might lose your place and find it difficult to get it back. That is the key difference.'

We ask Venkat about sledging.

Venkat laughs and says, 'It has been there from time immemorial. Coarse language was used even then, but folks did not get to see it, that's all! Ian Chappell, Tony Greig, they took sledging to a higher level. Nobody is a saint, they all yap. It is good we have a match referee to keep this kind of behavior down and

The authors after their illuminating conversation with Venkat
Photo Courtesy: S. Venkataraghavan

the fear of fines and suspension is a good deterrent. There is so much money in cricket today that fewer batters will walk when they know they are out. They would prefer to leave it to the umpires for if one gets dropped one stands to lose a lot of money.'

And among the nicest things Venkat then said, almost in reverie, was that although Indian players come from so many regions and languages and religions, none of these is ever a barrier. The bond is cricket and nothing else matters. To play for the country was an honor. I was paid Rs 200 for my first Test match and there was hardly any money those days but that did not matter. To wear the India cap was everything.

Venkat stands up and stretches to his full height, as our meeting draws to a close. Giri tells Venkat, you must be six feet? Venkat the precise engineer says no, I am five feet eleven and a half inches tall. Sometimes such sentences tell you more about a man than four hours of conversation.

EPILOGUE: THE ETERNAL ALLURE OF CRICKET

Cricket has moved at a frenetic pace since our book was first published in 2014. Virat Kohli, Joe Root, Ravichandran Ashwin, Nathan Lyon, Kane Williamson, and many other players, who now embellish the pantheon of all-time great cricketers had then just begun their careers.

So much has happened, so much has changed, that any attempt to synthesize all the developments in a concluding essay to this new edition, seemed daunting. And so, we ran an informal survey with a group of cricket lovers to validate and consolidate our thoughts on the most significant events and developments in the last 10 years. Here is our list:

1. Test cricket has always been seen as the pinnacle of the sport. The introduction of the World Test Championship or the WTC has now given a much greater salience to Test cricket.
2. Bazball: The new term in cricket lexicon to describe the style of play adopted by England after coach Brendon McCullum and captain Ben Stokes took charge. An unrecognizably ebullient England team are redefining the way to play Test matches. Attack, and if the team in trouble, Plan B is to attack some more. England in the last year has played the most exhilarating cricket in living memory. The openers hammer away at six an over and England rattles up 400 in a day. Will other

teams adopt a similar approach? What is clear is that the scoring rates which were already in an upward curve for the past 20 years—around 3.2 per over—will go up some more.

3. Fourth innings targets are being hunted down. In the history of Test cricket, there have been only 57 occasions when a team has scored at least 350 in the fourth innings. But 11 of these have been since 2014, five of them in a winning cause. And in case people think that such chases are difficult on turning pitches, four of these big chases have happened in the sub-continent. Stokes' team almost yearns for a fourth innings chase; even when they win the toss, they want to bat last. Indians are probably still hurting at how Johny Bairstow and Joe Root made a mockery of the 378-run target at Edgbaston in July 2022.
4. Just 30 years ago, only two out of three Tests provided a result. In the decade 2001–10, that improved to three out of four. But since 2016, almost 9 out of 10 (86 per cent of the games) have been decisive. The average duration of a Test match in these seven years has come down to around 3.5 days. One can read this in several ways: (a) the fear of losing is going down; (b) the WTC points for a draw is nearly as bad as losing, so teams are willing to take risks for a win; (c) the pitches are more bowler-friendly and most teams go with a five-member bowling attack; and (d) we should not be surprised if ICC reduces the playing time of Tests to four days.
5. Just 22 years back, Indian coach John Wright would draw a square on the practice pitch to explain to Harbhajan Singh, the best place to land the ball. Venkatesh Prasad would carry a paper in his pocket with handwritten field placing options. From that rudimentary situation to the hi-fi analytics today, is an incredible leap that only technology could have achieved. Video-analytics and

assorted data have become a core input to team strategy and for players to improve their skills and execution. But the real customers for analytics and infographics are the television audiences. Cricket—especially after IPL—is presented as spectacular family TV and smartphone entertainment. The major impetus for the analytics revolution with commerce as the driver happened with the 2015 World Cup.

6. The first day-night Test was played in 2015 in Adelaide. Since that inaugural game, 21 day-night Tests have been played and Pink Ball games are now a feature of most Test series across cricket-playing nations.
7. The Sandpaper Gate ball-tampering scandal was a train-wreck waiting to happen. The Australians were caught using abrasive paper to change the condition of the ball. Punitive actions, recrimination and remorse followed. In the aftermath, one saw the Australians gather themselves, raise their behavior on the ground even as they strove to retain the quality of their cricket. Has the game become better for the Sandpaper Gate?
8. The COVID-19 pandemic turned our lives upside down. Everyone lost a friend, a colleague or a relative. And yet, through the pandemic, cricket tried to provide some succor, some joy. For the first time, games were played to empty stadiums, with teams in their own sanitized bubbles. And with home umpires instead of neutral umpires. Remarkably, one of the greatest Test series ever was played during this period between hosts, Australia, and the Indian cricket team.
9. Cricket tragically lost Australian opener, Phil Hughes, to a bouncer despite the helmet. We now have the excellent concussion substitute rule. The first concussion substitute in Test cricket was at Lord's in the Ashes series in August 2019 when Marnus Labuschagne came in after Steve Smith was felled by a Jofra Archer delivery.

The amount of cricket that is being played through the year—all three formats included—means there is a game on, somewhere, every day. Fears that Test cricket may wither away seem to have lessened. The number of Tests in fact have gone up. In the years, 1981–2000, 634 Tests were played while the subsequent 20 years saw 873 Tests. Of the 74 Test players who have played 100 or more Tests, 23 made their debut in 2000 and later. The concern that the big three—Australia, England and India—will hog the Tests calendar and marginalize other nations, looms large, but the WTC, which has nine countries vying for the trophy, provides a countermeasure. In the past five years, the distribution of Tests among the nine countries playing the WTC is:

Country	England	India	Australia	South Africa	Sri Lanka	West Indies	New Zealand	Pakistan	Bangladesh
Tests played	66	51	46	42	42	41	40	39	33

Source: Data from espncricinfo.com. Analysis and tabular compilation by authors.

Rather than Tests, it is the 50-overs format that will get finessed out between Tests and T20. If commercial compulsions can be managed, the ICC could have fewer bilateral ODI and T20 series—they have ephemeral value—and instead create more multi-nation white ball tournaments. That way, meaningful spectacle and commerce could find a meeting ground.

The increasing dominance of IPL franchises in multiple countries, and the possibility of these franchises handing out year-long contracts could completely change the scenario. We might have a situation where the best cricketers are playing for their franchises while national teams are represented only by those who do not have such contracts.

Let us now turn our attention to the various aspects of the game. It will admittedly be a whistle-stop tour but hopefully we can capture the critical nuances of the game and the players who have made a name for themselves in these recent times.

Batting

A number of brilliant batters have emerged in the past 10 years to qualify for that modern phrase, G.O.A.T—Greatest Of All Time. Joe Root, Kane Williamson, Virat Kohli, Steve Smith and Babar Azam too, though his exploits are more recent. Smith is unconventional and may not please the purist, but his defense is impregnable and his is the wicket bowlers work hardest to get. The others are of course a picture of elegance and play gorgeous strokes on both sides of the wicket with their own distinctive stamp and style. All these batters are the fulcrum of their team's batting, but such is their greatness that they have never made it appear burdensome.

We must pause here to briefly discuss the unique but incredibly successful batting technique of Steve Smith. Though the shorter versions of cricket have brought many innovations to batting, the basic technique hasn't changed over decades in Test cricket. A still head and stance was considered absolutely 'de rigueur' by coaches and manuals along with the orthodox grip of the cricket bat. But, Smith has successfully defied the proven, accepted methods and devised his own novel and even outlandish way, with amazing results over the last many years in Test cricket. So what is Smith's way? As the bowler runs in, Smith starts moving to the off so that by the time the ball is delivered, he is not only covering all the stumps, but often exposing his leg stump! Woe betide the bowler who bowls on the leg stump, for the ball will be dispatched with certainty through mid-wicket or square leg. Anything outside the off stump will be left alone with that idiosyncratic twirl of the bat. Thus, risks eliminated. Smith maximizes the available scoring opportunities. Perfect drives through the off cordon combined with the predominant on-side strokes in an arc from long-leg to mid-on. He has found a way to tackle the short ball into his ribcage. His defense is solid; he judges length quickly and is balanced, as he plays back or forward with studious concentration. Smith is not attractive to watch; and with his antics and gesticulations, plain irritating for the bowler. He often remonstrates with himself and is in a cocoon, oblivious to others in the field. His batting against spin is more orthodox and sound in defense, as he nudges and pushes into the gaps and puts away bad ones efficiently. Add to this—self-belief, enormous patience, and an unflappable temperament. When opposing sides see Smith saunter in at no. 4, one can hear a collective sigh and a switch in tactics as if the fielding side has resigned itself to the notion that Smith is here to stay. And Smith is by no means a stonewaller, for once he gauges pace and bounce, his tempo gradually rises to respectable scoring rates. And to think that this man who averages nearly 60 in over 100 Tests, began his career as a leg-spin bowler who could also bat!

It has however been a challenging time for openers. Certainly, in the pace-friendly conditions of South Africa, England, New Zealand, and Australia, but also in countries like India and Sri Lanka, where spinners come into operation before the first drinks break, to severely Test their technique. The average opening partnership during 2018-22 is only 32.6, down from 38.9 during the 2008-12 period. The sturdy openers in recent times have been Dimuth Karunaratne, Dean Elgar, Usman Khawaja, Devon Conway and Kraigg Brathwaite. Rohit Sharma, after many years in the middle order, has made an inspired transition to an opener. His stylish stroke play is unaffected while a new compactness in defense has emerged.

The most interesting development is England's novel approach to batting. They have gone hammer and tongs from ball one since McCullum and Stokes took over the Test team. To watch England's opening, is like seeing Sehwag bat at both ends. If other teams emulate England, more than a few openers might hit centuries before lunch on the first day of a Test.

While many right handers have emerged to be counted among the greats, no left hander in recent times can be spoken of in the same breath as Harvey, Sobers or Gower. Australia and New Zealand though, have continued to produce prolific left handers in this period—David Warner, Khawaja, Travis Head, Tom Latham, Devon Conway and Henry Nicholls. India's Test results, ever since they played two left handers, have been impressive. In Australia, on that fabulous tour in 2020-21, they had Rishabh Pant, Ravindra Jadeja and Washington Sundar, and on every occasion, the left handers were critical in shaping the result of the game. In the home series against Australia in 2023, Jadeja and Axar Patel made an enormous difference with their left-handed batting after the top order regularly failed.

Bowling

We have always wanted the game to be even between bat and ball. Big bats and smaller boundaries loaded the game in favor of the batters. Happily, bowlers are enjoying the recent times. If nine out of 10 games are ending in a result and the average duration of a game is 312 overs (around 3.5 days), it means bowlers are taking 20 wickets.

This is the era of speed guns. Who will break 160 clicks? Thus, we have Haris Rauf, Mark Wood, Jofra Archer, Anrich Nortje, Umran Malik and a few others being discussed excitedly. But all this pales in front of the body of work that England's pace bowling pair of James Anderson and Stuart Broad have built over the last decade. Theirs has been the most enduring fast bowling partnership. Together, they have played 134 matches and taken over 1,000 wickets and are also no. 1 and 2 among fast bowlers at 685 and 576 wickets.

Australia has consistently had an enviable pace-bowling machine. And in recent years, even when their batting faltered, their formidable bowling combination of Pat Cummins, Josh Hazlewood, Mitch Starc, and Scott Boland backed by Nathan Lyon often won them games. That is why they ended up on top of the WTC 2023 table. Kagiso Rabada has realized in full measure the promise he showed as a lithe teenager, and is the world-class leader of the South African attack. India, during these years, developed and nurtured their relentless, penetrative pace brigade of Jasprit Bumrah, Ishant Sharma, Mohammad Shami, Mohammad Siraj and Umesh Yadav. It is the excellence of their fast bowlers that makes Shastri and Kohli, Dravid and Rohit, proclaim that they do not care what kind of pitches are provided when they play overseas.

It has been a good time for left-arm fast bowlers. Mitch Johnson of Australia was winding down his career with 355 Test wickets when Starc emerged. Starc is now a veteran with over 300 wickets. New Zealand's classical left-arm pacer, Trent Boult might have played his last Test, but he too has over 300 wickets in 78 Tests at an impressive 27.5. Though not of express pace, his compatriot, Neil Wagner is a speciality. His bouncers come at a line and height that force batters into errors. In recent times, no other bowler has more wickets with the short ball. India despite its fast-bowling riches has not got a left arm pacer since Zaheer Khan. But Pakistan does. First Mohammad Amir, who was banned for match fixing at 17, resurrected some years later and then retired in a huff. Then emerged Shaheen Shah Afridi. Just 23, he has already played 25 Tests for 99 wickets and is the spearhead of his nation's attack. He could be spoken of like Wasim Akram if he plays for another 10 years.

The story of off spin has seen great changes in the last few years. The obnoxious Doosra has almost gone. Bowlers will only invite scrutiny with it and face long bans if found to be bending their elbow beyond a permissible limit. Importantly, aspiring off spinners now have the best of role models in Lyon and Ashwin who have shown that the off spinner can have several variations without need for the dubious Doosra. Clean actions, flight and drift, a good rip with strong fingers for over spin and side spin, the floater, the faster leg cutter; there is enough and more in the armory. Today Lyon and Ashwin with over 470

Test wickets are only behind Muttiah Muralitharan among off spinners. During their overlapping careers, they have together taken 956 wickets. There has never been such a period for off spin in Test history.

Ashwin's spin twin Jadeja and Shakib Al Hasan of Bangladesh are the flagbearers for left-arm spin after Daniel Vettori of New Zealand called time and Rangana Herath signed off with 433 wickets. Lethal on helpful pitches, Jadeja is only behind Muralitharan among modern day spinners in home averages, even ahead of Ashwin. With his solid batting and cheetah-like fielding to go with his left-arm spin, Jadeja is the all-rounder extraordinaire of modern cricket. For the first time in cricket history, the top three all-rounders—Jadeja, Shakib and Ashwin—are all spin bowlers. Cast your mind back. Long ago, there was Wilfred Rhodes; then came Vinoo Mankad and Richie Benaud. The last time we had a bunch of all-time great all-rounders at the same time was when Ian Botham, Imran Khan, Kapil Dev and Richard Hadlee, all fast bowlers, played in the 1970-80s. The next set of top all-rounders, Jacques Kallis, Andrew Flintoff and Shaun Pollock were also pace bowlers.

Fielding and Wicket Keeping

The outfielding—boundary riding and catching—has undergone an unimaginable transformation since the advent of T20. Sliding stops had already become a feature, but the incredible catches on the line have elevated outfielding to a new level of athletic excellence. Catching in the slips has also improved, one aspect being the balls that come in the awkward area just below the chest. As a result of assiduous practice, slip fielders are now as adept at taking catches with fingers pointing up as they are at taking low catches. The one position where the quality of catching has not improved is at short leg to the spinners. Despite the legacy of Solkar, India has not committed to developing specialists for that position. They could learn from England and Australia, who have given that position the attention it deserves.

As a result, Peter Handscomb of Australia and Ollie Pope of England are currently the best in the world at short leg.

Two of the best keepers in this period have been Wriddhiman Saha of India and Ben Foakes of England. Cast in the classical mold, both have great hands and perfect footwork, staying low while standing up to spin. Often, the compulsions of team balance, means that a keeper who can bat better is preferred over the better keeper. Bairstow and Jos Buttler being preferred over Ben Foakes is an example. Pant is a rare jewel and has already scripted some famous wins for India in his short career. The audacity and brilliance of his batting is the reason he burst on the scene but he began as an ordinary keeper. His glove work has hearteningly improved because of assiduous coaching and his hard work and commitment to better fitness. One hopes he recovers from the injuries he sustained in the car accident for Pant is a once-in-a-generation athlete who can emulate his idols, M. S. Dhoni and Adam Gilchrist.

Captaincy

In the last 10 years, two captains who have had profound impact on the game are Eoin Morgan in white ball and Ben Stokes in Test cricket. After England's pusillanimous approach in the 2015 World Cup, Morgan was convinced that a new, fearless approach was the only way forward. His leadership—strategy and execution—transformed England's ODI team in the ensuing years and none was surprised when they won the 2019 World Cup.

Though Morgan transformed the white-ball team, England's red-ball team continued to play listlessly under Root. Remarkably, when Stokes took over in 2022, one saw how the same players became a completely different team. In coach McCullum, he has a kindred spirit. In these past 12 months, Stokes' captaincy—fearless, positive, liberating—has blown the mind away. If there was a survey done, with the question, 'Which Test team would you want to watch,' the unanimous answer would be England.

We have seen statesmen captains like Worrell, cerebral captains like Mike Brearley, charismatic captains like Richie Benaud. The exhilarating Stokes—early days, 13 Tests as captain with 10 wins—might end up as one of the finest Test captains the game has known.

What of Virat Kohli's impact as captain? Taking over from Dhoni, when the team was in a trough, Kohli captained India in 68 Tests over the next eight years. That is the highest by an Indian captain and the sixth most in Test history. His brand of passionate, aggressive captaincy (he can be infuriatingly boorish) and whimsical choices of playing XI (choosing Karn Sharma over Ashwin is just one example) has evoked extreme views. Critics point out that he did not win an ICC trophy and that after India was bowled out for 36 in Adelaide, it was under Rahane that India won that series in Australia. But against these, consider what he achieved: (a) a win percentage of 58.82 that is only below that of Steve Waugh and Ricky Ponting; (b) the first Indian captain to win a series in Australia; (c) India was no. 1 in ICC Test rankings for 42 consecutive months from October 2016 to March 2020; (d) India now competes on equal terms overseas on the basis of a world-class fast bowling unit; (e) new levels of physical fitness have been established and (e) India won 16 of 34 away Tests, a record better than any Indian captain and also superior to his contemporaries, Steve Smith (6 out of 15) and Joe Root (10 out of 33). That is some legacy.

This is a section where we share our observations and analysis on the technical aspects of the game. The caveat is that some of these will come across as mere opinions, to be contested and even rejected. Still, that kind of debate is the very essence of cricket conversations!

More batters, because of T20 cricket, are bottom handed

and adopt a more open chested stance. And with all the training to play big hits to clear the field, there is an increased tendency to hit across the line. As a result, the bat does not come down straight; we see more batters bowled off stump. This was not a common occurrence earlier for the batters with tight technique. That is why, left-arm fast bowlers are enjoying more success. If they get their inswinger on the right line and length, they have every chance of getting the batter bowled or LBW, as the batter plays around his front pad.

Another fallout is that batters find it challenging to build an innings patiently, especially in bowler-friendly conditions. Pujara and Khawaja who play only red ball cricket find this easier. Only the exceptional among the multi-format players—such as Smith, Root, Williamson, Kohli and Babar Azam—easily switch across formats because they have the technique and temperament.

Most batters, particularly Indian batters brought up on Indian pitches, have a forward-press and pre-commit to the front foot. That is why bowlers like Anderson have our batters in all sorts of trouble. The absence of a strong back foot play means that as fine a batter as Kohli rarely plays the cut even on the bouncier pitches of Australia and South Africa. Quality spinners can only be countered by quick feet, soft hands, and the ability to play off front and back foot. The sweep cannot be the only answer to a spin Test. In earlier days, one could say Indians play spin better, but on recent evidence that is not the case. They have been as vulnerable to spin as batters from other countries.

Having said this, one admires the audacity of stroke play and the very approach to batting. A reverse sweep to get to a ton is not just the preserve of the irrepressible Pant but also the classical Root. Classical batting seems to co-exist beautifully with innovative new strokes. Even purists will accept that the ramp over third man is as gorgeous as the pristine cover drive.

A quick look at DRS and LBW trends. LBW dismissals,

which were around 15.2 in the 1970–2000 period, rose to 17.3 by 2012, within four years of the introduction of DRS. One might have thought that in subsequent years, with the maturity of DRS and the umpires' willingness to give batters LBW while playing well forward to spin, the percentage of LBW dismissals would have risen further. However, they have since, only risen marginally to 17.5 per cent. One reason is that, with the advent of DRS, batters now adopt the 'bat in front of pad instead of bat besides the pad' approach to spin. That has helped keep LBW in check but the bowled/caught at slip dismissals have risen.

Off spinners are bowling a lot more from around the wicket—not only to the left handers but also the right handers. In the recent India–Australia series, Ashwin, Lyon and Todd Murphy bowled around 70 per cent of their deliveries from around the wicket. Maybe because the pitches were turning a lot.

The scrambled seam! We have grown up admiring the fast bowler's skill to bowl with a bolt upright seam. Which makes the recent development of fast bowlers using the scrambled seam most interesting. Not surprisingly, it is the veteran Anderson, who has shown how effective it can be. Those brought up on the importance of an upright seam, now realize that the scrambled seam is lethal because the batter cannot easily judge whether the ball will go out or come back after pitching.

Are fast bowlers less inclined to pitch the ball up for fear of giving easy boundaries? One remembers even the very quick Bob Willis and Dale Steyn would pitch the ball up to give it maximum chance to swing. Is the yorker and bouncer being used less for the same fear of leaking runs? Remember how Waqar Younis and Wasim Akram would polish of the tail with toe-crushing yorkers?

We said earlier that short leg is the one position where standards have stagnated or even dropped. Protective gear (helmet, shin guards, box and all) is absolutely necessary at that suicidal position and that perhaps restricts the movements, however good the fielder may be.

While there is a huge improvement in the athleticism of cricketers, is all the gym work perversely impacting fast bowlers' fitness? Why are so many fast bowlers breaking down regularly, not just in India but across the world? Kapil Dev, Hadlee, Ambrose, Botham, Marshall and Walsh never missed games for any extended period. This puzzles us as much as it disturbs us. Is bowling fitness—the ability to bowl without injury through the year and career—more achievable through well-supervised bowling practice rather than hours at the gym that might strengthen some muscles and yet rob bowlers of some essential flexibility?

If all this is food for thought and makes for a good chat among cricket lovers, we are content.

Cricket is not played in a vacuum. It is a microcosm of society and in its own way the game—and all sports—is a reflection of our society and its mores and values. If we have seen jingoism go through the roof over the last 30 years in our country, that is also a reflection of the trajectory of society and nation.

If Australia and South Africa ensure that there is always a Test match on Boxing Day but India has given up holding a Test match on Pongal at Chennai, it reflects these countries' respective views on tradition. If the museums at MCG and Lord's are a treasure trove of cricket history and the Eden Gardens or Feroze Shah Kotla at Delhi do not have anything remotely comparable, it reflects the respect we have for history and for preserving and archiving it for posterity. If we name our stadiums after administrators and politicians while SENA countries retain their original names and commemorate their cricketing legends fittingly, that is also a pointer to society and what it values.

But we believe things could change. The most unlikely events or people can well trigger the change. At Eden Gardens, in a game between Kolkata Knight Riders and Chennai Super Kings, the stadium was awash with yellow T-shirts, with hardcore KKR supporters cheering Dhoni, for he has transcended team loyalties. It was the same a few years ago at the Chinnaswamy Stadium when AB de Villiers came out to bat for South Africa. He received the most rousing reception from the Bengaluru crowds for he was their darling at the Royal Challengers Bangalore. From here to the next stage of being more appreciative of opposing teams, graciously applauding the skills of their players may not be a big leap. Does it reflect the more confident, self-assured India of the 2020s, and its growth from the early stages of liberalization and globalization in the 1990s? On the other hand, a recent malaise is the mindless trolling on social media of the sportsperson and every public figure. The irate fan who threw stones at Dhoni's home is gone but the social media bully has taken his place.

That India has failed to win an ICC title for the past ten years—including two consecutive WTC finals—weighs heavily on the team. But in terms of sheer consistency, theirs have been the best Test team. Over the past seven years, the team has been no. 1 in ICC Test rankings for 64 months; the next closest are Australia and New Zealand with 8 months each on the top.

When we wrote *From Mumbai to Durban*, we chose 28 of India's greatest Tests since Independence. If we were to write that book today, at least seven Tests that India has played since 2014 would replace them. Cast your mind back to the game at Adelaide in 2014 that India lost. It was Kohli's first Test as captain—he hit centuries in both innings—and when India was set a target of 364, he announced that India would go for a win rather than a draw. Dhoni told him it will not be possible. To which Kohli is believed to have replied, 'Only if we try, we can know, na?' The win in 2018 at Johannesburg on an impossibly hostile pitch is one for the ages, as India's pacers outgunned the hosts' pace battery. And has there ever been a greater Test series in cricket history than the one India played in Australia during the COVID-19 pandemic? For Ajinkya Rahane's team to win at Melbourne and draw the Sydney game was nothing short of heroic. But to triumph at Brisbane's 'Gabba the fortress', against a full-strength Australia with an all-novice bowling attack and a total experience of four Tests, may perhaps have no parallel in cricket history.

Finally, to end on a personal note. We are both long in the tooth. The elder has watched cricket since 1955 and played with Salim Durani and contemporaries. The younger, no spring chicken, watched his first Test in 1964. Neither of us have played white ball cricket. Readers would have realized that for us, red ball cricket holds the greater charm. But we must also tell the reader that in these last 10 years, we realized that the acrobatic catch on the boundary, the audacious ramp to a bouncer over third man and the masterly spell of off spin from round the wicket to right handers that we see in Tests, are skills honed by white ball cricket.

ACKNOWLEDGEMENTS

We thank Kasturi & Sons for allowing us to print selected photographs from the fabulous collection in their archives.

The statistical data for our essays have been sourced from the ESPNcricinfo.com website. Stats and analysis were also provided by Deepu Narayanan of cricbuzz.com.

The illustrations in the book have been done by V. Balaji of Chennai.

A number of essays in this collection were first published in espncricinfo.com, firstpost.com, *The Hindu Business Line*, *The Times of India*, and *Huffington Post* (details below). We thank them for permission to use them in our book. While some of the essays have been reproduced virtually unchanged, the others have been updated, expanded or rewritten.

Firstposts.com

- Chapter 1: First published as 'Close encounters on the cricket field/India's best fielders before the ODI era'
- Chapter 4: First published as 'Men of Dravid's ilk—their country's most trusted batsmen'
- Chapter 5: First published as 'Tyson, Holding, Donald: The true terror of the fast bowler'
- Chapter 9: First published as 'The link between Dhoni, Brearley and Bradman'
- Chapter 11: First published as 'The ballad of the big-hitters of cricket'

- Chapter 16: First published as 'From Viswanath to VVS: Stylists who make cricket magical'
- Chapter 17: First published as 'Left-arm spin: Its place in cricket history'
- Chapter 18: First published as 'Is batting average the clue to finding the next Dhoni?'
- Chapter 20: First published as 'Davo, Akram, Zaheer: What is the legacy of left-arm bowlers?'
- Chapter 25: First published as 'Proved without a doubt, India is the true home of spin'
- Chapter 31: First published as 'Why Laker, Prasanna remain better off-spinners than Murali, Bhajji'

Espncricinfo.com

- Chapter 2: First published as 'The Lesser Known Facets of Kapil's Brilliance'
- Chapter 3: First published as 'Fab four—then and now'
- Chapter 6: First published as 'Leg Spinners—A statistical assessment/ Leg Spinners: Stories and Anecdotes'
- Chapter 13: First published as 'Dissecting the LBW'
- Chapter 14: First published as 'Dashing Durani'
- Chapter 21: First published as 'A salute to wicket keepers'
- Chapter 23: First published as 'Dashing openers—A priceless tribe'
- Chapter 24: First published as 'The Chinaman bowler—odd man in/ Mystery and Magic: Iverson, Ramadhin, Gleeson and Mendis'
- Chapter 26: First published as 'Nobility in a hard game/ Courage in a hard game'
- Chapter 27: First published as 'The Sublime Left Handers'
- Chapter 30: First published as 'For an Even Game between Bat and Ball'

The Times of India

- Chapter 10: First published as 'Hurray for the system that got Team India there'
- Chapter 12: First published as 'The Seventeenth Man'
- Chapter 19: First published as 'Running the numbers: How data and analytics influence cricket', Part 1 and 2
- Chapter 28: First published as 'Captains Courageous/ Captains of Strategy'

The Hindu Business Line

- Chapter 7: First published as 'The many stories of Bishan Singh Bedi'

Huffington Post

- Chapter 22: First published as 'What made M. S. Dhoni one of a kind in contemporary Indian cricket'

We can never adequately express our gratitude to the many people who gave us their unconditional love and support. Be it the sharing of anecdotes and stories or providing us photographs, helping with the analysis or going through the manuscript, they somehow found the time to help us. This is the kinship of cricket lovers. We could not have moved one page without them. To all of them, thank you very much.

BIBLIOGRAPHY

Arlott, John. *Jack Hobbs: Profile of 'The Master'*. London: Penguin Books Ltd, 1981

Atherton, Mike. *Glorious Summers & Discontents*. London: Simon & Schuster, 2011

Bailey, Trevor. *Sir Garry: A Biography*. Kolkata: Collins, 1976

Bala, Rajan. *The Covers are Off*. New Delhi: Rupa & Co, 2004

Barnes, Simon. *A Book of Heroes: Or a Sporting Half Century*. London: Short Books Ltd, 2010

Berry, Scyld. (ed). *Wisden Cricketers' Almanack*. London: John Wisden & Co, 2010

Bharatan, Raju. *Indian Cricket: The Vital Phase*. New Delhi: Bell Books, Vikas Publishing House, 1977

Bhattacharya, Rahul. *Pundits From Pakistan*. New Delhi: Penguin Random House India, 2012

Bird, Dickie. *My Autobiography*. London: Hodder & Stoughton, 1997

Bose, Mihir. *A History of Indian Cricket*. London: Andre Deutsch, 1990

——. *The Magic of Indian Cricket: Cricket and Society in India*. Oxon: Routledge, 2006

Bowes, Bill. Express Deliveries. London: The Sportsman's Book Club, 1958

Boycott, Geoffrey. *The Best XI*. London: Penguin Books, 2009

Brearley, Mike. *The Art of Captaincy*. London: Channel 4 Books, Pan Macmillan Ltd, 2001

Cardus, Neville. *Close of Play*. London: Collins, 1957

——. *Cardus on Cricket*. London: Souvenir Press Ltd, 1977

Chopra, Aakash. *Out Of The Blue: Rajasthan's Road to the Ranji Trophy*. Noida: HarperCollins Publishers India, 2011

Davidson, Alan. *Fifteen Paces*. London: The Sportsman's Book Club, 1965

Evans, Godfrey. *The Gloves Are Off*. London: The Sportsman's Book Club, 1961

Fingleton, J.H.W. *The Immortal Victor Trumper*. Sydney: Collins, 1978

Gavaskar, Sunil. *Idols*. New Delhi: Rupa & Co, 1983

Giridhar, S. and V. J. Raghunath. *From Mumbai to Durban: India's Greatest Tests*. New Delhi: Juggernaut Books, 2016.

Guha, Ramchandra. *A Corner of a Foreign Field: The Indian History of a British Sport*. London: Pan Macmillan, 2011.

——.(ed). *The Picador Book of Cricket*. London: Picador, 2001

——.The Commonwealth of Cricket: A Lifelong Love Affair with the Most Subtle and Sophisticated Game Known to Humankind. Noida: HarperCollins Publishers India, (2020)

Haigh, Gideon. *On Warne*. Edinburgh: Penguin, 2012

——.*Stroke of Genius: Victor Trumper and the Shot that changed cricket*. London: Simon & Schuster, 2016

Harvey, Neil. *My World of Cricket*. Melbourne: Hodder &Stoughton, 1963

Holding, Michael. *Why We Kneel, How We Rise*. London: Simon & Schuster, (2021)

James, C. L. R. *Beyond a Boundary*. London: Yellow Jersey Press, 2005

Karunatilaka, Shehan. *Chinaman: The legend of Pradeep Mathew*. Noida: Penguin Random House India, 2011

Kesavan, Mukul. *Men in White: A Book of Cricket*. New Delhi: Penguin Books India, 2007

Laker, Jim. *Over to me*. London: Frederick Muller Ltd, 1960

Landsberg, Pat. The Kangaroo Conquers. London: Museum Press, 1955

Majumdar, Boria. *Twenty-two Yards to Freedom: A Social History of Indian Cricket*. London: Penguin/Viking, 2004.

Mailey, Arthur. *10 for 66 and All That*. Sydney: Allen & Unwin, 2008

Mallett, Ashley. *Chappelli Speaks Out*. Sydney: Allen & Unwin, 2005

Marks, Vic. *The Wisden Illustrated History of Cricket*. London: Queen Anne Press, 1989.

Memon, Ayaz. *Indian Innings: The journey of Indian Cricket from 1947*. Chennai: Westland Sport, 2021

Menon, Suresh. *Bishan: Portrait of a Cricketer*. Gurgaon: Penguin India, 2011

Miller, Keith and R. S. Whittington. *Keith Miller Companion*. London: The Sportsman's Book Club, 1955

Moyes, A. G. J. *The Changing Face of Cricket*. London: The Sportsman's Book Club, 1966

Mukherjee, Sujit. *The Romance of Indian Cricket*. Delhi: Hind Pocket Books, 1968

Noble, M. A. *Gilligan's Men*. London: The Sportsman's Book Club, 1955

Pataudi, M.A.K. *Tiger's Tale*. London. Stanley Paul, 1969

Ramaswami, N.S. *From Porbander to Wadekar*. New Delhi. Abhinav Publications, 1975

Ramchand, Partab. *The Gentle Executioners: Story of Indian Spinners*. London: Konark Publishers, 2004

Robinson, Ray. *On Top Down Under: Australia's Cricket Captains*. Melbourne: Cassell, 1975

——.*The Wildest Tests*. Melbourne: Pelham, 1972

Ross, Alan. (ed). *The Penguin Cricketer's Companion*. Melbourne: Penguin, 1981

Ross, Gordon. *The Surrey Story*. London: The Sportsman's Book Club, 1958

Sridhar, R with R. Kaushik. *Coaching Beyond: My Days with the Indian Cricket Team*. New Delhi: Rupa Publications, 2023

Sundaresan, Bharat. *The Miracle Makers: Indian Cricket's Greatest Epic*. Gurgaon: Penguin Random House India, 2023

Tyson, Frank. *A Typhoon called Tyson*. London: The Sportsman's Book Club, 1962

Upton, P. *The Barefoot Coach: Life-changing Insights from Coaching the World's Best Cricketers*. Chennai: Westland Sport, 2019

Wadekar, Ajit. *My Cricketing Years*. New Delhi: Rupa & Co, 1973

Wright, Graeme. (ed). *A Wisden Collection*. London: Bloomsbury, 2004

Wright, John with Sharda Ugra and Paul Thomas. *John Wright's Indian Summers*. New Delhi: Penguin/Viking, 2006

INDEX